THE FABER BOOK OF SMOKING

James Walton was born in Merseyside in 1962, but didn't start smoking until 1991. Since 1994 he has worked for the *Daily Telegraph*, first as deputy literary editor, now as the television critic. He also writes and presents Radio Four's literary quiz, *The Write Stuff*. This is his first book.

'You don't have to be a smoker to enjoy this book: one of its strengths is the confidence it has to include fascinating snippets which are only tangential to smoking, like the heart-warming fan mail between Groucho Marx and T. S. Eliot. If you are a smoker, though, you will love it. And if, best of all, you are a lapsed smoker, you will devour it rather as a prisoner might a particularly juicy porn mag after ten years in solitary confinement.' James Delingpole, *Spectator*

'As anthologies go, Walton's could not be improved on . . . His amiable introduction and chapter prefaces are down-to-earth, even-handed, alert to fun; but his choices, and where he places them, illuminate both sides of a debate that has often been conducted in farcical terms.' Robert Potts, *Times Literary Supplement*

'Even a vehement anti-smoker would enjoy this book . . . If you read all of it, the funny, sad, angry, calm, annoying, poetic and downright idiotic bits, with contributions by the likes of Mark Twain, Adolf Hitler, Churchill, 'Bridget Jones', Martin Amis and the late Dennis Potter, then maybe more smokers and anti-smokers will come to an understanding and mutual tolerance. Whether this is an epitaph to smoking remains to be seen. I will always remember it as a three-pipe and five-coronas delight.' *Daily Express*

THE FABER BOOK OF
SMOKING

EDITED BY

James Walton

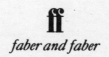

faber and faber

First published in 2000
by Faber and Faber Limited
3 Queen Square London WC1N 3AU
This paperback edition first published in 2001

Phototypeset by Intype London Ltd
Printed in England by Clays Ltd, St Ives Plc

A CIP record for this book
is available from the British Library

ISBN 0-571-120750-2

2 4 6 8 10 9 7 5 3 1

To Mum, Dad and Helen
(I'll give up one day, I promise.)

In ancient times, when the land was barren, the Great Spirit sent a beautiful, naked girl to save humanity. Wherever her right hand touched the earth, there grew potatoes. Wherever her left hand touched the earth there grew corn. And in the place where she had sat, there grew tobacco.

Huron myth

[On the phone to Sir Walter Raleigh]

Things are fine here, Walt . . . Did we get the what? That boatload of turkeys. Yeah, they arrived fine, Walt. As a matter of fact, they're still here, Walt. They're wandering all over London as a matter of fact . . . See, that's an American holiday, Walt. What is it this time – you got another winner for us, do ya? . . . Tobacco. What's tobacco, Walt? . . . It's a kind of leaf. And you bought eighty tons of it. Let me get this straight, Walt – you bought eighty tons of leaves. This may come as kind of a surprise to you, Walt, but come fall in England we're kind of up to our – it isn't that kind of a leaf? What is it, a special food of some kind, is it, Walt? . . . Not exactly. It has a lot of different uses. Like what are some of the uses, Walt? . . . Are you saying 'snuff'? What's snuff? . . . You take a pinch of tobacco [*laughing*] and you shove it up your nose. And it makes you sneeze. I imagine it would, Walt, yeah. Golden-rod seems to do it pretty well over here . . . It has some other uses, though. You can chew it or put it in a pipe, or you can shred it and put it on a piece of paper and roll it up and – don't tell me, Walt, don't tell me – you stick it in your ear, right, Walt? . . . Oh, between your lips? Then what do you do to it, Walt? . . . You set fire to it, Walt? Then what do you do, Walt? . . . You inhale the smoke? You know, Walt, it seems offhand that you could stand in front of your fireplace and have the same thing going for you . . .

Bob Newhart, *The Introduction of Tobacco to Civilisation* (comic monologue), 1963

The progress of the tobacco trade . . . is certainly one of the most curious that commerce presents. That a plant originally smoked by a few savages, should succeed, in spite of the most stringent opposition in Church and state, to be the cherished luxury of the whole civilised world; to increase with the increase of time, and to end in causing so vast a trade and so large an outlay of money; is a statistical fact, without an equal parallel.

F. W. Fairholt, *Tobacco: Its History and Associations*, 1859

. . . the tobacco years have been world history's grandest – and most terrible – hitherto, in terms of effort, conflict, achievement, transformation in every field. To all this, tobacco's contribution is impossible to measure, but it has been immense.

V. G. Kiernan, *Tobacco: A History*, 1991

Contents

[ix]

CONTENTS

Introduction

In 1957, Sir Compton Mackenzie – then 74 and at the height of his reputation; now probably best known for *Whisky Galore* – published his 81st book, *Sublime Tobacco*. Its purpose was simple: to demonstrate through careful historical analysis that smoking is 'one of the greatest boons ever conferred upon humanity'. The proofs turn out to be wide-ranging. The American Civil War, for instance, was won by the North largely because General Grant chain-smoked ('Cigars . . . kept his nerves . . . calm and steady') and General Lee didn't smoke at all. Mackenzie knows 'with absolute certainty that the harder I work, the more I need to smoke, because tobacco is the handmaid of literature'. Such is the bonding effect of cigarettes that if they 'disappeared from the earth, the world would go to war again within a comparatively short lapse of time'.

But, before it settles down to the task in hand, *Sublime Tobacco* has a 62-page prologue entitled 'My Smoking Life'. This makes melancholy reading for today's smoker. Most obviously, the simple pride Mackenzie takes in having got through half a ton of tobacco since his first cigarette at the age of four is unthinkable now. (For the record, he lived until 1972.) We also learn that Mackenzie would no more have dreamed of puffing away at one brand of cigs in every smoking circumstance – as most of us do these days – than a knowledgeable drinker would stick with a pint of lager whatever the occasion or the accompanying food. Whether he plumped for a cigar, a pipe or a cigarette depended on the situation – and, in any case, was only the prelude to deciding what blend of tobacco it should contain. (In fact, Mackenzie's tolerance of cigarettes at all is unusual for 'real' smokers of his generation, many of whom regarded fags as gourmets would later regard fast-food.) Lastly, there's the glamour and exoticism of the whole thing: how Mackenzie as a boy saw the Empress of Austria smoking on a beach in Cromer; his casual comparison of antelope, kangaroo and monkey skins as the best material for tobacco pouches; the time he used a spot of nonchalant puffing to avert a rebellion in

Greece. ('Such is the power of a cigarette at the right moment.')
Nowhere does Mackenzie mention those key components of a smoking
life nowadays: the fetid train carriage; the anxious patched-up prep-
arations for plane flights; the frozen huddle outside the office building;
the exile to back-garden or doorstep when visiting friends' houses.
(Pneumonia and piles will surely be added to the list of smoking-
related diseases soon.)

In retrospect, then, *Sublime Tobacco* marks a turning point in
smoking history. On the one hand, its account of an unrecognisable
smoking world was published comfortably within living memory. On
the other, it was also published in the same year that the Medical
Research Council in Britain first accepted a 'causal link' between
cigarettes and lung cancer. As you might imagine, Mackenzie gave the
blasphemy short shrift. Nonetheless, as you might further imagine,
Sublime Tobacco was the last example of a once-familiar literary
genre: the utterly respectable book which praises smoking to the skies.
(Others earlier in the century had included *The Mighty Leaf, The
Soverane Herbe* and – my own favourite title – *St Nicotine*.) Such
innocence would never be possible again.

And yet, Mackenzie's scepticism about the latest anti-smoking attack
was perhaps less bone-headed than it appears. Wild claims – often
based not so much on science as on visceral disgust – had been made
about the dangers of tobacco from the time it first appeared in Europe.
How could he know that this time the arguments would turn out to
be right? Mackenzie understood there's something about people
smoking that its opponents (Hitler is an example he unsurprisingly
dwells on) just hate – and that they just hated long before anything
had been proved. Nor has their attitude always been rational, based on
such fair-enough factors as smelly clothes and discoloured wallpaper.
Despite the claims of pro-smoking groups today, it seems to go well
beyond a Puritan distaste at the pleasures of others. Even now that
all doubt about tobacco's dangers has been removed, remnants of
evangelical exaggeration surely remain in the anti-smoking case.

But far more irrational, of course, is the fact that smoking hasn't
come remotely close to dying out in the half-century since its perils
became public knowledge. Just look around any pub. The reason given
for this by anti-tobacco campaigners – particularly in American courts
– is straightforward enough: teenagers are ensnared by cunning advertising, and by the time they want to give up as adults, they're hopelessly

addicted. It's a central premise of this book, however, that smoking is a more complicated, perverse and, above all, *mysterious* activity than that.* When I first proposed the idea for this anthology to Faber, I thought that one of its uses might well be as an epitaph on a 500-year-long habit. I'm afraid I even imagined future generations – puzzled by the clouds billowing from their ancestors in films and photographs – turning to this book for enlightenment. Well, having finished the research, I'm not so sure they'll need to. Smoking, I would now suggest, may be here to stay. After all, not only did it spread around the planet with lightning speed; not only has the desire for tobacco played a significant part in the history of the world ever since; but the habit has also survived onslaughts even fiercer than those of today – not least being punishable by torture and death. Remember, too, that despite Hitler's massive anti-smoking efforts, the main form of currency among the ruins of Berlin in 1945 was cigarettes.

The book that follows splits, neatly I like to think, into two parts. (I'm also quite chuffed it ended up with 20 chapters, one for every cigarette in a pack.) The first – in the possibly misguided belief that anybody reads anthologies in the correct page-order – tells the basic story of smoking from Columbus's arrival in the New World to the tobacco battles of today. The second picks out such recurring themes as Giving Up; Smoking, Sex and Seduction; and Poisoning Cats (a strangely persistent one, that) – and follows them through the centuries. I appreciate that many entries could have appeared in one of several different chapters, but I thought I'd spare you an intricate system of cross-referencing. I've also spared you anything that made my own eyes glaze over when I was researching. There's little here, for example, about the cultivation and yearly cycle of the tobacco plant – or about its different varieties and where they're grown. More questionably, some might think, I've only included a few snippets about the spiritual significance of smoking to the pre-Colombian peoples of the Americas – honestly, it's not as fascinating as it sounds. An easier decision was to restrict the book to *tobacco*-smoking: other smokable substances are definitely a whole other subject.

A few omissions – among those not caused by incompetence or bad

---

* A friend of mine once told me how the doctors in a leading British heart hospital explained to her that her partner had been rendered inoperable by his smoking. The doctors then went off for a cigarette break.

luck* – are due to surprising non-existence: annoyingly, the famous moments in *Now, Voyager* where Paul Henreid lights two cigarettes in his mouth and hands one to Bette Davis aren't in the published screenplay. They must have been improvised on set. Then, there's the price of copyrights and considerations of length. (Faber, for some reason, wanted me to 'live in the real world' – a place, inexplicably, where 1,000-page anthologies don't exist.) The development of the tobacco trade in Colonial America, for instance, could be the subject of a book on its own. I've therefore opted not to go into vast detail about it – partly on those grounds, and partly because this is *The Faber Book of Smoking*, not *The Faber Book of Tobacco Production, Manufacture and Export*. It's essentially about the habit itself, rather than about the agricultural evolution which made the habit possible. Even so, I should say in passing that both George Washington and Thomas Jefferson were tobacco farmers, that tobacco was an important factor in the rise of slavery and that in the Southern States, the American War of Independence was known as The Tobacco Wars. You could argue, in other words, that the United States as it now is would be unimaginable without smoking.

In his preface to *A History of Smoking* (1930), E. C. Corti wrote: 'As for my own personal attitude, it would afford me the liveliest pleasure should the reader, after finishing my book, find himself unable to decide whether I am a smoker or not!' Well, I wondered about taking a Corti line; but in these confessional times, it seemed better to come clean. I reckon I've smoked around 40,000 cigarettes while working on this book. (Sadly, it hasn't taken me 15 years.) On the other hand – apart from the occasional unconvincing attempt as a teenager – I didn't begin puffing until I was 29, and so have spent most of my adult life as a non-smoker. I think I took up the habit for two reasons. First, as a result of an uncharacteristically successful diet in the early Nineties. (Some people give up smoking and start eating a lot. I gave up eating a lot and started smoking.) Second, because non-smokers were becoming increasingly irritating, and the only way I could dis-

---

* (One for the reviewers:) 'With probably the single exception of religion, there is no subject on which so much printer's ink and paper has been expended as on tobacco and the practice of smoking . . . It is improbable that any man ever will . . . devote himself to the truly Herculean task of sifting and sorting the huge mass of Nicotian printages' – W. A. Penn, 1901.

tance myself from them was to light up. My mother smoked all through my childhood. Friends at university and beyond must have smoked as well. And yet, I can honestly say I never really noticed. I certainly couldn't say for sure which friends smoked and which didn't. Nonetheless, here were non-smokers going into operatic coughing-fits at the slightest wisp of tobacco-smoke, and wasting any amount of moral indignation on the subject. Now, of course, I know that some people really are affected by smoke. I also realise that the raised consciousness of its presence could be considered – in many quarters *is* considered – a good thing. I'm just saying how it struck me at the time. These days, while theoretically a mutual-tolerance man, in practice I'm as cowed as the next smoker. I would maintain, though, that as love–hate relationships go, the one with cigarettes is up there with the best. You meet some interesting people, your days are punctuated with little treats, and – unlike non-smokers – you get to give and receive gifts all the time.

But fortunately, this being an anthology, the idea of the book isn't to create a single central argument. Instead, it's to reflect, as accurately as I can, the various viewpoints held on the subject over the years. There are plenty of extracts here I agree with, plenty that I don't – and plenty (often the most entertaining) that now look plain bonkers. With a bit of luck, this combination should provoke in the reader the twin realisations I had myself while researching: that certain aspects of smoking have changed unexpectedly drastically, others unexpectedly not at all. Obviously, too, I'd like to provide a good read, some laughs, some firm nods of recognition from smokers and non-smokers alike and some thoughts along the lines of, 'Blimey! Smoking was linked to low birth-weight in the early 1600s?' As for the best smoking writers in history, I think I'd confer a shared prize on Mark Twain, Raymond Chandler and Martin Amis – with an honourable mention to J. M. Barrie. The best single novel on the subject must be Christopher Buckley's *Thank You for Smoking*. And, in the interests of balance, the Maddest Smoking Claims Ever Made Award is a tie between the Rev. J. Q. A. Henry for his tale of the 'bloodless boy' in *The Deadly Cigarette* (see Chapter Five) and W. A. Penn for his memorable assertion that: 'All the alleged harm of cigarettes is due to bad paper, the deadliest thing a smoker can consume'.

Which brings us on finally to what I suspect might be the most ticklish aspect of this whole enterprise. Naturally, the dangers of smoking can be found in the pages that follow; but so, too, can its pleasures. Putting in any kind of good word for tobacco these days risks asking for trouble. Yet, clearly any anthology that didn't record the delight and relief, the stimulation and relaxation that this peculiar, dual-acting drug has brought to so many millions of people over so many hundreds of years would be – at the very least – dishonest.

Note: Wherever possible, I've tried to put the date of each individual entry. When this plan has failed, there are only the dates of the author. In most cases, spelling and punctuation have been modernised.

The Way We Smoke Now

5 July [1989] A middle-aged couple walking along the cliffs in Wales are 'brutally murdered'. The dead man's brother, unable to believe it could have happened to them, says, 'They were perfect parents, church goers, *non-smokers*.'

Alan Bennett, *Writing Home*, 1994

On the wall was a sign bearing the saddest words Keith had ever read: NO SMOKING.

Martin Amis, *London Fields*, 1989

The new morality

We have problems here of high smoking and alcoholism. Some of these problems are things we can tackle by impressing on people the need to look after themselves better. That is something which is taken more seriously down South . . . I honestly don't think the problem has anything to do with poverty . . . The problem very often for people is, I think, just ignorance.

Edwina Currie, health minister, in a speech at Newcastle-upon-Tyne, 23 September 1986

Something is happening to America, not something dangerous but something all too safe. I see it in my lifelong friends. I am a child of the 'baby boom,' a generation not known for its sane or cautious approach to things. Yet suddenly my peers are giving up drinking, giving up smoking, cutting down on coffee, sugar, and salt. They will not eat red meat and go now to restaurants whose menus have caused me to stand on a chair yelling, 'Flopsy, Mopsy, Cottontail, dinner is served!' This from the generation of LSD, Weather Underground, and Altamont Rock Festival! And all in the name of safety! Our nation has withstood many divisions – North and South, black and white,

[1]

labor and management – but I do not know if the country can survive division into smoking and non-smoking sections.

P. J. O'Rourke, *Republican Party Reptile: Essays and Outrages*, 1987

Of the pressures facing the successful novelist in the mid-1990s Richard Tull could not easily speak. He was too busy with the pressures facing the unsuccessful novelist in the mid-1990s – or the resurgent novelist, let's say (for now): the *unproved* novelist. Richard sat in Coach. His seat was non-aisle, non-window and above all non-smoking. It was also non-wide and non-comfortable . . .

While it would always be true and fair to say that Richard felt like a cigarette, it would now be doubly true and fair to say it. He felt like a cigarette. And he felt like a cigarette. His mouth was plugged with a gum called Nicoteen. And he wore circular nicotine patches, from the same product stable, on his left forearm and right bicep. Richard's blood brownly brewed, like something left overnight in the teapot. He was a cigarette; and he felt like one. And he still felt like a cigarette . . . What he was doing was practising non-smoking. He knew how Americans treated smokers, people of smoke, people of fire and ash, with their handfuls of dust. He knew he would be asked to do an awful lot of it: non-smoking. So he felt like a cigarette, and he felt like a drink – he felt like a lot of drinks. But he didn't drink and he didn't smoke. All he had was the plastic bottle of mineral water that Gina had made him bring.

Martin Amis, *The Information*, 1995

Parents exposing their children to second-hand smoke is the most common form of child abuse in America.

John Banzhaf III, tobacco activist, quoted in *Time* magazine, 25 October 1993

The Sands of Iwo Jima was a little dated, but it was a good, big-hearted movie. And there was this . . . transfiguring moment where Wayne, having brought his men through hell to victory, exults, 'I never felt so good in my life. How about a cigarette?' And just as he's offering the pack around to his men, a Jap sniper drills him, dead. Without realizing it, Nick took out a cigarette and lit up.

'Da-ad,' Joey said.

Obediently, Nick went outside on the balcony.

Christopher Buckley, *Thank You for Smoking*, 1995

[2]

[Indiana, USA]

When Janice Bone was called into her boss's office only days after starting work as a secretary in an engineering company, the last thing she imagined was that she had failed the mandatory drugs test. But so it proved.

Heroin addict? Crack victim? Acid casualty? Not a bit of it. The routine urine sample taken by the company doctor had shown up traces of the six cigarettes she had smoked the previous weekend. She was fired on the spot.

Giles Coren, 'Sacked for fishin' and smokin'', *Daily Telegraph*, 27 August 1997

One began to suspect that the attack on smoking in America – the industrial world's leading moral exporter – was escalating rather out of hand when in 1996 the attorney general of Texas announced, apparently in all seriousness, that 'history will record the modern-day tobacco industry alongside the worst of civilisation's evil empires'; when a *New York Times* book reviewer suggested that 'only slavery exceeds tobacco as a curse on American history'; when an anti-tobacco activist and plaintiff called tobacco firms 'the most criminal, disgusting, sadistic, degenerate group of people on the face of the earth.' Not long ago an earnest young American assured this newspaper that breathing other people's smoke is morally equivalent to being sprayed with machine-gun fire. Your correspondent (a non-smoker) was reduced to an undignified gape.

'Blowing smoke', *The Economist*, 20 December 1997

A smoker plans to take his former employer to an industrial tribunal, claiming he was sacked for allegedly lighting a cigarette in his car after work.

John Dixon, 54, lost his job as a supervisor at Parkside Flexible Packaging in Leeds, which has a no-smoking policy, after managers videoed a flash in his car as he drove off at the end of his shift.

Mr Dixon, of Outwood, near Wakefield, West Yorks, said he was shown the video nine weeks later and told the 'most reasonable conclusion' for the flash was that he was lighting a cigarette. He denied smoking.

Daily Telegraph, 28 August 1998

[3]

CATHERINE (Sharon Stone): What are you going to do? Charge me
with smoking?
Basic Instinct, 1991

Welcome operates a no-smoking policy, so only non-smokers should
apply.
Welcome Food Ingredients advert in *Job Hunters' Guide*, 10 April 1999

'Brunel Quits Smoking after 141 Years' – headline on a story that
Isambard Kingdom Brunel's trademark cigar had been airbrushed from
a photograph in a . . . tourist brochure.*
Mail on Sunday, 11 October 1998

As soon as I looked at the front page of the October/December 1997
edition of Christian Aid News, I saw advertisements for cigarettes.
The adverts appeared in a photograph of an Indian railway station at
rush hour. The images of people were blurred, showing urgent movement, and the station's adverts for Wills cigarettes were in turn very
clear.

Christian Aid should not – inadvertently or otherwise – promote
cigarette sales.
Letter to *Christian Aid News*, summer 1998

It's ten miles to Gloucester and he isn't sober. But Frank can't be sure
he'd have got it right in Cheltenham. He's out of practice. No whores
since Mel's been in his life. Honour, partly. Love, partly. But mainly
no need of them. Why go to whores to have himself disprized when
he's got Mel?

It's also more difficult now than it was in his heyday to be certain
that the nodding dolly propping up a lamppost with a fag between
her fingers is in fact on the job. There's every chance that she's a

---

* Not a new phenomenon: 'That formidable scholar Dr Samuel Parr, who was the nearest
thing to Dr Johnson that the Whigs could produce, was a tremendous smoker. He maintained
that tobacco preserved the memory, and as Dr Parr could remember being suckled by his
mother his opinion must be respected. Parr's biographer was inclined to attribute
his failure to be offered a bishopric to his smoking. 'His pipe might be deemed in these
fantastic days a degradation at the table of the palace.' There is a portrait of Parr in the
Combination-room at St John's College, Cambridge, in which the pipe he was holding
has been painted out.' Compton Mackenzie, *Sublime Tobacco*, 1957 (For the reasons
behind smoking's unrespectability in the eighteenth century, see Chapter Three.)

company director just slipped out of a strictly non-smoking office to have a puff. Go anywhere you like in the West End during business hours and you see them, loitering on street corners and in doorways, one leg up behind, sucking hard on a Marlboro, and nodding with the stress of the job – whores for all the world. As always, it's morality that makes for harlotry. True, there's little likelihood of his hitting on a company director out smoking in a doorway in Cheltenham at one in the morning, but better to be safe than sorry. Gloucester has a meaner reputation. You can't come to grief in Gloucester. That's to say you can come to grief in Gloucester.

Howard Jacobson, *No More Mister Nice Guy*, 1998

So the Age of Tobacco is passing away (unless the reckless human race is dooming itself to pass away first), bequeathing to posterity a rich store of relics. Museums hold an immense array of pipes, snuff-boxes, and so on, to feed our curiosity and let our minds stray to departed owners who little knew that their treasures would one day repose in glass cases, under our gaze. Even fragments of old clay pipes turned up by the spade or washed up in Thames mud can make us think of the wisps of smoke that once stole through them, and guess at the wisps of thought that passed through their smokers' minds.

Tobacco faces banishment, but this ought not to mean oblivion. It has meant very much to legions of human beings, brought untold comfort to sufferers, performed innumerable small acts of kindness. It has allayed fears, consoled misfortune, lulled anger, called spirits from the vasty deep. A devotee who has abandoned its aid may well say with Macduff:

> I cannot but remember such things were,
> That were most precious to me.

It is time for us to take leave of tobacco, but it should not be an ungrateful farewell.

V. G. Kiernan, *Tobacco: A History*, 1991

The last cigarette smokers in America were located in a box canyon south of Donner Pass in the High Sierra by two federal tobacco agents in a helicopter who spotted the little smoke puffs just before noon. One of them, Ames, the district chief, called in the ground team by air-to-ground radio. Six men in camouflage outfits, members of a crack anti-smoking joggers unit, moved quickly across the rugged terrain, surrounded the bunch in their hideout, subdued them with tear gas, and made them lie face down on the gravel in the hot August sun. There were three females and two males, all in their mid-forties. They had been on the run since the adoption of the Twenty-eighth Amendment.

Ames, a trim, muscular man in neatly pressed khakis who carried a riding crop, paced back and forth along the row of prisoners, their shoe soles motionless. 'What are you people using for brains? Can't you read?' he snapped, flicking the crop at their ankles. He bent down and snatched up an empty Marlboro pack and thrust it in the face of a pale, sweaty man whose breath came in short, terrified gasps. 'Look at this! This warning has been there for decades! Want me to read it to you? Want me to give you the statistics? What does it take to make you understand? Look at me! Speak up! I can't hear you!'

In fact, the smokers had been very subdued since long, long before the acrid tear-gas fumes drifted into their hideout, a narrow cave near the canyon mouth. They knew the end was near. Days before, they had lost radio contact with the only other band of smokers they knew of: five writers holed up in an Oakland apartment. It had been three weeks since the Donner group's last supply drop from the air, forty pounds of barbecued ribs, ten Picnic Tubs of Jimbo deep-fried chicken, and six cartons of smokes, all mentholated. Agents who searched the cave found exactly two cigarettes. There was not a single shred of tobacco found in any of the thousands of discarded butts. The two cigarettes were hidden in the lining of a sleeping bag, and the general disorder in the cave – clothing and personal effects strewn from hell to breakfast – indicated that some smokers had searched frantically for a smoke that very morning. Blackened remnants of what appeared to be cabbage leaves lay in the smoldering campfire.

'Move 'em out of here!' Ames said. 'They disgust me.'

*

Among the personal effects were four empty packs, carefully slit open, the blank insides covered with handwriting. An agent picked them up and put them in a plastic bag, for evidence. They read:

Dear Lindsay & Matt –
This is to let y. know I'm OK & w. friends tho how this w. reach you I dont know. 5 of us are in the mts (dont know where). I never

thot it wld come to this. All those yrs as ashtrays vanishd fr parties & old pals made sarc remarks & FAA crackd down & smoke sect. became closet, I thot if I just was discreet & smokd in prv & took mints I'd get by but then yr dad quit & I had to go undergrnd. Bsmnt, gar., wet twls, A/C, etc. Felt guilty but contd, couldnt stop. Or didnt. Too late for that now. Gotta go on midnt watch. More soon.

Love,
Mother.

My Dear Children –
Down to 1 cart. PlMls. Not my fav. Down to 1 cg/day. After supper. Hate to say it but it tastes fant. So rich, so mild. I know you never approvd. Sorry. In 50s it was diffrnt, we all smokd like movie stars. So gracefl, tak'g cg from pk, the mtch, the lite, one smooth move. Food, sex, then smoke. Lng drags. Lrnd Fr. exh. Then sudd. it was 82 and signs apprd (Thanx for Not S). In my home! Kids naggng like fishwives & yr dad sudd. went out for track. I felt *ambushed*. Bob Dylan smokd, Carson, Beatles. I mean WE'RE NOT CRIMINALS. Sorry. Too late now. More soon.

Love,
Mother.

Dear Kids –
This may be last letter, theyre closing in. Planes o'head every day now. Dogs in dist. Men w. ldspkrs. Flares. Oakland chapt got busted last pm. Was w. them on radio when feds came. Reminded me of when yr dad turnd me in. After supper. Knew he was a nut but didnt know he was a creep. Cops surr. hse, I snk away thru bushes. No time to say g-b to y. Sorry. Wld you believe I quit twice yrs ago, once fr 8 mo. I'm not a terrible wom. y'know. Sorry. Know this is hard on y. Me too. We're down to 2 pks & everybody's tense. Got to go chk perimtr. Goodbye.

Love,
Mother.

Dear L & M –
This is it. They saw us. I have one left and am smokng it now. Gd it tastes gd. My last cg. Then its all over. I'm OK. I'm ready. Its a better thng I do now than I hv ever done. I love you both . . .

*

The five smokers were handcuffed and transported to a federal deten-
tion camp in Oregon, where they were held in pup tents for months.
They were charged with conspiracy to obtain, and willful possession
of, tobacco, and were convicted in minutes, and were sentenced to
write twenty thousand words apiece on the topic 'Personal Integrity'
by a judge who had quit cigarettes when the price went to thirty-five
cents and he could not justify the expense.

The author of the letters was soon reunited with her children, and
one night, while crossing a busy intersection near their home in
Chicago, she saved them from sure death by pulling them back from
the path of a speeding car. Her husband, who had just been telling
her she could stand to lose some weight, was killed instantly, however.

Garrison Keillor, *We Are Still Married*, 1989

It is understandable that the man who, on any attempt at smoking, is
made to realize that he is allergic to the weed will be no advocate on
its behalf, but most non-smokers are wonderfully tolerant about it . . .

Sidney Russ, *Smoking and Its Effects: With Special Reference to Lung Cancer*, 1955

The old defiance

Will lit a cigarette, and Fiona made a face and wafted the smoke
away. Will hated people who did that in places where they had no
right to do so. He wasn't going to apologize for smoking in a pub; in
fact, what he was going to do was single-handedly create a fug so
thick that they would be unable to see each other.

Nick Hornby, *About a Boy*, 1998.

[Dennis Potter's Last Interview]

DENNIS POTTER: You don't mind this cigarette? I just . . . now . . . I
mean, I always have smoked, but . . .

MELVYN BRAGG: *Why should I mind?*

DP: Well, people do nowadays. You get so bloody nervous smoking.

MB: *It's all right, I'm a very passive smoker.*

DP: Thank God I don't have to go to America any more . . . because
I remember asking a waiter in America at breakfast for an ashtray

as he was turning away, and it was just as though I'd shot him in the back. It's easier to pull a gun in America than a cigarette out of your pocket. But I like to go in the . . . there is a remnant left on the train – I do, of course, travel first class; I mean, I enjoy money and spending it . . . money, I like it . . . but in the remnant of the first-class train, InterCity, there is one bit for smokers, and if I . . . I love to see . . . if I see people sitting there without a cigarette, I love to say, 'You do know this is a smoking compartment, don't you?' Because I've so many, you know . . . 'You do know you're not allowed to smoke here.' But of course now I'm just virtually chain-smoking, because there's no point in . . . There's so many things, like I can't keep food down any more – I can't have a meal, my digestive system's gone, but I can drink things, and those prepared, those horrible chemical things with all the minerals and stuff in them, but I can add a dash of this and that to it, which I do, and . . . like cream, like cholesterol, aawww! I can break any rule now, you know, I can do it . . . but the cigarette, well, I love stroking this lovely tube of delight. Look at it (*laughter*).

MB: *I've packed in. Now stop, or I'll be smoking again in a minute, Dennis, with you.*

Dennis Potter, *Seeing the Blossom*, 1994

Smokers for Celibacy

Some of us are a little tired of hearing that cigarettes kill.
We'd like to warn you about another way of making yourself ill:

we suggest that in view of AIDS, herpes, chlamydia, cystitis and NSU,
not to mention genital warts and cervical cancer and the proven
   connection between the two,

if you want to avoid turning into physical wrecks
what you should give up is not smoking but sex.

We're sorry if you're upset,
but think of the grisly things you might otherwise get.

We can't see much point in avoiding emphysema at sixty-five
if that's an age at which you have conspicuously failed to arrive,

and as for cancer, it is a depressing fact

that at least for women this disease is more likely to occur in the
   reproductive tract.

We could name friends of ours who died that way, if you insist,
but we feel sure you can each provide your own list.

You'll notice we don't mention syphilis and gonorrhea;
well, we have now, so don't get the idea

that, just because of antibiotics, quaint old clap and pox
are not still being generously spread around by men's cocks.

Some of us aren't too keen on the thought of micro-organisms
   travelling up into our brain
and giving us General Paralysis of the Insane.

We're opting out of one-night stands:
we'd rather have a cigarette in our hands.

If it's a choice between two objects of cylindrical shape
we go for the one that is seldom if ever guilty of rape.

Cigarettes just lie there quietly in their packs
waiting until you call on one of them to help you relax.

They aren't moody: they don't go in for sexual harassment and
   threats,
or worry about their performance as compared with that of other
   cigarettes,

nor do they keep you awake all night telling you the story of their
   life,
beginning with their mother and going on until morning about their
   first wife.

Above all, the residues they leave in your system are thoroughly
   sterilised and clean,
which is more than can be said for the products of the human
   machine.

Altogether, we've come to the conclusion that sex is a drag.
   Just give us a fag.

Fleur Adcock, *Time Zones*, 1991

I do not know how anyone gets to bed with anyone without fags. They are such handy little gifts! All that delicate potential for bridging silences, confirming tastes, offering and accepting, exchanges, confessions of needs, touchings, longings and ambitions! And fags are now the perfect way to tell who among a gang of people is worth meeting: if you want to filter out the people who believe in Eternal Life Assurance, then smoking is your thing, be it workplace, plane, train or party: it is the surest statistical indicator that whoever it is belongs to the blessed tribe of the slightly fucked up. This is especially true of Americans: if ever you meet an educated Yank who smokes and does not appear to be completely MAF (Mad As Fuck), shift into Friendship-Offering Mode without delay, it is almost sure to be worth it.

James Hawes, *A White Merc with Fins*, 1996

ANNETTE INSDORF: It's also one of the very few American films of recent years in which the characters take pleasure in smoking. And there's no one walking into the frame telling them not to do it.

PAUL AUSTER: Well, the fact is that people smoke. If I'm not mistaken, more than a billion people light up around the world every day. I know the anti-smoking lobby in this country has grown very strong in the last few years, but Puritanism has always been with us. In one way or another, the teetotalers and zealots have always been a force in American life. I'm not saying that smoking is good for you, but compared to the political and social and ecological outrages committed every day, tobacco is a minor issue. People smoke. That's a fact. People smoke, and they enjoy it, even if it isn't good for them.

AI: You won't get an argument from me.

PA: I'm just guessing now, but maybe all this is connected to the way the characters act in the film . . . to what you might call an undogmatic view of human behavior. Does this sound too far-fetched? I mean, no one is simply one thing or the other. They're all filled with contradictions, and they don't live in a world that breaks down neatly into good guys and bad guys.

'The Making of *Smoke*', in *Smoke and Blue in the Face: Two Films by Paul Auster*, 1995

Smoking, once again, is hot in the entertainment media. Half the movies released between 1990 and 1995 featured a major character who chose to light up on screen, a significant increase compared with 29 percent in the 1970's, according to a recent study at the University of California, San Francisco. And the trend appears to be accelerating. In her syndicated column earlier this month, Hillary Rodham Clinton noted that 77 percent of all films last year had scenes depicting smoking, as did every film nominated for best picture at the Academy Awards. She went on to denounce films that 'equate smoking with status, power, confidence and glamour.' Mrs Clinton cites these facts in order to blame Hollywood for an increase in teen-age smoking, 'despite,' she says, 'the best efforts of parents and teachers to educate children about the dangerous effects of tobacco.'

There can be no doubt about those efforts. In the last four and a half years, American teenagers have been the object of the most sustained and systematic anti-smoking campaign ever mounted, directed at them from their earliest age by every adult institution of authority, particularly by the Clinton White House. Yet teen-age smoking during the same period has increased alarmingly. The President himself announced a 30 percent increase in smoking among 10th graders and 40 percent among 9th graders. Children are smoking more and starting earlier.

Who can doubt that they are being influenced by the new aura of cool that surrounds smoking in the media? When television isn't preaching the evils of tobacco, it's putting cigarettes in the hands of unlikable characters, the ones we love to hate. On the silver screen, the sexiest, most bewitching stars make smoking look glamorous again. Somewhere along the way, all that preaching has backfired.

Richard Klein, 'After the Preaching, the Lure of the Taboo', *New York Times*, 24 August 1997

The first non-smoking bar in Paris has been greeted with a mass boycott. A week after La Belle Hortense removed its ashtrays, turnover has plunged by 90 per cent, but owner Xavier Denamur insists they will be sticking to their *non-fumeur* policy.

Evening Standard, 8 June 1999

As ever, Torquil was already installed at the bar and half way into his drink – whisky, judging by the smell on his breath. He offered Lorimer one of his cigarettes and was politely turned down. Lorimer ordered a triple vodka and soda with plenty of ice – Rintoul's last words were still echoing in his inner ear.

'That's right, you don't smoke,' Torquil said incredulously. 'Why not? Everybody smokes.'

'Well, not everybody. Two-thirds of us don't.'

'Rubbish. All smoking statistics are lies, I tell you, Lorimer. Every government in the world lies about them, they have to. Smoking's on the increase worldwide and it suits them fine, though they daren't admit it. So they routinely churn out these figures. But take a look around you.'

'You're probably right,' Lorimer conceded. True enough, of the fifty or so people in El Hombre Guapo, ninety-eight per cent were smoking and the other two per cent looked like they were about to smoke any minute, rummaging in pockets and handbags for their cigarettes.

William Boyd, *Armadillo*, 1998

Friday, November 28th William is a lovely boy – especially when slightly sedated by prescription drugs. I am writing this in the hospital restaurant – Nightingales. I am alone in the seventy-seat non-smoking section. Whereas the small smoking section is crammed full of doctors and nurses.

Sue Townsend, *Adrian Mole: The Cappuccino Years*, 1999

PART ONE

The History of Smoking

CHAPTER ONE

The First Accounts

My dear friend,
My Greenhouse fronted with Myrtles, and where I hear nothing but the pattering of a fine shower and the sound of distant thunder, wants only the fumes of your pipe to make it perfectly delightfull. Tobacco was not known in the Golden age. So much the worse for the Golden age. This age of Iron or Lead would be insupportable without it, and therefore we may reasonably suppose that the Happiness of those better days would have been much improved by the Use of it.

William Cowper, Letter to William Bull, 3 June 1783

One of the great advantages of compiling a smoking anthology is that because tobacco was unknown to Europeans until the discovery of the New World you don't have to start with Homer, *Beowulf* or Chaucer. You do, however, have to start with amateur anthropologists of the fifteenth and sixteenth centuries – some of whom are far from reliable. Oviedo, for example, not only gives us the first of the many false derivations of the word tobacco, but also – unless tobacco strength has decreased alarmingly since he wrote of its stupor-inducing properties – may have been confusing it with other drugs. Or he may have been out to stop this pagan habit from spreading because it *was* pagan. Certainly Las Casas, an early champion of Indian rights, denounced Oviedo as a murderer, pillager and all-round enemy of the native people.

From the early accounts, though, two indisputable facts do emerge. First, the five main ways we now know of taking tobacco – by pipe, cigar, cigarette, chewing and as snuff – were all present and correct in the Americas when the first Europeans landed. Tobacco enemas were there too, but fortunately don't qualify for this book, although they were used in Europe to loosen the bowels, and to treat cholera until well into the nineteenth century – hence their mention in the 1857 *Lancet* debate in Chapter Four. (In eighteenth-century Britain, incidentally, there was a short-lived vogue for blowing tobacco smoke up the patient's bottom with a pair of bellows as an aid to artificial respiration in drowning cases.)

Second, the Spanish on the whole ended up in the Southern Americas, where the proto-cigar predominated; the British in the North, where the Native-Americans used pipes. As a result, for more than 200 years, while the Spanish puffed cigars, smoking in Britain essentially meant pipe-smoking. It wasn't until the Peninsula War took the rest of Europe to Spain that cigars became more widespread.

But I can't put it off any longer. Here come those fifteenth- and sixteenth-century anthropologists . . .

We found a man in a canoe going from [the island of] Santa Maria to Fernandia. He had with him . . . some dried leaves which are in high value among them, for a quantity of it was brought to me at San Salvador.

Christopher Columbus, Journal entry for 15 October 1492 (three days after his first landing at San Salvador)

[Columbus sends two men* inland]

The Spaniards upon their journey met with great multitudes of people, men and women with firebrands in their hands and herbs to smoke after their custom.

Christopher Columbus, Journal entry for 6 November 1492

[And the fuller version . . .]

These two Christians found on the way . . . many people, the men with a half burned wood in their hands and certain herbs in order to take their smokes, which are some dry herbs put in a certain leaf, also dry, in the manner of a musket made of paper, like those the boys make on the day of the Passover of the Holy Ghost, and having lighted one part of it, by the other they suck, absorb or receive that smoke inside with the breath, by which they become benumbed and almost drunk, and so it is said that they do not feel fatigue. These muskets, as we will call them, they call tobacco (*tabacos*) . . .

Bishop, Bartolomé de Las Casas, *History of the Indies, c.* 1535

Among other evil practices, the Indians have one that is especially harmful, the inhaling of a certain kind of smoke which they call

---

* One was Rodrigo de Jérez, later imprisoned by the Spanish Inquisition for smoking.

tobacco, in order to produce a state of stupor ... The caciques employed a tube, shaped like a Y, inserting the forked extremities in their nostrils and the tube itself in the lighted weed; in this way they would inhale the smoke until they became unconscious and lay sprawling on the earth like men in a drunken slumber. Those who could not procure the right sort of wood took their smoke through a hollow reed (*cañuela*); it is this that the Indians call *tabacco*, and not the weed nor its effects, as some have supposed. They prize this herb very highly, and plant it in their orchards or on their farms for the purpose mentioned above.

I cannot imagine what pleasure they derive from this practice, unless it be the drinking which invariably precedes the smoking. I am aware that some Christians have already adopted the habit, especially those who have contracted syphilis, for they say that in the state of ecstasy caused by the smoke they no longer feel their pain. In my opinion the man who acts thus merely passes while still alive into a deathly stupor. It seems to me that it would be better to suffer the pain, which they make their excuse, for it is certain that smoking will never cure the disease. Lately too many of the negroes who live in this town, and indeed in all parts of the island, have acquired the habit. They grow the plant on their owners' farms and inhale its smoke, for they say that if they take tobacco when their day's work is over they forget their fatigue. It seems to me that here we have a bad and pernicious custom.

Gonzalo Fernandez de Oviedo y Valdes, *Historia general y natural de las Indias*, 1535

[In Brazil]

There is another secret herb which they name in their language *Petun*, the which most commonly they bear about them, for that they esteem it marvellous profitable for many things ... They gather this herb very charily, and dry it within their little cabanes or houses. Their manner to use it is this; they wrap a quantity of this herb being dry in a leaf of a Palm tree which is very great, and so they make rolls of the length of a candle, and then they fire the one end, and receive the smoke thereof by their nose and by their mouth. They say it is very wholesome to cleanse and consume the superfluous humours of the brain. Moreover being taken after this sort, it keepeth the parties from hunger and thirst for a time, therefore they use it ordinarily. Also when they have any secret talk or counsel among themselves, they draw this smoke, and then they speak. The which they do customably one after another in the councils of war . . . The women use it by no means. If that they take too much of this perfume, it will make them light in the head, as the smell or taste of strong wine. The Christians that do now inhabit there are become very desirous of this herb and perfume, although that the first use thereof is not without danger, before that one is accustomed thereto, for this smoke causeth sweats and weakness, even to fall into a syncope, the which I have tried myself.

Frère André Thevet, *Les Singularités de la France Antarctique, autrement nommé Amérique*, 1557 (trans. Thomas Hacker as *The New Found Worlde*, 1568)

[In Canada, 1535–6]

Furthermore they have a plant, of which a large supply is collected in summer for the winter's consumption . . . They hold it in high esteem, though the men alone make use of it in the following manner. After drying it in the sun, they carry it about their necks in a small skin pouch in lieu of a bag, together with a hollow bit of stone or wood . . . Then at frequent intervals they crumble this plant into powder, which they place in one of the openings of the hollow instrument, and laying a live coal on top, suck at the other end to such an extent, that they fill their bodies so full of smoke, that it streams out of their mouths and nostrils as from a chimney. They say it keeps them warm and in good health, and never go about without these things . . . We made a trial of this smoke. When it is in one's mouth, one would think one had taken powdered pepper, it is so hot.

The Voyages of Jacques Cartier, trans. H. P. Biggar, 1924

There is an herb which is sowed apart by itself and is called by the inhabitants *Uppówoc*. In the West Indies it hath divers names, according to the several places and countries where it groweth and is used: the Spaniards generally call it *Tabacco*. The leaves thereof being dried and brought into powder, they use to take the fume or smoke thereof by sucking it through pipes made of clay into their stomachs and head; from whence it purgeth superfluous steam and other gross humours, openeth all the pores and passages of the body; by which means the use thereof not only preserveth the body from obstructions, but also if any be, so that they have not been of too long continuance,

in short time breaketh them; whereby their bodies are notably preserved in health, and know not many grievous diseases wherewithal
we in England are oftentimes afflicted.

This *Uppówoc* is of so precious estimation amongst them, that they
think their gods are marvellously delighted therewith. Whereupon
sometime they make hallowed fires and cast some of the powder
therein for a sacrifice; being in a storm upon the waters, to pacify
their gods, they cast some up into the air and into the water: so a
weir for fish being newly set up, they cast some therein and into the
air: also after an escape from danger, they cast some into the air
likewise: but all done with strange gestures, stamping, sometime
dancing, clapping of hands, holding up of hands, and staring up into
the heavens, uttering therewithal and chattering strange words and
noises.

We ourselves during the time we were there used to suck it after
their manner, as also since our return, and have found many rare and
wonderful experiments of the virtues thereof, of which the relation
would require a volume of itself: the use of it by so many of late, men
and women of great calling as else, and some learned Physicians also,
is sufficient witness.

Thomas Hariot, *A Brief and True Account of the New Found Land of Virginia*, 1588

[The only mention of tobacco in the books of Sir Walter Raleigh]

Those called Cupuri and Macureo are for the most part Carpenters
of *Canoas*, for they make the most and fayrest houses, and sell them
into Guiana for golde, and into *Trinedado* for *Tobacco*, in the excessive
taking whereof they exceed all nations, and notwithstanding the moist-
ness of the aire in which they live . . . in all my life either in the Indies
or in Europe did I never beholde a more goodlie or better favoured
people, or more manlie.

*The Discoverie of the Large Rich and Bewtiful Empire of Guiana, with a relation of
the Great and Golden Citie of Manoa (which the Spaniards call El Dorado)*, 1595

[And a final prophecy]

[Tobacco] is planted, gathered, seasoned, and made up fit for the
Merchant in short time, and with easy labour. But when we first
arrived in Guiana we altogether wanted the true skill and knowledge
how to order it, which now of late we happily have learned of the

Spaniards themselves whereby I dare presume to say . . . that only this commodity Tobacco (so much sought after and desired) will bring as great a benefit and profit to the undertakers,* as ever the Spaniards gained by the best and richest Silver mine in all their Indies considering the charge of both.

Robert Harcourt, *A Voyage to Guiana*, 1613

* The people who undertake the business (obviously).

CHAPTER TWO

Arrival in Europe to Global Domination

For you see many sailors, all of whom have returned from
[the New World] carrying small tubes . . . [which] they light
with fire, and, opening their mouths wide and breathing in,
they suck in as much smoke as they can . . . in this way they
say their hunger and thirst are allayed, their strength is
restored and their sprits are refreshed; they asseverate that
their brains are lulled by a joyous intoxication.

Matthias de l'Obel, botanist, 1570

A scrupulously observed, but ultimately pointless, tradition of tobacco histories is to agonise for page after page as to who first brought the 'Indian weed' into Britain/Europe/popular use, before deciding that nobody knows and that it doesn't matter much anyway. Stow's *Annales of England*, under the year 1614, might appear to clear the question up – at least as far as Britain and popular use are concerned. First it states that 'Tobacco was first brought, and made known in England by Sir John Hawkins about the year one thousand five hundred sixty five, but not used by Englishmen in many years after, though at this day commonly used . . .' It then adds in a marginal note that 'Sir Walter Raleigh was the first that brought tobacco into use, when all men wondered what it meant.' Unfortunately, this seems no less based on guesswork, hearsay and wishful thinking than any later attempts to nail the culprits or honour the heroes, according to taste.

Raleigh, of course, remains the choice of British legend, and was certainly linked to smoking from its earliest times – not least by James I. Yet, as you can see from the J. M. Barrie passage below, even by 1890 these claims were known to be largely mythical.* Other candidates have included Sir Francis

---

* Naturally, Compton Mackenzie saw the myth as further proof of how great smokers are: 'It is a tribute to the larger view of life that smokers in general were able to take compared with non-smokers that they recognised who it was that more than anybody made tobacco a vital contribution to the greatness of that magical alloy of peoples we call British. Whatever the meticulous and grudging historian may declare, it is to Sir Walter that we owe the popularity of tobacco.'

Drake, Ralph Lane (the first governor of Virginia), Thomas Hariot and any number of unnamed sailors. In fact, nobody knows and it doesn't matter much anyway.

What does seem clear – albeit in the usual messy and overlapping way of its history – is that tobacco was initially seen as medicinal in Europe. Only later did its use, like that of many new drugs over the centuries, move from the pharmaceutical to the recreational. And tobacco's reputation as a curative was created by two men in particular. While serving as the French Ambassador to the king of Portugal from 1559 to 1561, Jean Nicot was given both a tobacco plant and stories of its healing properties. He used poultices of it to treat the ulcers and wounds of his domestic staff with apparent success, then presented some seeds to Catherine de Medici, the Queen Mother, in Paris, where more miracle cures were soon reported – and where the French Court's taste for snuff soon developed. (Nobody there appears to have thought of smoking the stuff.) Nicot was commemorated immediately in the Latin name given to the plant, and again when the alkaloid present in tobacco was discovered in 1828.

The other champion of the new herb's powers was Nicolas Monardes, a Seville doctor, whose 1571 work, translated into English as *Joyfull Newes Out of the Newe Founde Worlde*, listed more than twenty ailments, including cancer, which could be cured by tobacco. It was thanks to Monardes that the early supporters of smoking in Britain tended to defend it not as harmless but as a panacea. His influence may also explain why for a while tobacco could be bought only from apothecaries, and why the first two references to it in English Literature proper – in Spenser and Lyly – are medicinal. (It should perhaps be borne in mind that Spenser and Raleigh were close friends.)

But not everybody saw it that way. Most famously, in 1604, James I published *A Counterblaste to Tobacco*. (It should definitely be borne in mind that James and Raleigh were sworn enemies – note the King's attack on tobacco's 'hated' father, and the fact that he later had Raleigh executed.) Originally, this was an anonymous work, but once its true, if unsurprising, authorship was revealed, royal favourites queued up to echo their master – led by Joshua Sylvester, the court poet, whose *Tobacco Battered* runs to more than 800 lines. Even Ben Jonson joined in the sycophancy when *The Gipsies Metamorphosed* was performed for His Majesty. Among all the talk of humours, though, the anti-tobacco case of the early sixteenth century had some surprisingly modern objections, up to and including the low birth-weight of children. The fad for smoking among London gallants also came in for much satire from poets and playwrights, and in many cases was seen as evidence of the national decline. None of which prevented the King from realising that a profit could be made. Introducing the first tax on tobacco, the same year as *A Counterblaste*, he achieved another first – by arguing that his primary motive was a concern for public health. In 1624, the year before his death, tobacco became a royal monopoly.

Meanwhile, in other parts of the world, rulers did more than publish pamphlets and impose taxes to stop their subjects from taking up the new habit. They were no more successful than James. And smoking started to spread faster than ever during the Thirty Years' War (1618–48), which set the pattern of soldiers learning about the habit from each other. (As I've already said, cigars were spread by the Peninsula War. As I will say, the Crimean War and the First World War both gave cigarettes an important boost.)

The following chapter attempts to trace all these developments – and to continue the story until the end of the eighteenth century when tobacco was big business and smoking seemed to have routed its enemies forever. In passing, I've included a few of the many theories about why, when his contemporaries wrote so much on the subject, Shakespeare doesn't mention tobacco once; accounts of how tobacco-growing in England was stamped out at the request of the Virginian settlers; and evidence of the widespread belief that smoking could prevent the plague.

———

Many hundreds of volumes have been written about the glories of the Elizabethan age, the sublime period in our history. Then were Englishmen on fire to do immortal deeds. High aims and noble ambitions became their birthright. There was nothing they could not or would not do for England. Sailors put a girdle round the world. Every captain had a general's capacity, every fighting-man could have been a captain. All the women, from the Queen downwards, were heroines. Lofty statesmanship guided the conduct of affairs, a sublime philosophy was in the air. The period of great deeds was also the period of our richest literature. London was swarming with poetic geniuses. Immortal dramatists wandered in couples between stage-doors and taverns.

All this has been said many times, and we read these glowing outbursts about the Elizabethan age as if to the beating of a drum. But why was this period riper for magnificent deeds and noble litera-ture than any other in English history? We all know how the thinkers, historians, and critics of yesterday and to-day answer that question; but our hearts and brains tell us that they are astray. By an amazing oversight they have said nothing of the Influence of Tobacco. The Elizabethan age might be better named the beginning of the smoking era. No unprejudiced person who has given thought to the subject can question the propriety of dividing our history into two periods – the pre-smoking and the smoking. When Raleigh, in honour of whom England should have changed its name, introduced tobacco into this country, the glorious Elizabethan age began. I am aware that those hateful persons called Original Researchers now maintain that Raleigh was not the man; but to them I turn a deaf ear. I know, I feel, that with the introduction of tobacco England woke up from a long sleep. Suddenly a new zest had been given to life. The glory of existence became a thing to speak of. Men who had hitherto only concerned themselves with the narrow things of home put a pipe into their mouths and became philosophers. Poets and dramatists smoked until all ignoble ideas were driven from them, and into their place rushed such high thoughts as the world had not known before. Petty jealousies no longer had hold of statesmen, who smoked, and agreed to work together for the public weal. Soldiers and sailors felt when engaged with a foreign foe, that they were fighting for their pipes. The whole country was stirred by the ambition to live up to tobacco.

J. M. Barrie, *My Lady Nicotine*, 1890

Tobacco the healer

[Belphoebe tends the injured Timias]

Into the woods thenceforth in hast she went,
To seeke for hearbes, that mote him remedy;
For she of harbes had great intendiment,
Taught of her Nymphe, which from her infancy
Her nourced had in trew Nobility:
There, whether it diuine *Tobacco* were,
Or *Panachœa*, or *Polygony*,
She found, and brought it to her patient deare
Who al this while lay bleeding out his hart-bloud neare.

Edmund Spenser, *The Faerie Queene*, Book III, 1590

Who has ever found a more sovereign remedy against coughs, rheum in the stomach, head and eyes? . . . In few, I think there is nothing that harms a man from his girdle upward, but may be taken away with a moderate use of *Tobacco*, and in those parts consist the chief reasons of our health, for the stomach and head being clear and void of evil humours, commonly the whole body is the better.

Anthony Chute, *Tobacco*, 1595*

> PANDORA [who has just wounded her lover with a spear]:
> Gather me balme and cooling violets,
> And of our holy herb nicotian,
> And bring withall pure honey from the hive,
> That I may here compound a wholesome salve,
> To heal the wound of my unhappy hand.
>
> John Lyly, *The Woman in the Moon*, 1597

[Tobacco] cureth any grief, dolour, imposture, or obstruction proceeding of cold or wind, especially in the head or breast. The fume taken in a pipe is good against rheums, catarrhs, hoarseness, ache in the head, stomach, lungs, breast: also in want of meat, drink, sleep or rest.

Henry Buttes, *Dyets Dry Dinner*, 1599

> I sing the loves of the superior powers,
> With the fair mother of all fragrant flowers:
> From which first love a glorious Simple springs,
> Belov'd of heav'nly Gods, and earthly Kings.
> Let others in their wanton verses chant
> A beauteous face that doth their senses daunt,
> And on their Muses' wings lift to the sky
> The radiant beams of an enchanting eye.
> Me let the sound of great *Tobacco*'s praise
> A pitch above those lovesick poets raise:
> Let me adore with my thrice-happy pen
> The sweet and sole delight of mortal men,
> The Cornucopia of all earthly pleasure,
> Where bankrupt Nature hath consum'd her treasure,
> A worthy plant springing from Flora's hand,

---

* The first work in English devoted to tobacco. Chute's authorship was proved in a 1931 essay in *Review of English Studies* by Robert J. Kane. Kane's essay also proves that in 1931 it was still permissible to use 'the divine weed' and 'the divine herb' as synonyms for tobacco in academic writing.

The blessed offspring of an uncouth land.
Breath-giving herb, none other I invoke
To help me paint the praise of sugared smoke . . .
Teach me what power thee on earth did place,
What God was bounteous to the human race,
On what occasion, and by whom it stood,
That the blest world received so great a good . . .

Who takes this med'cine need not greatly care,
Who *Galenists*, who *Paraclesians* are:
Nor need he seek their *Rosaries*, their *Summes*,
Their *Secrets*, their *Dispensatoriums*:
Nor fill his pocket with their costly bills,
Nor stuff his maw with their unsavoury pills,
Nor make huge pitfalls in his tender veins,
With thousand other more than hellish pains,
But by this herb's celestial quality
May keep his health in mirth and jollity:
It is the fountain whence all pleasure springs,
A potion for imperial crowned Kings:
He that is master of so rich a store,
May laugh at Croesus, and esteem him poor,
And with his smoky sceptre in his fist
Securely flout the toiling alchemist,
Who daily labours with a vain expense
In distillations of the quintessence,
Not knowing that this golden herb alone
Is the philosopher's admired stone . . .
It is the sponge that wipes out all our woe:
'Tis like the thorn that doth on *Pelion* grow,
With which whoe'er his frosty limbs anoints,
Shall feel no cold in his benumbed joints;
'Tis like the river, which whoe'er doth taste,
Forgets his present griefs and sorrows past . . .

Sir John Beaumont, *The Metamorphosis of Tobacco*, 1602

The debate begins

A woeful exclamation late I heard,
Wherewith Tobacco takers may be fear'd:
One at the point with pipe and leaf to part,
Did vow Tobacco worse than death's black dart:
And prov'd it thus: You know (quoth he) my friends
Death only stabs the heart, and so life ends:
But this same poison, steeped India weed,
In head, heart, lungs, doth soot and cobwebs breed.
With that he gasp'd and breath'd out such a smoke
That all the standers-by were like to choke.

Samuel Rowlands, *Epigram 18*, in *The Letting of Humors Blood in the Head-Vaine*, 1600

The first full-length attack on smoking in England was *Work for Chimney-Sweepers or A Warning to Tobacconists**(1601) by 'Philarates', who listed, and then amplified, eight objections to tobacco, including the clincher that 'the first author and finder hereof was the Devil'. All eight points were denied, one by one, in the genial *A Defence of Tobacco: With a Friendly Answer to the late printed Book called* Work for Chimney-Sweepers (1602) – usually ascribed to a doctor called Roger Marbeck. He concluded that, rather than tobacco coming from the Devil, 'it were more charitable to think that it came from God, who is the author of all good gifts'. Here's a brief flavour of the debate:

And if any man be so far blinded by tobacco that he will not admit for true that the vapour or fume thereof ascending to the brain is dark and swart of colour . . . let him but cast his eyes on the smoke issuing forth of the nostrils of the tobacconists, or the smoky tincture left in the tobacco pipe after the receipt thereof, and he shall easily reclaim his error. This swart and sootish tincture cleaveth so fast to the inward part of the pipe as hardly by any means but by the extreme heat of the fire it may be cleared from thence. And no doubt the like impression doth the same leave in our brains and in the cavities thereof.

Work for Chimney-Sweepers

* *Tobacconist* was the usual word for tobacco-smoker in the early days. It didn't come to mean a seller of tobacco until the middle of the seventeenth century.

As for the reason that you bring, to prove tobacco to leave in our brain a black, swart sootish tincture, because it doth all to be-black the pipe wherein it is taken; o Lord, it is a very weak reason. For between your dead and senseless pipes, made of earth or otherwise; and the lively cavities, passages and pipes of our breathing and living bodies, there is no likelihood or comparison to be made.

And for the proof hereof, let us not stand now upon making of school syllogisms: but let us fall to a flat demonstration: and one demonstration, you know very well, is worth five syllogisms. My demonstration, then, at a word is this: look but into the throats and nostrils of all the great tobacco takers: view them well, I say, and pry into their noses as much as you please, and I will lay what wager you will, that you shall find them as fair nosed gentlemen, and as clean mouthed and throated, as any man alive, I will warrant you.

A Defence of Tobacco

The King joins in

That the manifold abuses of this vile custom of Tobacco taking, may the better be espied, it is fit, that first you enter into consideration both of the first original thereof, and likewise of the reasons of the first entry thereof into this Country. For certainly as such customs, that have their first institution either from a godly, necessary, or honourable ground, and are first brought in, by the means of some worthy, virtuous, and great Personage, are ever, and most justly, holden in great and reverent estimation and account, by all wise, virtuous, and temperate spirits: so should it by the contrary, justly bring a great disgrace into that sort of customs, which having their original from base corruption and barbarity, do in like sort, make their first entry into a Country, by an inconsiderate and childish affectation of novelty as is the true case of the first invention of Tobacco taking, and of the first entry thereof among us.

['The first invention']

Tobacco . . . was first found out by some of the barbarous Indians . . . And now good Countrymen, let us (I pray you) consider, what honour or policy can move us to imitate the barbarous and beastly manners of the wild, godless, and slavish Indians, especially in so vile and stinking a custom? ... Why do we not as well imitate them in walking naked as they do? In preferring glasses, feathers, and such toys to gold and precious stones, as they do? Yea, why do we not deny God and adore the Devil as they do?

['The first entry among us']

Now to the corrupted baseness of the first use of this Tobacco, doth very well agree the foolish and groundless first entry thereof into this Kingdom. It is not so long since the first entry of this abuse amongst us here ... both the first Author, and the form of the first introduction of it, amongst us. It was neither brought in by King, great Conqueror, nor learned Doctor of Physic.

With the report of a great discovery for a Conquest, some two or three savage men, were brought in, together with this Savage custom. But the pity is, the poor wild barbarous men died, but that vile barbarous custom is yet alive, yea, in fresh vigour; so as it seems a miracle to me, how a custom springing from so vile a ground, and brought in by a father so generally hated, should be welcomed upon so slender a warrant.

[Passive smoking]

And for the vanities committed in this filthy custom, is it not both great vanity and uncleanness, that at the table, a place of respect, of cleanliness, of modesty, men should not be ashamed, to sit tossing of Tobacco pipes, and puffing of the smoke of Tobacco one to another, making the filthy smoke and stink thereof, to exhale athwart the dishes, and infect the air, when very often, men that abhor it are at their repast? Surely Smoke becomes a kitchen far better than a dining chamber, and yet it makes a kitchen also oftentimes in the inward parts of men, soiling and infecting them, with an unctuous and oily kind of Soot as hath been found in some Tobacco takers, that after their death were opened.

[And the big finish . . .]

Have you not reason then to be ashamed, and to forbear this filthy novelty so basely grounded, so foolishly received and so grossly mistaken in the right use thereof? In your abuse thereof sinning against God, harming yourselves both in persons and goods, and taking also thereby the marks and notes of vanity upon you: by the custom thereof making yourselves to be wondered at by all foreign civil Nations, and by all strangers that come among you, to be scorned and condemned. A custom loathsome to the eye, hateful to the nose, harmful to the brain, dangerous to the lungs, and in the black stinking fume thereof, nearest resembling the horrible Stygian smoke of the pit that is bottomless.

James I, *A Counterblaste to Tobacco*, 1604

Although the use of the smoking apparatus, that funnel, or (as it is generally called) pipe, has developed into a regular custom among our better classes, just as once it was fashionable in Athens to play on the double flute, yet as Alcibiades and Pallas Athene rejected the double pipe, so our heroes and heroines ought to despise, break, and cast away these foul, ugly, and stinking tobacco-pipes. But why should I cite Alcibiades or Pallas, when here we have King James, far mightier, wiser and more learned than Alcibiades, and his lady, the Queen, as wise as Pallas Athene, both of whom not only mislike but even hate such stench and dirt.

Dr Warner, the King's physician. Closing speech at a debate on smoking in which the King participated, Oxford, 27 August 1605. (Undergraduates were forbidden to smoke while James was in the city)

Two smoky engines, in this later age
(Satan's short circuit; the more sharp his rage.)
Have been invented by too-wanted wit,
Or rather, vented from th'infernal pit,
Guns and Tobacco-pipes, with fire and smoke,
(At least) a third part of mankind to choke:
(Which haply th'Apocalypse foretold)
Yet of the two, we may (think I) be bold,
In some respects, to think the last the worst,
(However both in their effects accurst.)
For Guns shot fromward, only at their foen;
Tobacco-pipes, homeward, into their own.

Joshua Sylvester (*c.* 1563–1618), a court poet of James I,
Tobacco Battered

[The Devil breaks wind]

And there he made such a breach with the wind,
   The hole too standing open the while,
That the scent of the vapour before and behind,
   Hath foully perfumed most part of the isle.

And this was tobacco, the learned suppose,
   Which since in country, court, and town,
In the devil's glister-pipe smokes at the nose,
   Of polecat and madam, of gallant and clown.

From which wicked weed, with swine's flesh and ling,
   Or any thing else that's feast for the fiend:
Our captain, and we cry, God save the king,
   And send him good meat, and mirth without end.

Ben Jonson, *A Masque of the Gipsies Metamorphosed*, 1621.
(These three stanzas were added to the original manuscript,
presumably to impress the King, before whom the Masque was
performed)

———————

[Smoking may reduce the birth-weight of your child]

   'Tis true, tobacconists; why do you swell
   With anger at the truth? Ere seven years end
   Tobacco will the baneful force extend.
   It breeds a wheezing in a narrow breast,
   The hectic fever or thick phlegm at least.
   A bastard heat within the veins it leaves,
   Which spoils the infant if the wife conceives.

   Sir William Vaughan, *Three Hundred Thousand
   Pounds Ye Yearly Spend*, 1626

And where there have been many great inquests
To find the cause why bodies still grow less,
And daily nearer to the Pygmies' size;
This among many probabilities,
May pass for one; that their progenitors
Did gladly foment their interiors

[33]

With wholesome food, unmixed, moderate,
And timely liquors duly temperate:
But nowadays their issue inly choke
And dry them up (like herrings) with this smoke:
For, herrings in the sea are large and full,
But shrink in bloating and together pull.

Joshua Sylvester (c. 1563–1618), *Tobacco Battered*

[Peer group pressure]

Yet 'tis now almost a wonder to behold,
How generally now both young and old
Suck on that foreign weed. For so they use it,
Or rather (to speak right) so they abuse it,
In too oft taking; that a man would think
It were more needful than their meat or drink:
But what's their reason? Do not ask them why,
For neither can they tell you that, nor I:
Unless't be this: So they have seen some do:
And therefore they forsooth must use it too.

George Wither (1588–1667), *Of Vanity: Satire I*, from his
Juvenilia, 1633

Some do this plant with odious crimes disgrace,
And call the poor *Tobacco* homicide,
They say that it, O what a monstrous case!
Forestalls the life, and kills man in the seed,
It smoketh, blacketh, burneth all the brain,
It dries the moisture treasure of the life,
It cureth not, but stupifies the pain,
It cuts our days before Atropus' knife.
Good lady, look not to these raving speeches,
You know by proof that all these blames are lies,
Forged by scurvy, lewd, unlearned leeches,
As time hath taught, and practice that all tries.
Tobacco neither altereth health nor hue,
Ten thousand thousands know that it is true.

William Barclay, *To Philoclea*, 1614

[34]

Here lies Wat Moone, that great tobacconist,
Who died too soon, for lack of *Had I wist.**
Henry Parrot, *Cures for the Itch*, 1626

A request to the reader

Rather than my leaves should tobacco light,
I pray thee with them make thy backside bright.
Robert Hayman, *fl.* 1628

———————

Gallants, tobacco and national decline

What gallant's that whose oaths fly through mine ears?
How like a lord of Pluto's court he swears
How brave in such a bawdy house he fought,
How rich his empty purse is outside wrought,
How Dutchman-like he swallows down his drink
How sweet he takes tobacco till he stink:
How lofty-spirited he disdains a Boor,
How faithful-hearted he is to a whore
How cock-tail proud he doth his head advance,
How rare his spurs do ring the morris-dance.
Now I protest by Mistress Susan's fan,
He and his boy will make a proper man.
Samuel Rowlands (?1570–?1630), *Epigram* 32

Our gold goes out so fast, for foolish foreign things,
Which upstart gentry still into our country brings;
Who their insatiate pride seek chiefly to maintain
By that which only serves to uses vile and vain:
Which our plain fathers earst would have accounted sin,
Before the costly coach, and silken stock came in;
Before that Indian weed so strongly was embrac'd;
Wherein such mighty sums we prodigally waste.
Michael Drayton, *Poly-Olbion*, 1613

* Known.

[35]

Tria mala

The whore, tobacco and strong waters meet,
Like three grand plagues in almost every street.

Henry Parrot, *Cures for the Itch*, 1626

The true sack drinker

Sobriety and study breeds
Suspicion in our thoughts and deeds,
The downright drunkard no man heeds:
Let me have sack, tobacco store,
A drunken friend, a little whore,
Provided, I will ask no more.

Anon., in John Gamble, editor, *Songbook*, 1659

Look to the towered chimneys which should be
The windpipes of good hospitality.
Through which it breatheth to the open air,
Betokening life and liberal welfare.
Lo, there th'unthankful swallow takes her rest,
And fills the tunnel with her circled nest,
Nor half that smoke from all his chimneys goes
As one tobacco-pipe drives through his nose.

Joseph Hall (1574–1656), *Satire II*

They say old hospitality kept chimneys smoking still,
Now what our chimneys want of that, our smoking noses will.
Much victuals serve for gluttony, to fatten men like swine,
But he's a frugal man indeed, that with a leaf can dine.
And needs no napkin for his hands, his fingers' ends to wipe,
But keeps his kitchen in a box, and roast meat in a pipe.
This is the way to help dear years, a meal a day's enough,
Take out tobacco for the rest, by pipe or else by snuff,
And you shall find it physical; a corpulent fatman,
Within a year will shrink so small that one his guts may span.

Samuel Rowlands (?1570–?1630), *The Devil's Health-Drinker*

[Seeing both sides]

Tobacco! divine, rare, super-excellent tobacco! which goes far beyond all the panaceas, potable gold, and philosopher's stones; a sovereign remedy to all diseases; a virtuous herb, if it be well qualified, opportunely taken, and medicinally used; but as it is commonly abused by most men, who take it as tinkers do ale, 'tis a plague, a mischief, a violent purge of goods, lands, health, hellish, devilish, and damned tobacco, the ruin and overthrow of body and soul.

Robert Burton, *The Anatomy of Melancholy*, 1621 (revised until 1651)

A popular legend*

I remember a pretty jest of tobacco which was this. A certain Welchman coming newly to London, and beholding one to take tobacco, never seeing the like before, and not knowing the manner of it, but perceiving him vent smoke so fast, and supposing his inward parts to be on fire; cried out, 'O Jhesu, Jhesu man, for the passion of Cod hold, for by Cod's splud ty snowt's on fire,' and having a bowle of beere in his hand, threw it at the other's face, to quench his smoking nose.

Barnaby Rich, *Irish Hubbub*, 1619

Tarlton (as other Gentlemen used) at the first comming up of tabacco, did take it more for fashions sake than otherwise, and being in a roome, set between two men overcome with Wine, and they never seeing the like, wondered at it; and seeing the vapour come out of Tarlton's nose, cryed out, Fire, Fire, and threw a cup of Wine in Tarlton's face. Make no more stirre, quoth Tarlton, the fire is quenched: if the Sheriffes come, it will turne to a fine, as the custome is. And drinking that againe, Fie, says the other, what a stinke it makes, I am almost poisoned. If it offend, saies Tarlton, let every one take a little of the smell, and so the savour will quickly goe: but Tabacco whiffes made them leave him to pay all.

Tarlton's Jests, 1638 (Richard Tarlton, a celebrated stage comedian, died in 1588)

---

* The variation of this legend, featuring Sir Walter Raleigh being drenched by his servant, did not appear in print until 1708, in a magazine called *The British Apollo*.

Shakespeare's surprising reticence

It is a curious fact that no allusion to 'divine Tobacco,' as Spenser calls it, is to be found in the works of Shakespeare, though Ben Jonson and his contemporaries indulge in jests at the expense of the lately-imported weed, which was smoked under the very noses of the players by the gilded youth of the period, who were wont to take up their positions upon the stage, where stools were placed for them, and smoke incessantly during the whole performance.

Shakespeare being the favourite playwright of James I, whose hatred of smoking is well-known, it is not surprising that he failed to notice it favourably in the days of that monarch; but that the companion of Raleigh and Bacon at the 'Mermaid' should have nothing to say upon the subject is an enigma which some future Shakespearean scholar may perhaps unravel.

Tobacco Talk and Smokers' Gossip: an Amusing Miscellany of Fact and Anecdote, 1884

Shakespeare never mentions or alludes to smoking, though the practice was pursued in his own theatre, the Globe. Not a single passage in his works can be construed into reference to tobacco. Still, we think of him as a great smoker, and imagine him meditating and maturing many a thought and fancy over a pipe of Virginia. Cannot you trace the broad-minded, generous, intuitive views of Shakespeare to tobacco? Much of Hamlet's melancholy and indecision would have been dissipated had he but smoked. Perchance Shakespeare abstained from the weed to appreciate his hero's despair and vacillation of mind, or drew upon the experiences of his pre-smoking days for example. Yes, Shakespeare was a smoker – decidedly a good smoker.

W. A. Penn, *The Soverane Herbe: A History of Tobacco*, 1901

Tobacco conquers Britain anyway

There is not so base a groom that comes into an ale-house to call for his pot, but he must have his pipe of tobacco; for it is a commodity that is nowe as vendible in every tavern, wine, and ale-house, as either wine, ale, or beer; and for apothecaries' shops, grocers' shops, chandlers' shops, they are (almost) never without company, that from morning till night are still taking of tobacco. What a number are there besides, that do keep houses, set open shops, that hath no other trade to live by, but by the selling of tobacco.

I have heard it told, that now very lately there hath been a catalogue of all those new erected houses that have set up that trade of selling tobacco in London, and near about London; and if a man may believe what is confidently reported, there are found to be upward of seven thousand houses that doth live by that trade.

Barnaby Rich, *Honestie of this Age*, 1614

Global persecution

[Turkey]

Murad IV (1623–40) went for the smokers tooth and nail, and tried moreover to close the coffee-houses which often harboured them, and could be suspected by a nervous police of being a resort of malcontents and plotters. A veritable persecution was launched, and there were many who proved as ready to die for their nicotine as others have been for their country or faith. Katib Chelebi (d. 1657), the judicious Turkish writer, commented in an essay on tobacco that as Murad's severity increased, 'so did people's desire to smoke . . . "Men desire what is forbidden", and many thousands of men were sent to the abode of nothingness.' When Murad was on campaign against Baghdad, 15 or 20 officers were found guilty of smoking at one halting-place; they were put to death by torture in his presence. Some soldiers, Chelebi says, kept short pipes in their sleeves or pockets, and, with what seems almost incredible hardihood, 'found an opportunity to smoke even during the executions'.*

V. G. Kiernan, *Tobacco: A History*, 1991

[Russia]

The Russians have long been addicted to smoking, even a poor man preferring to spend his last penny on tobacco rather than on bread.

---

* Pleasingly, a brand of cigarettes, launched after the First World War by Lorillard, was given the name Murad.

However, it soon became evident that the people, so far from being benefited, got great harm from the practice. The ordinary citizen, his servants, his serfs, all alike would neglect their work; owing to the carelessness of smokers many houses were burned to the ground, while even in the churches the sacred icons, which should be honoured only with incense and sweet perfumes, stank of tobacco smoke. Consequently in 1634 the sovereign, at the instigation of the Patriarch, issued an order strictly forbidding the use or sale of tobacco, as well as all private traffic in brandy and beer. Offenders are usually sentenced to slitting of the nostrils, the bastinado, or the knout; those convicted of taking snuff have their noses torn away. We ourselves have met with many victims of each of these forms of torture, which were inflicted alike on men and women.

The knout seemed to me a barbarous method of punishment; I saw it inflicted, in September 1634, on eight men and one woman who had been convicted of selling tobacco and spirits. These persons were made to strip to the loins, in the presence of the tribunal; then one after another was hoisted on to the back of the executioner's assistant, around whose neck the culprit's arms were fastened, his legs being tied together by a rope held by another attendant, so that he could move neither hands nor feet. The executioner then took his stand behind the victim at a distance of three paces and plied the long stout whip with such force that the blood flowed freely after every stroke; at the end of the knout are three thongs, the length of a finger, made of hard untanned elk-skin, which cut like a knife. In the case of grave offenders the victims are sometimes whipped to death; in this instance each man received from twenty to twenty-six strokes; the woman endured sixteen, after which she lost consciousness. Not a finger's breadth of skin was left on their backs, which looked like the flayed carcase of an animal.

Adam Olearius, *Beschreibung der Moskowitischen und Persienischen Reise*, Hamburg edition, 1696

[India and Persia]

The Mogul emperor of Hindustan, Jāhangīr, displayed comparative restraint. Under his ruling smokers were merely to have their lips slit. He noted, casually, in his memoirs:

As the smoking of tobacco has taken very bad effect upon the health and mind of many persons I ordered that no one should practice the habit. My brother Shah Abbas, also being aware of its evil effects, has issued a command against the use of it in Iran.

It was this same Abbas who became the terror of those who continued to defy his commands. There are eyewitness accounts of the torture or cruel death inflicted by the shah's orders upon smokers, foreign tobacco merchants, and unfortunate travelers in the Persian domain. His antagonism to smoking could, on occasion, be more subtle. An English visitor reported that he had once beguiled his courtiers, knowing they were secretly using the pipe, by inviting them to a feast where he served what he called the most excellent tobacco available. He listened to their servile flattery of the fare he had provided, and when they had done cried in anger, 'Cursed be that drug that cannot be discerned from the dung of horses.'

Jerome E. Brooks, *The Mighty Leaf: Tobacco through the Centuries*, 1953

Shah Abbas was succeeded by Shah Sefi in 1629. He, like his grandfather, was subject to sudden attacks on tobacco. Jean Tavernier, a translation of whose *Six Voyages*, which began in 1631, was published in English in 1676, writes of Persia:

The plains are planted with tobacco which is transported into Turkey, for which they have a very great trade.

In spite of this smokers were not safe.

The Persians both men and women are so addicted to take tobacco, that to take their tobacco from them, is to take away their lives. So that if the King should prohibit Tobacco for any time, he should lose a good part of his revenue. However, Shah Sefi in a humour having once forbidden tobacco to be taken in any part of his dominion his spies (that are in every city) found in the Indian inn two rich merchants of that nation smoking their noses. Immediately they were seized, bound and carried to the King, who commanded forthwith that justice should be done upon them, which was that they should pour melted lead down their throats till they were dead.

Compton Mackenzie, *Sublime Tobacco*, 1957

[The Catholic Church]

Whereas the churches are houses of prayer consecrated to the service of God, and therefore in every way to be considered holy, We to whom the care of all the churches in the world has been entrusted are bound to see that all unseemly and profane behaviour be excluded from them; and whereas information has lately reached Us from the Dean and Chapter of the metropolitan church in Sevilla that in those parts the use of the herb commonly called tobacco has gained so strong a hold on persons of both sexes, yea, even priests and clerics, that – We blush to state – during the actual celebration of Holy Mass, they do not shrink from taking tobacco through the mouth or nostrils, thus soiling the altar linen and infecting the churches with its noxious fumes, sacrilegiously and to the great scandal of the pious . . . it therefore behoves Us, in order to purge our churches of this shameless abuse, to prohibit and interdict all persons of either sex, clergy or laity, collectively and individually, from using tobacco or snuff in any form whatever in the churches of the said diocese of Sevilla, their vestibules, vestries, or immediate surroundings; and all persons thus offending shall be punished by immediate excommunication, *ipso facto*, without further ado, in accordance with the terms of the present interdict.

Urban VIII, Papal Bull, 1642

We have been greatly pained to learn that there are certain persons, clergy as well as laity, so unmindful of the reverence due to consecrated places that they do not hesitate to smoke or snuff up the herb commonly known as tobacco even in the church of the Prince of the Apostles, in the city to which the faithful of every nation in the world are wont to resort from motives of devotion, thereby causing deep distress to all pious souls.

Innocent X, Papal Bull, 1650

[Switzerland]

In 1661 the Communal Fathers of Berne legislated against tobacco. The canton regulations were based upon the Ten Commandments, to each being added in explanation the crimes which it was held to comprehend. Under the seventh, 'Thou shalt not commit adultery,' was comprehended the sin of smoking. This prohibition was renewed in 1675, and to punish breaches of the law a Chambre du Tabac was instituted; this tribunal existed until the middle of the eighteenth century.

W. A. Penn, *The Soverane Herbe: A History of Tobacco*, 1901

Tobacco conquers the world anyway

[Bigger than Jesus]

... Multitudes them daily, hourly, drown
In this black sea of Smoke, tossed up and down
In this vast ocean, of such latitude
That Europe only cannot all include,
But out it rushes, over-runs the Whole,
And reaches, well-nigh round, from Pole to Pole;
Among the Moors, Turks, Tartars, Persians,
And other Ethnics (full of ignorance
Of God and Good); and, if we shall look home
To view (and rue) the State of Christendom;
Upon this point, we may this riddle bring;
The subject hath more subjects than the king:
For Don Tobacco hath an ampler reign
Than Don Philippo, the Great King of Spain
(In whose dominions, for the most, it grows).
Nay, shall I say (O horror to suppose!)
Heathenish tobacco (almost everywhere)
In Christendom (Christ's outward kingdom here)
Hath more Disciples than Christ hath (I fear)
More suit, more service (bodies, souls and good)
Than Christ, that bought us with his precious blood.

Joshua Sylvester (*c.* 1563–1618), *Tobacco Battered*

[Japan, 1614]

... at least 150 persons have been apprehended for buying and selling tobacco, contrary to the emperor's command, and are in jeopardy of their lives. Large quantities of tobacco had been burnt.

Richard Cocks, *Diary* (edited by E. M. Thompson, 1883)

[Japan, 1615]

... the King had ordered no tobacco to be drunk in his government ... It is strange to see how these Japanese, men, women, and children, are besotted in drinking that herb; and not ten years since it was in use first.

Calendar of State Papers, Colonial, East Indies

[Seventeenth-century China]

If a person smokes when he is hungry, he feels as though he has taken plentiful food; and when he smokes after eating sufficiently, it affords good digestion in a most satisfactory manner. For this reason many people use it as a substitute for wine and tea, and never get tired of it, even when smoking all day long.

A Chinese herbal, written between 1644 and 1661, quoted by B. Laufer in *The Introduction of Tobacco into Europe*, 1924

[Seventeenth-century Holland]

I cannot refrain from a few words of protest against the astounding fashion lately introduced from America – a sort of smoke-tippling, one might call it, which enslaves its victims more completely than any other form of intoxication, old or new. These madmen will swallow and inhale with incredible eagerness the smoke of a plant they call *Herba Nicotiana*, or tobacco.

J. Joachim von Rusdorff, *Metamorphosis Europae*, 1627

[Tobacco] is like Elias' cloud, which was no bigger than a man's hand, that hath suddenly covered the face of the earth; the low countries, Germany, Poland, Arabia, Persia, Turkey, almost all countries, drive a trade of it; and there is no commodity that hath advanced so many from small fortunes to gain great estates in the world.

Seamen will be supplied with it for their long voyages. Soldiers cannot but want it when they keep guard all night, or upon other hard duties in cold and tempestuous weather. Farmers, ploughmen, porters, and almost all labouring men plead for it, saying they find great refreshment by it, and very many would as soon part with their necessary food as they would be totally deprived of the use of tobacco.

Scholars use it much, and many grave and great men take tobacco to make them more serviceable in their callings. Tobacco is grown to be not only the physick, but even the meat and drink of many men, women, and children. In a word, it hath prevailed so far, that there is no living without it.

If we reflect upon our forefathers, and that within the time of less than one hundred years, before the use of tobacco came to be known amongst us, we cannot but wonder how they did to subsist without it; for were the planting or traffick of tobacco now hindered, millions of this nation in all probability must perish for the want of food, their whole livelihood almost depending upon it. So many druggists, grocers, tobacco-shops, taverns, inns, alehouses, victuallers, carriers, cutters, and dryers of tobacco, pipe-makers, and the like, that deal in it, will prove no less.

Dr Everard, *Panacea, or the Universal Medicine; being a Discovery of the Wonderful Virtues of Tobacco taken in a Pipe; with its Use and Operation both in Physick and in Chyrurgery,* 1659

Later in the century

The suppression of English-grown tobacco

[A hangman writes]

The very planting of tobacco hath proved the decay of my trade, for since it hath been planted in Gloucestershire, especially at Winchcombe, my trade hath proved nothing worth . . . Then 'twas a merry world with me, for indeed before tobacco was there planted, there being no kind of trade to employ men, and very small tillage, necessity compelled poor men to stand my friends by stealing of sheep and other cattle, breaking of hedges, robbing of orchards and what not.

Harry Hangman's Honour, or Gloucestershire Hangman's Request to the Smokers and Tobacconists of London, 11 June 1655

[1658]

. . . This morning I got together 36 horse, and went to Cheltenham early, and found an armed multitude guarding the tobacco field. We broke through them and went into the town, but found no peace officer, but a rabble of men and women calling for blood for the tobacco, so that had there been any action, blood would have been spilt. The soldiers stood firm, and with cocked pistols, bade the multitude disperse, but they would not, and 200 more came from Winchcombe... Ten men could not in 4 days destroy the good tobacco about Cheltenham... I was forced to retreat; the justices [of the peace] rather hinder than help us.

Letter of a government agent, *Calendar of State Papers, Domestic Series*

[1667]

Up, and all the morning at the office. At noon home to dinner, W. Hewer and I and my wife, when comes my cozen, Kate Joyce, and an aunt of ours, Lettice, formerly Haynes, and now Howlett, come to town to see her friends, and also Sarah Kite, with her little boy in her armes, a very pretty little boy. The child I like very well, and could wish it my own. My wife being all unready, did not appear. I made as much of them as I could such ordinary company; and yet my heart was glad to see them, though their condition was a little below my present state, to be familiar with. She tells me how the lifeguard, which we thought a little while since was sent down into the country about some insurrection, was sent to Winchcombe, to spoil the tobacco there, which it seems the people there do plant contrary to law, and have always done, and still been under force and danger of having it spoiled, as it hath been oftentimes, and yet they will continue to plant it. The place, she says, is a miserable poor place.

Samuel Pepys, *The Diary of Samuel Pepys*, 19 September 1667

Tobacco seen as a protection against the plague

Nor indeed were those persons affected who smoked tobacco, especially if they smoked in the morning, a time when the body is more susceptible to outer influences than it is later in the day. For the smoke of the plant secures those parts which lie most open, namely, the mouth, nostrils, etc., and at once intercepts and keeps the contagion that floats in the air from the brain, lungs, and stomach. It also stirs the blood and spirits all over, and makes them throw off any contagion that may adhere to them.

Dr Willis, physician-in-ordinary to Charles II, *A Plain and Easy Method of Preserving (by God's Blessing) Those that are Well from the Infection of the Plague*, 1666

This day, much against my will, I did in Drury Lane see two or three houses marked with a red cross upon the doors, and 'Lord have mercy upon us' writ there; which was a sad sight to me, being the first of the kind that, to my remembrance, I ever saw. It put me into an ill conception of myself and my smell, so that I was forced to buy some roll-tobacco to smell to and chaw, which took away the apprehension.

Samuel Pepys, *The Diary of Samuel Pepys*, 7 June 1665

The supper being finished, they set on the table half a dozen pipes and a pacquet of tobacco for smoking, which is a general custom, as well among the women as men, who think that without tobacco, one cannot live in England, because they say it dissipates the evil humours of the brain.

Whilst we were walking about the town, he asked me if it was the custom in France, as in England, that when the children went to school, they carried in their satchel, with their books, a pipe of tobacco, which their mother took care to fill early in the morning, it serving them instead of a breakfast; and that at the accustomed hour, every one laid aside his book to light his pipe, the master smoking with them, and teaching them how to hold their pipes and draw in the tobacco; thus accustoming them to it from their youth, believing it absolutely necessary for a man's health.

Monsieur Jorevin de Rochefort. His travels were printed in Paris in 1672, and translated in the *Antiquarian Repertory*, vol ii

[Compulsory smoking at Eton]

Jan. 21 [1721]. I have been told, that in the last great plague at London none that kept tobaconist's shops had the plague. It is certain, that smoaking it was looked upon as a most excellent preservative. In so much, that even children were obliged to smoak. And I remember, that I heard formerly Tom Rogers, who was yeoman beadle, say, that when he was that year, when the plague raged, a school-boy at Eaton, all the boys of that school were obliged to smoak in the school every morning, and that he was never whipped so much in his life as he was one morning for not smoaking.

Thomas Hearne (1678–1735), *Reliquiae Hernianae*

Strength to strength

When William and Mary came to the throne after the expulsion of King James II tobacco received its biggest stimulus ever. As a Dutchman with Dutch troops and Dutch courtiers all of whom smoked far larger pipes than were common in England King William III had every reason to approve of tobacco. The English government had passed a law appropriating the entire tobacco revenue to pay for the cost of his expeditionary force from Holland.

This is the first time that tobacco paid for the armed forces.

Charles Graves, *A Pipe-Smoker's Guide*, 1969

The sin of the kingdom in the intemperate use of tobacco, swelleth and increaseth so daily, that I can compare it to nothing but the waters of Noah, that swell'd fifteen cubits above the highest mountains. So that if this practice shall continue to increase as it doth, in an age or two it will be as hard to find a family free, as it was so long time since one that commonly took it.

. . . But above all, that this practice should overgrow all the powers of reason, religion, and experience amongst most part of the godly, is yet to be admired: that a thing should grow to that height in their affections (that is not naturally pleasant) is a wonder: that they should suffer such an unnatural fire to be kindled in their nature, that proves in the event to be such a world of iniquity, and puts them in such a ferment and disorder, may make us cry out with the prophet Jeremiah, chap. 2, v. 12, 'Be astonished, Oh ye heavens, at this! be ye horribly afraid, be ye very desolate, saith the Lord of Hosts!'

Laurence Spooner, *A Looking-Glass for Smokers*, 1703

By the beginning of the eighteenth century the whole world had surrendered to tobacco. Every one smoked.

E. C. Corti, *A History of Smoking*, 1930 (trans. Paul England, 1931)

CHAPTER THREE

Sneezing for Pleasure: The Rise of Snuff

We talked of change of manners. Dr. Johnson observed, that our drinking less than our ancestors was owing to the change from ale to wine. 'I remember, (said he,) when all the *decent* people in Lichfield got drunk every night, and were not the worse thought of. Ale was cheap, so you pressed strongly. When a man must bring a bottle of wine, he is not in such haste. Smoking has gone out. To be sure, it is a shocking thing, blowing smoke out of our mouths into other people's mouths, eyes, and noses, and having the same thing done to us. Yet I cannot account, why a thing which requires so little exertion, and yet preserves the mind from total vacuity, should have gone out. Every man has something by which he calms himself: beating with his feet, or so.

James Boswell, *The Tour to the Hebrides*, 19 August 1773

The chief received wisdoms about snuff in Britain run as follows: that it was basically an eighteenth-century interruption to the history of smoking; that its rise was inspired largely by snobbery and Francophilia; and that for decades it replaced the pipe completely. All of these assertions are simplifications, along the lines of referring to 'the Swinging Sixties' or saying that in the 1970s 'everybody' wore platform shoes. For one thing, snuff had been taken long before 1700,* and obviously didn't die out in 1800. (Nor, as we shall see, did the distaste for smoking.) For another, plenty of people simply carried on puffing.

Nonetheless, as shorthand histories go, the traditional one isn't madly inaccurate. Snuff *did* take off in the eighteenth century – partly because of the fashion for French habits among the trend-setting classes, partly because smoking had become so widespread as to be considered vulgar, and partly because in 1702 the British fleet near Cadiz plundered several thousand barrels of choice Spanish snuff, and on the way home captured more in Vigo. (Back in Britain, the booty was given out to the sailors, who soon spread its fame.) For reasons the next chapter will explore, smoking *did* make a gradual but

* See, for example, the mention by Samuel Rowlands in the last chapter.

ultimately spectacular comeback after 1800. Even more importantly, though, the received wisdoms about snuff – just like those about the Swinging Sixties and platform shoes, in fact – were received almost immediately. They would therefore have been readily recognisable to people from the eighteenth century. Hence the passages below in which the stout British habit of pipe-smoking is contrasted with the snuffing of effete and Frenchified fops. Hence, the clear belief of many writers that snuff had triumphed forever over its smellier, more anti-social and – in an age before matches or lighters – less convenient rival.

All of which is why I've decided to tackle the tricky question of what to do about snuff (it's tobacco, but it isn't smoked) in this book by confining it chiefly to this chapter, and so by treating it just in relation to the business of smoking – a business to which, however many qualifications recent scholarly works have made on the subject, it was a serious threat only in the eighteenth century.

Snuff spreads

> . . . Now 'tis by every sort
> And sex adored, from Billingsgate to court.
> But ask a wench, 'how oysters sell?' – if nice,
> She begs a pinch before she sets a price.
> Go thence to 'Change, inquire the price of Stocks;
> Before they ope their lips they open first the box.
> Next pay a visit to the Temple, where
> The lawyers live, who gold to heaven prefer;
> You'll find them stupify'd to that degree,
> They'll take a pinch before they'll take their fee.
> Then make a step and view the splendid court,
> Where all the gay, the great, the good resort;
> E'en they, whose pregnant skulls, though large and thick,
> Can scarce secure their native sense and wit,
> Are feeding of their hungry souls with pure
> Ambrosial snuff.

> Anon., *Pandora's Box: A Satyr against Snuff*, 1719

The world has taken up a ridiculous fashion – the excessive use of snuff. All nations are snuffing. All classes snuff, from the highest to the lowest. I have sometimes wondered to see how lords and lackeys,

High Society and the mob, woodchoppers and handymen, broom-squires and beadles, take out their snuff-boxes with an air, and dip into them. Both sexes snuff, for the fashion has spread to the women; the ladies began it, and are now imitated by the washerwomen. People snuff so often that their noses are more like a dust-heap than a nose; so irrationally that they think the dust an ornament, although, since the world began, all rational men have thought a dirty face unhealthy; so recklessly that they lose the sense of smell and their bodily health. They snuff without need, at all times, in all places, without rest, as though their fate and fortune, their name and fame, their life and health, even their eternal salvation depended on it.

Do but notice what grimaces snuff-takers make, how their whole features are convulsed, how they dip into their snuff-boxes in measured rhythm, cock up their noses, compose their mouths, eyes, and all their features to a pompous dignity, and, as they perform the solemn rite of snuff-taking, they look as if they scorned the whole world, or were bent on some enterprise of which they might say, like Bouflet, 'I will make the whole world tremble!'

I have found by certain experiments that such men have the idea that, in the moment when they sniff the snuff up their noses, they are as men inspired, transformed into mighty kings and princes, or at least made royal and princely at heart.

Johann Heinrich Cohausen, *Lust of the Longing Nose*, 1720

[Sexy snuff]

With Snuff the beauteous Celia shades her face,
And adds a foil to every obvious grace.
Her lips o'erspread with dusky Vigo, speak
The brighter colour on her lovely cheek;
Nay, underneath the tawny shade they wear,
The lips themselves more beautiful appear.
For beauty mask'd, like the great few who shun
The praise and honour by their merits won,
By how much it denies its own applause
Or seems but so to do, a greater draws.
For, apt to imagine more than is conceal'd,
The fancy heightens every charm that's veil'd.

James Arbuckle, *Snuff*, 1719

[51]

[The Pope's blessing: snuff permitted in St Peter's . . .]

. . . To provide for the needs of everybody's conscience, and especially for the good order of the basilica, which is seriously compromised by the frequent walking out of those who can't abstain from the use of tobacco which is so widespread today, partly due to the opinion of physicians who recommend it as a remedy against many infirmities, especially for those people who are obliged to frequent cold and humid places in the early morning hours.*

A proclamation of Pope Benedict XII, 1725

> Let foolish Indians be no more our scorn,
> Who truck their gold or gems for beads or horn;
> The gay polite of sage Britannia's land
> Will part with Sterling in exchange for sand.
> With what disdain the Belles would glance askew,
> Were leaf not powder proffer'd to their view!
> Tho' still the thing's the same, the title only new:
> For fav'rite snuff, disguise it as you will,
> In spite of art remains tobacco still:
> As when a Fair is lur'd to sin and shame,
> Tho' coach'd or carted, prais'd or damn'd by Fame;
> Tho' Miss or Duchess, lowly-born or great,
> With cinders on her head, or coronet;
> Down to Nell Gwyn, from Rosamond or Shore,
> Whate'er her title be, in English she's a whore . . .
>
> Strange is the pow'r of snuff, whose pungent grains
> Can make fops speak, and furnish Beaus with brains;
> Nay, can enchant the Fair to such degree,
> Scarce more admir'd could French romances be,
> Scarce scandal more belov'd, or darling flattery.
> Whether to th'India-house they take their way,
> Loiter i' th' park or at the toilet stay,
> Whether at Church they shine or sparkle at the play.
> Nay farther yet, perhaps their Snuff they keep,
> Take it in bed, and dream on't when asleep.

* The papacy opened a tobacco factory of its own in 1779, and in 1851 the dissemination of anti-tobacco literature became an imprisonable offence in the Papal States.

For sure, unless the Beau may claim a part,
Snuff is the topmost trifle of the heart.
Nor care of cleanliness, nor love of dress,
Can save their clothes from brick-dust nastiness . . .

Samuel Wesley (1691–1739), *Snuff: a Satire*

The pipe versus snuff

Says the Pipe to the Snuff-box, I can't understand
What the ladies and gentlemen see in your face,
That you are in fashion all over the land,
And I am so much fallen into disgrace.

Do but see what a pretty contemplative air
I give to the company, – pray do but note 'em, –
You would think that the wise men of Greece were all there,
Or, at least, would suppose them the wise men of Gotham.

My breath is as sweet as the breath of blown roses,
While you are a nuisance where'er you appear;
There is nothing but sniveling and blowing of noses,
Such a noise as turns any man's stomach to hear . . .

William Cowper, 'To the Rev. Mr Newton, Rector of St Mary Woolnoth', 1782

The Bag-Wig and the Tobacco-Pipe

A bag-wig of a jauntee air,
Trick'd up with all a barber's care,
Loaded with powder and perfume,
Hung in a spendthrift's dressing-room:
Close by its side, by chance convey'd,
A black Tobacco-pipe was laid;
And with its vapours far and near,
Outstunk the essence of Monsieur;
At which its rage, the thing of hair,
Thus, bristling up, began declare.
'Bak'd dirt! that with intrusion rude
Breakst in upon my solitude,
And whose offensive breath defiles

[53]

The air for forty thousand miles –
Avaunt – pollution's in thy touch –
O barb'rous English! horrid Dutch!
I cannot bear it – Here, Sue, Nan,
Go call the maid to call the man,
And bid him come without delay,
To take this odious pipe away.
Hideous! sure some one smoak'd thee, Friend,
Reversely, at his t'other end.
Oh! what mix'd odours! what a throng
Of salt and sour, of stale and strong!
A most unnatural combination,
Enough to mar all perspiration –
Monstrous! again – 'twou'd vex a saint!
Susan, the drops – or else I faint!'

The pipe (for 'twas a pipe of soul)
Raising himself upon his bole,
In smoke, like oracle of old,
Did thus his sentiments unfold.
'Why, what's the matter, Goodman Swagger,
Thou flaunting French, fantastic bragger?
Whose whole fine speech is (with a pox)
Ridiculous and heterodox.
'Twas better for the English nation
Before such scoundrels came in fashion,
When none sought hair in realms unknown,
But every blockhead bore his own.
Know, puppy, I'm an English pipe,
Deem'd worthy of each Briton's gripe,
Who, with my cloud-compelling aid
Help our plantations and our trade,
And am, when sober and when mellow,
An upright, downright, honest fellow.
Tho' fools, like you, may think me rough,
And scorn me, 'cause I am in buff,
Yet your contempt I glad receive,
'Tis all the fame that you can give:
None finery or fopp'ry prize;

But they who've something to disguise;
For simple nature hates abuse,
And Plainness is the dress of Use.'

Christopher Smart (1722–71)

[The balanced approach]

Thus dost thou every taste and genius hit,
In smoke thou'rt wisdom; and in snuff thou'rt wit.

Anon., 1731, in John Brand, *Popular Antiquities of Great Britain*, 1854

The unreconstructed pipeman

While all the world was snuffing my uncle Toby continued to smoke his pipe, thus displaying in his unobtrusive manner his scorn of the daintier Nicotian custom.

Laurence Sterne, *Tristram Shandy*, 1759–67

Criticks avaunt; *Tobacco* is my theme;
Tremble like hornets at the blasting steam,
And you, court-insects, flutter not too near
Its light, nor buzz within the scorching sphere,
Pollio, with flame like thine, my verse inspire,
So shall the Muse from smoke elicit fire.
Coxcombs prefer the tickling sting of snuff;
Yet all their claim to wisdom is – a puff:
Lord *Foplin* smokes not – for his teeth afraid:
Sir *Tawdry* smokes not – for he wears brocade;
Ladies, when pipes are brought, affect to swoon;
They love no smoke, except the smoke of town;
But courtiers hate the puffing tribe, – no matter,
Strange if they love the breath that cannot flatter!
Its foes but shew their ignorance; can he
Who scorns the leaf of knowledge, love the tree?
The tainted templar (more prodigious yet)
Rails at *Tobacco*, tho' it makes him – spit.
Citronia vows it has an odious stink;

She will not smoke (ye gods!) but she will drink:
And chaste *Prudella* (blame her if you can)
Says, pipes are us'd by that vile creature Man:
Yet crowds remain, who still its worth proclaim,
While some for pleasure smoke, and some for fame:
Fame, of our actions universal spring,
For which we drink, eat, sleep, smoke, – ev'ry thing.

Isaac Hawkins Browne (1705–60), *A Pipe of Tobacco: in
Imitation of Six Several Authors*, Imitation IV (of Edward Young)

See! Stretch'd on nature's couch of grass.
The foot-sore traveller lies!
Vast treasures let the great amass;
A leathern pouch, and burning glass,
For all his wants suffice.

For him the sun its power displays,
In either hemisphere;
Pours on Virginia's coast its blaze,
Tobacco for his pipe to raise;
And shines to light it – here!

Samuel Bishop (1731–95), *Epigram CXIII*

Postscript

Snuff was Granny T's one horrible vice, and she indulged it with no
moderation. A fine brown dust coated all her clothes and she had
nostrils like badger-holes. She kept her snuff in a small round box,
made of tin and worn smooth as a pebble. She was continually tapping
and snapping it open, pinching a nailful, gasping *Ah!*, flicking her
fingers and wiping her eyes, and leaving on the air a faint dry cloud
like an explosion of fungoid dust.

The snuff-box repelled and excited us boys and we opened its lid
with awe. Reeking substance of the underworld, clay-brown dust of
decay, of powdered flesh and crushed old bones, rust-scrapings, and
the rubbish of graves. How sharp and stinging was this fearful spice,
eddying up from its box, animating the air with tingling fumes like a

secret breath of witchery. Though we clawed and sniffed it we could not enjoy it, but neither could we leave it alone.

'You at me snuff agen, you boys? I'll skin yer bottoms, I will!'

We looked up guiltily, saw her cackling face, so took a big pinch between us. With choking tears and head-rocking convulsions we rolled across the floor. The old lady regarded us with pleasure; our paroxysms shook the house.

'That'll learn you, I reckon; you thieving mites. Here, give it to me, I'll show 'ee.'

She took up the box and tapped the lid, then elegantly fed her nose. A shudder of ecstasy closed her eyes. She was borne very far away.

Laurie Lee, *Cider with Rosie*, 1959

CHAPTER FOUR

The Return of Smoking – and of Smoking Debates

> Smoking has had its vicissitudes, as well as other fashions. In Elizabeth's day, when it first came up, it was a high accomplishment; James (who liked it none the better for its being of Raleigh's invention) indignantly refused it the light of his countenance; ... it prevailed more or less during the reign of the first two Georges; grew thin, and died away under George the Third; and has lately reappeared, with a flourish of Turkish pipes, and through the milder medium of the cigar, under the auspices of his successor.
>
> Leigh Hunt (1784–1859), writing in the 1830s, *The Wishing-Cap Papers*

So why did smoking make such a comeback in the nineteenth century? Well, Hunt's isn't a bad summary. The three influences seem to have been fashion, again – in Britain, the Revolutionary and Napoleonic Wars had made French ways suddenly less attractive – improved pipe technology and the coming of the cigar.

Hunt's 'Turkish pipes' are a reference to the 1830s' fad for hookahs, but the traditional clay version was under attack from other materials, too. Eighteenth-century Europe had already given birth to the meerschaum pipe, made from a porous Asia Minor stone, whose name is the German for 'seafoam'. A few decades later, the bizarre discovery of the briar took place. As for cigars, they made some impact – particularly in America – after the British occupation of Cuba during the Seven Years' War (1756–63). Even so, it wasn't until Europe's soldiery got their hands on them while in Spain for the Peninsula War (1808–14) that cigars spread all over the continent – Britain imported 26 pounds of cigars in 1800, 250,000 pounds in 1830. The return of smoking was by no means instantaneous, though, and for decades the habit remained not quite respectable: in G. V. Cox's *Recollections of Oxford* (1868), Archbishop Denison recalled, 'When I went up to Oxford, 1823–24, there were two things unknown at Christ Church, and I believe very generally in Oxford – smoking and slang.'

Meanwhile, over the Atlantic something not at all respectable was taking place: the rise of tobacco-chewing. Looking back, the American tobacco historian, Jerome E. Brooks, is clearly puzzled and disgusted. Dickens, there at the time, is just disgusted. Even so, chewing was still the favourite American way to take tobacco in 1900 (44 per cent of the market), spittoons weren't removed from Federal buildings until 1945 and 'non-smoking tobacco', as it's now coyly known, sells steadily in the South today. As you can see, this book deals with chewing in the same way that it dealt with snuff – through a few passages about its golden age and a quick reminder that the habit didn't end there.

Back in Britain, smoking was so established by the mid-nineteenth century that it was time for the first serious debates on the subject since the days of James I. In April 1853, the British Anti-Tobacco Society was formed from the kind of alliance of scientists and crusading evangelicals that, some people* would say, has stayed in place ever since. The same year saw Professor Lizars's full-scale attack and soon *The Lancet* was the battleground for the warring parties. The magazine itself turned more anti-smoking as a result. It came out strongly against juvenile smoking, which was to become the focus of anti-tobacco campaigners once they realised their more ambitious hopes were getting nowhere. On the whole, however, *The Lancet* continued to make the distinction between the use and abuse of tobacco – in direct parallel to the use and abuse of alcohol – that had been around since the early 1600s and that more or less remained the consensus until after the Second World War.

Perhaps the strangest aspect of the 1857 debate, then, was how short-lived its effects were. Smoking continued to grow in popularity and acceptability for the rest of the century. The compulsory provision of smoking carriages replaced a much-ignored ban on British trains in 1868. (John Stuart Mill's last speech in the House of Commons was in favour of the measure.) Anti-tobacco groups became ever tinier and pro-tobacco poetry ever more wildly sentimental. (There are some classic examples in Chapter 16.) Finally, so the often-repeated – but, as far as I can see, untraceable – story goes, at the first official dinner of his reign in 1901, Edward VII uttered four words which could never have passed Victoria's tobacco-despising lips: 'Gentlemen, you may smoke.' At which point, I should say that one significant aspect of Victorian smoking is largely missing from the following extracts. For most of the nineteenth century, the habit was considered – to an extent unknown before or since – an exclusively male activity. Chapter Eight will fill this gap.

---

* Me in the Introduction to this book, for instance.

The revival of smoking

I have sometimes asked myself whether if British statesmen had continued to smoke their pipes instead of surrendering to snuff the
American Colonies would ever have been lost. Snuff tempted men to
action, even precipitate action. What George III and Lord North
required was the sedative pipe, or the even more soothing cigar. What
the churchwarden and the cutty [clay pipes] had failed to do against the
influence of snuff, the cigar was to achieve.

Compton Mackenzie, *Sublime Tobacco*, 1957

> Sublime Tobacco! which from East to West
> Cheers the tar's labour or the Turkman's rest;
> Which on the Moslem's ottoman divides
> His hours, and rivals opium and his brides;
> Magnificent in Stamboul, but less grand,
> Though not less loved, in Wapping or the Strand;
> Divine in hookas, glorious in a pipe,
> When tipped with amber, mellow, rich, and ripe;
> Like other charmers, wooing the caress,
> More dazzlingly when daring in full dress;
> Yet thy true lovers more admire by far
> Thy naked beauties – Give me a cigar!

Lord Byron,* *The Island*, 1823

[The coming of briar]

The discovery of the ideal pipe material, the so-called briar-root, was
quite accidental, as such discoveries so often are. It was incidental to
the revival of the cult of the great Napoleon in the second decade
following his death in 1821, when the disasters of 1814 were forgotten. Those who wished to honour their late Emperor were not
content to visit the tomb at the Invalides, whither his ashes had been
brought from St. Helena, but made a pilgrimage also to the birthplace
of the Little Corporal in Corsica. Among these pilgrims was a French
pipe-maker, who during his stay had the misfortune to break or lose

---

* Sadly, given the ringing defiance here, Byron took to cigars mainly to take his mind off
food when he was trying to lose weight.

his meerschaum pipe. He commissioned a Corsican peasant to carve him another, and this was done, the pipe proving such a success that its possessor secured a specimen of the wood from which it was made and brought it home with him. This wood, noted locally for its hardness and fine grain, was the root of the tree-heath, or bruyère, to give it its French name, and from this date, somewhere in the early fifties, it was destined to supersede all other pipe materials.

Alfred Dunhill, *The Pipe Book*, 1924

'A very warm evening, sir,' said a passenger seated at his right; puffing, while he spoke, from a short German pipe, a volume of smoke into Philip's face.

'Very warm. Be so good as to smoke into the face of the gentleman on the other side of you,' returned Philip petulantly.

'Ho, ho!' replied the passenger, with a loud, powerful laugh – the laugh of a strong man. 'You don't take to the pipe yet; you will by and by, when you have known the cares and anxieties that I have gone through. A pipe! – it is a great soother, a pleasant comforter! Blue devils fly before its honest breath! It ripens the brain – it opens the heart; and the man who smokes, thinks like a sage and acts like a Samaritan!'

Edward Bulwer-Lytton, *Night and Morning*, 1851

> Some sing about love in their season of roses,
> But love has in sorrow no blossoms to wear;
> So I'll sing tobacco, that cheers and composes,
> And lulls us asleep in our trouble and care.
> So here's to tobacco, the Indian weed,
> The peaceful companion through trouble and strife;
> May it prove every smoker's best friend in his need,
> And be to his heart a restorer through life.
>
> There's the husbandman hourly tormented with care,
> By his daily companion, a troublesome wife;
> But a pipe of tobacco will soothe his despair,
> And bring him sunshine in the shadows of life.
> Then here's to tobacco, the Indian weed,
> May it bless honest smokers with peace to the end,
> For such a companion is friendship indeed,
> Since it proves in the midst of all trouble a friend.

The statesman, the lawyer, the parson will find,
When business oppresses and sorrow grows ripe,
To steer clear of follies and strengthen the mind,
There's nothing like leisure and smoking a pipe.
So here's to that cheering tobacco once more;
May each honest smoker prove blest with the weed,
May it mend broken hopes and lost pleasures restore,
And always prove dear as a friend in his need.

John Clare (1793–1864), 'Song on Tobacco'

The juicy habit

During the colonial period chewing had been a common practice in the Connecticut Valley where locally it was called 'fudgeon.' Transatlantic sailors chewed in every port. The habit was, therefore, not entirely a novelty to residents of the United States. What was a novelty was its spontaneous appearance, from about the third decade of the nineteenth century, throughout the States. There appears to be no traceable reason for its sudden spread across a good part of the land. It was not owing to any scarcity of tobacco; no part of the globe had more abundant quantities of that commodity in natural and in manufactured forms . . . It was not imitative of the habit of any conspicuous individual or group. Nor can the wide adoption of the quid in the United States at that time be regarded as a rebellion against European manners. The habit was not a revolt – it was merely revolting. Chewing was adopted neither as a substitute for food nor as an aid to health. But its users thought it served both, thus regarding it as a kind of *tertium quid*. This was the era of bad taste when a general sloppiness in American manners was painfully evident. It was a time when a sturdy citizen could (in a phrase quoted by a journalist) stand in his doorway, bite his morning 'chaw' and spit eighteen feet without trespassing on his neighbor.

The juicy habit was in widest evidence during the years of which the Jacksonian period was the center. It may be that the exciting events of those times demanded that the jaws be kept well lubricated for the requirements of argument and oratory. Legislators were notorious chewers and the habit identified them as of the common people in the log cabin era. It may be that the intrusion of the frontier upon urban areas and the casual and rough manners of the backwoods had a dynamic effect upon a mixed society whose social habits were diverse and unstandardized. Whatever the reason, the fact remains that a very large part of the population of the United States became ruminating animals. After the habit began slowly to diminish (in the post-Civil War period) the rhythmic exercise of the jaw, so peculiarly American, was not to be seen again en masse until the introduction of a new tidbit, the sweetened chicle known as chewing gum.

Jerome E. Brooks, *The Mighty Leaf: Tobacco through the Centuries*, 1953

As Washington may be called the head-quarters of tobacco-tinctured saliva, the time is come when I must confess, without any disguise, that the prevalence of those two odious practices of chewing and expectorating began about this time to be anything but agreeable, and soon became most offensive and sickening. In all the public places of America, this filthy custom is recognised. In the courts of law, the judge has his spittoon, the crier his, the witness his, and the prisoner his; while the jurymen and spectators are provided for, as so many men who in the course of nature must desire to spit incessantly. In the hospitals, the students of medicine are requested, by notices upon the wall, to eject their tobacco juice into the boxes provided for that purpose, and not to discolour the stairs. In public buildings, visitors are implored, through the same agency, to squirt the essence of their quids, or 'plugs,' as I have heard them called by gentlemen learned in this kind of sweetmeat, into the national spittoons, and not about the bases of the marble columns. But in some parts, this custom is inseparably mixed up with every meal and morning call, and with all the transactions of social life. The stranger, who follows in the track I took myself, will find it in its full bloom and glory, luxuriant in all its alarming recklessness, at Washington. And let him not persuade himself (as I once did, to my shame) that previous tourists have exaggerated its extent. The thing itself is an exaggeration of nastiness, which cannot be outdone . . .

The Senate is a dignified and decorous body, and its proceedings are conducted with much gravity and order. Both houses are handsomely carpeted; but the state to which these carpets are reduced by the universal disregard of the spittoon with which every honourable member is accommodated, and the extraordinary improvements on the pattern which are squirted and dabbled upon it in every direction, do not admit of being described. I will merely observe, that I strongly recommend all strangers not to look at the floor; and if they happen to drop anything, though it be their purse, not to pick it up with an ungloved hand on any account.

It is somewhat remarkable too, at first, to say the least, to see so many honourable members with swelled faces; and it is scarcely less remarkable to discover that this appearance is caused by the quantity of tobacco they contrive to stow within the hollow of the cheek. It is strange enough too, to see an honourable gentleman leaning back in his tilted chair with his legs on the desk before him, shaping a convenient 'plug' with his penknife, and when it is quite ready for use, shooting the old one from his mouth, as from a pop-gun, and clapping the new one in its place.

I was surprised to observe that even steady old chewers of great experience, are not always good marksmen, which has rather inclined me to doubt that general proficiency with the rifle, of which we have heard so much in England. Several gentlemen called upon me who, in the course of conversation, frequently missed the spittoon at five paces; and one (but he was certainly short-sighted) mistook the closed sash for the open window, at three. On another occasion, when I dined out, and was sitting with two ladies and some gentlemen round a fire before dinner, one of the company fell short of the fireplace, six distinct times. I am disposed to think, however, that this was occasioned by his not aiming at that object; as there was a white marble hearth before the fender, which was more convenient, and may have suited his purpose better.

Charles Dickens, *American Notes*, 1842

[Postscript: George Babbitt on holiday with his friend Paul]

They stood on the wharf before the hotel. He winked at Paul and drew from his back pocket a plug of chewing-tobacco, a vulgarism forbidden in the Babbitt home. He took a chew, beaming and wagging his head as he tugged at it. 'Um! Um! Maybe I haven't been hungry for a wad of eating-tobacco! Have some?'

They looked at each other in a grin of understanding. Paul took the plug, gnawed at it. They stood quiet, their jaws working. They solemnly spat, one after the other, into the placid water. They stretched voluptuously, with lifted arms and arched backs. From beyond the mountains came the shuffling sound of a far-off train. A trout leaped, and fell back in a silver circle. They sighed together.

Sinclair Lewis, *Babbitt*, 1922

The revival of debating

The constitutional effects of Tobacco . . . are numerous and varied, consisting of giddiness, sickness, vomiting, dyspepsia, vitiated taste of the mouth, loose bowels, diseased liver, congestion of the brain, apoplexy, mania, loss of memory, amaurosis [blindness], deafness, nervousness, palsy, emasculation and cowardice.

John Lizars, senior operating surgeon to the Royal Infirmary of Edinburgh, *Practical Observations on the Use and Abuse of Tobacco*, 1853

Mania is a fearful result of the excessive use of Tobacco – two cases of which I have witnessed since the publication of this treatise. I have also to mention, that a gentleman called on me, and thanked me for the publication of my Observations on Tobacco, and related to me, with deep emotion, what had occurred in his own family from smoking Tobacco. Two amiable younger brothers had gone deranged, and committed suicide. There is no hereditary predisposition to mania in the family. At a meeting of the Medical and Chirurgical Society of London, on 2nd May 1854, a paper was read, entitled, 'Additional Remarks on the Statistics and Morbid Anatomy of Mental Diseases,' by Dr Webster, wherein he cites, among the causes, the great use of Tobacco, which opinion he supported by reference to the statistics of insanity in Germany.

Loss of memory takes place in an extraordinary degree in the smoker, much more so than in the drunkard, evidently from Tobacco acting more on the brain than Alcohol. The cure consists in '*throwing away Tobacco for ever.*'

John Lizars, *Practical Observations on the Use and Abuse of Tobacco*, 5th edition, 1856

At Manchester, last week, a meeting was held, over which Canon STOWELL presided, of 'the British Anti-Tobacco Society.' The members of this body, we suppose, do not smoke. Tobacco does not agree with them. There are a great many people with whom the Indian herb does not agree. They dislike the smell of smoke – it makes them sick. With such people we have no quarrel. But we have a right to hint to them that their dislike of tobacco should not teach them to violate truth and charity. Still less should they elevate their biliary idiosyncrasies into conscientious scruples; and least of all ought they, as religious people, to libel their neighbours and brethren, who may perhaps be just as good Christians as themselves. At this meeting, certain 'sentiments' were moved 'in favour of abolishing the use of tobacco, as being injurious to the human body – as tending to create drunkards – and pledging the meeting to use all efforts to discourage smoking.' Among such efforts, that of telling little fibs about smoke and smokers is not to be neglected.

. . . This is only an impertinent interference with Christian liberty and our neighbour's taste. An Anti-STOWELL Society would be quite as useful, and perhaps more sensible. There are – we own that we are of the party – many to whom pride and ignorance, bad logic and cant, are as insufferable as tobacco is to Mr STOWELL.

The Saturday Review, 14 June 1856

To stay the torrent of vice and immorality which everywhere abounds, to train our young people for God and godliness, to fill our Sunday-schools and places of worship, and to raise the masses from the depths of degradation, we must begin with *the* stepping-stone to other evils – *the* evil of smoking.

Thomas Reynolds (Secretary of the Anti-Tobacco Society), *A Lecture on the Great Tobacco Question*, delivered in the Mechanics Institute, Salford, 1857

The Lancet joins in

A lecture on general paralysis by Samuel Solly – surgeon to St Thomas's Hospital and supporter of Lizars – was carried in *The Lancet* of 13 December 1856 and contained the following remarks: 'There was another habit, also, in which my patient indulged, and which I cannot but regard as the curse of the present age. I mean smoking . . . I know of no *single* vice which does so much harm as smoking.' On 27 December, a letter from J. A. McDonagh appeared, suggesting that Solly had overstated the case, and inviting an exchange of opinions on the subject. There followed for the next three months an avalanche of correspondence from doctors all over the world, in what was initially called 'The Tobacco Controversy: Is Smoking Injurious?' and soon became 'The Great Tobacco Question'.

Some of the points made now seem oddly prophetic, others less so – but the debate was nothing if not wide-ranging. Smoking was blamed for impotence, the decline of Turkey and causing leeches applied to the bodies of its practitioners to drop off dead. For neither the first nor last time, Thomas Hobbes and Isaac Newton were brought forward as examples of 'inveterate smokers' who were both clever and long-lived. A doctor at the Devon County asylum asserted that far from causing insanity, smoking 'is more likely to prevent it, by blunting the keen edge of bodily distress and mental grief'. (As conclusive proof, he cited 'the preponderance of lunatics of the female sex'.) Yet, perhaps the most surprising thing to us now – apart from the fact that *The Lancet* at the time was also discussing the dangers of food additives and whether homeopathy was real medicine – is that among the dozens of diseases ascribed to smoking by various correspondents, lung cancer does not feature once. On the other hand, the letter from H.G.W. is likely to be a chilling reminder for fans of cigarettes that this is largely because pipes and cigars were not inhaled. Here are a few of those 1857 highlights:

This tobacco controversy may – I sincerely trust it will – lead to directors of Insurance Companies taking the precaution of inquiring from the party proposing an insurance, or through his agents and medical referees, – if he is an habitual and inveterate smoker?

J. B. Neil, *The Lancet*, 10 January 1857

Mr Neil says, 'the Turks never use cigars or short clay pipes, both of which are much stronger than their long hookahs, by using which last the smoke becomes cool *before it reaches the lungs.*' Now, exclusively for Mr Neil's information, I will remark, *en passant*, that the smoke never reaches the lungs at all, but simply goes into the mouth and out again. It is to be regretted that he did not inform himself on such a simple point before venturing to join in the discussion. I rather think a man would soon discontinue smoking if the undiluted tobacco-smoke came in contact with the delicate lining membrane of the air-cells of the lungs, or with that of the bronchial tubes . . .

H. G. W., *The Lancet*, 24 January 1857

The advocates of smoking plead for it because it soothes them when they are troubled in mind – angry, irritable, and petulant in their families; thus meeting a moral evil with a physical remedy. Would it not be far more manly, far nobler, far more in accordance with the precepts of Christianity, if, instead of smoking away our griefs and stifling in the pipe our angry passions, we met our difficulties with a manly front, and conquered our evil tempers by the force of our better nature? Are not all troubles sent by an all-wise Providence to improve the character, and, by self-control, raise the soul above the influence of the carnal nature? Do we not pervert the streams which are intended to purify us by taking the opiate draught of smoke, instead of submitting to the rod, and rising strengthened by the chastisement?

Samuel Solly, *The Lancet*, 14 February 1857

[Three Doctors in favour]

What medical man in practice has not been told by some of his patients of the relief they obtained by smoking in asthma, chronic bronchitis, constipation and several forms of neuralgia?

J. A. McDonagh MRCS, *The Lancet*, 17 January 1857

The man who is himself a smoker, and will presume to vindicate such a habit, unquestionably calls down upon himself a certain amount of obloquy, and exposes himself to the imputation of vulgarity. Despite such disadvantages, it is the duty of the medical man to give an impulse to 'the onward march of truth,' and to contribute, as far as he is enabled, to the welfare of his fellow mortals by an honest avowal of his opinions . . .

I am sorry to be obliged to dissent from the opinions of such a high authority as Mr. Solly. I think he has advanced very little in the way of argument to lessen the confidence of tobacco smokers in the occasional value to be obtained from this extensively-diffused habit. I am, of course, speaking of its *use* not its *abuse*. I look upon *moderation* as the quintessence of most of our social habits, and believe that too rigid preceptors frequently defeat the best-intentioned inculcations for the promotion of morality and virtue. I cannot help thinking that a custom so extensively diffused has originated, not in mere caprice, nor from a spirit of puppyism – a desire to appear manly, but from some instinctive deep-seated requirement of man's corporeal organisation. Whether in the wild, in the wigwam, or in the mart of civilisation, the custom is so prevalent that it is absolutely, from its very diffusiveness, astounding. Compare with it the limited extent to which Christianity or Mohemmedanism, or any other form of worship, has been diffused, and the means adopted for their propagation, and the contrast will at once be obvious; and this notwithstanding the bulls of popes, the counterblasts of kings, the knouts of emperors, and the dogmatic precepts of physiological or psychological professors.

P. J. Hynes, MD, *The Lancet*, 21 February 1857

Unhappily, if a man smokes, by some, whatever disease he has is laid to its charge, and he is treated somewhat as the women of old used to be when tested for withcraft: hands and feet tied, and thrown into the water; if they swam, they were taken out and burned for witches; if not they were drowned and there was an end of them. So, if a man is ill, and has smoked, tobacco caused it; if he survives and lives long, 'tis in spite of it, and because he has a 'constitution like a horse' . . .

Smoking promotes kindly feeling, good temper (witness, no one is ever in a passion with a pipe in his mouth), equanimity of mind; and is not the last a boon, and ought not physicians, knowing the power of mind over matter, minister to it? and yet some would transport men caught in *flagrante delicto* of smoking, forgetting perhaps that they are already so.

T. Abbleby Stephenson, MRCS (Eng), LSA, *The Lancet*, 4 April 1857

[Imagine that]

The Lancet of last week contains many important letters on the abuse of tobacco-smoking, and its ill effects on the health of those devoted to the useless practice. Mr Solly's views are well worthy the *serious* consideration of medical students, who alas! are, as far my experience goes, devoted to this vile and useless habit.

M.D., *The Lancet*, 7 March 1857

If the various positions of Mr. Solly and his friends of the 'Lancet' were well founded, it would follow that every third man at least of our population must have been suffering from all manner of diseases for the last two centuries – since the consumption of tobacco has kept pace with the increase of population: nay, it also follows that, instead of increasing in population at a great ratio, as proved beyond a doubt, we have been suffering from sterility! And this in the face of the well-known fact that the population increased last year at the rate of one thousand per day. And insanity, too, is ascribed to tobacco – whilst it is well known that the female lunatics exceed the male by a considerable number. In short, nothing but the most glaring improbabilities are adduced, and the assertions are such as Mr. Solly may make when he pleases to his pupils without fear of contradiction. I cannot but look upon the whole excitement as an exhibition of ill-conditioned prejudices – from whatever motive proceeding I know not; – but if Mr. Solly gave up smoking, as he says, because he believed that it impaired his nervous energy, I am sorry to feel compelled to say that his letters in the 'Lancet' evince very considerable nervous weakness – indeed, such a weakness as would believe implicitly in the existence of witches and hobgoblins.

Andrew Steinmetz, *Tobacco: Its History, Cultivation, Manufacture and Adulterations*, 1857

Time, careful and truthful observation, can alone finally demonstrate the correctness or the shallowness of the opinions I have advanced...

Samuel Solly, *The Lancet*, 7 February 1857

Later Victorian respectability

Tobacco

Horace, you were born too soon!
Half the things beneath the moon,
That make living light to men,
Known are now and known were then.
Dewy eyes and waving hair,
All the sweets of dark and fair,
Garden shades, Falernian wine,
Talk and friendship, nights divine,
These and many more were thine.
But our Raleigh was not born,
Who bade sorrow cease to mourn,

Softened joy, tempestuous rage,
Mellowed youth and brightened age:
Taught us talk was made for two,
Not to turn, as boys will do
And at times the elders too,
Flowing, cheerful dialogue
Into fearful monologue.
Moan, ye wits! ye smokers, moan!
Had Tobacco but been known,
When the centuries were young,
When our Horace lived and sung;
Straight his style he would have took,
Added to his odes a book;
How Prometheus but began
Half the kindly task for man;
Raleigh gave us life indeed,
Heavenly fuel in the weed,
For the fire that filled the reed.
How Augustus thronèd high
Round the tables in the sky,
When the goddesses are gone,
And the couches closely drawn,
Not alone his nectar sips,
But between his purple lips
Hangs his hookah, pleased and proud,
Jove-like to compel a cloud.

William John Courthope (later Professor of Poetry at Oxford),
1865

. . . the marvellous successes of the German soldiers on a diet of black bread, pease-pudding, and twelve cigars a day, has created a strong reaction in favour of the weed, so long abused by the unimaginative as the food of dreamers, and reviled as noxious by those who have no mind to use it.

British Medical Journal, 10 September 1870

A Winter Evening Hymn to My Fire

Nicotia, dearer to the Muse
Than all the grape's bewildering juice,
We worship, unforbid of thee;
And as her incense floats and curls
In airy spires and wayward whirls,
Or poises on its tremulous stalk
A flower of frailest reverie,
So winds and loiters, idly free,
The current of unguided talk,
Now laughter-rippled, and now caught
In smooth dark pools of deeper thought.
Meanwhile thou mellowest every word,
A sweetly unobtrusive third;
For thou hast magic beyond wine
To unlock natures each to each;
The unspoken thought thou canst divine;
Thou fill'st the pauses of the speech
With whispers that to dreamland reach,
And frozen fancy-springs unchain
In Arctic outskirts of the brain.
Sun of all inmost confidences,
To thy rays doth the heart unclose
Its formal calyx of pretences,
That close against rude day's offences,
And open its shy midnight rose!

James Russell Lowell (1819–91)

[1884]

The long season finally wound down with an end-of-term beano, Smokers v. Non-smokers, played for the benefit of the Cricketers' Fund at Lord's on 15 and 16 September. The main concern was to divide the Australians equally, and the qualifications of the abstainers were not too closely inspected. Bonnor hit a whirlwind century for the Non-smokers, which included some clattering blows off Spofforth, and was then seen perambulating round the boundary puffing on a cigar. His 124 out of the 156 made while he was at the crease was the highlight of the match, though Peate in one spell for the Smokers took 6 for 10 in thirteen overs. Grace showed the benefit of clean lungs – or, as he believed, one clean lung* – bowling thirty-four tight overs and taking 5 for 29.

Simon Rae, *W. G. Grace: A Life*, 1998

LADY BRACKNELL (*pencil and note-book in hand*): I feel bound to tell you that you are not down on my list of eligible young men, although I have the same list as the dear Duchess of Bolton has. We work together, in fact. However, I am quite ready to enter your name, should your answers be what a really affectionate mother requires. Do you smoke?

JACK: Well, yes, I must admit I smoke.

LADY BRACKNELL: I am glad to hear it. A man should have an occupation of some kind.

Oscar Wilde, *The Importance of Being Earnest*, 1895

After he had done eating – and he made a heavy meal – the Invisible Man demanded a cigar. He bit the end savagely, before Kemp could find a knife, and cursed when the outer leaf loosened.

It was strange to see him smoking: his mouth and throat, pharynx and nares, became visible as a sort of whirling smoke cast.

'This blessed gift of smoking,' he said, and puffed vigorously.

H. G. Wells, *The Invisible Man*, 1897

There is no diminutive of tobacco; it is wholly superlative; there are no degrees of comparison in its use. The millionaire, the pauper, the brawny labourer, the learned scholar, the wildest savage, the oldest and the youngest alike enjoy tobacco. It matters not whether they live in the farthest north with sunless days and perpetual frost, in the fair fields of favoured lands, or in the sweltering heat and rich luxuriance of the tropics, tobacco is ever the same to its devotees, be they black or white, red or yellow, man or woman. Tobacco knows not colour, sex nor creed, country; age nor race. On the world-wide empire of tobacco the sun never sets. In all the intermediate states of light and darkness there rises the incense of tobacco and the red glow of count-

---

* Grace was always convinced that a bout of pneumonia he contracted at the age of 14 had cost him a lung.

less pipes. The Occident world smokes, and when it slumbers the Orient takes up the pleasant task, pouring forth incense in praise of tobacco's joys and inspiration. If ever the Utopian dream of the brotherhood of man be realized, tobacco will have had no small share in its realization. Tobacco draws men together and binds them in the common bond of sympathy as smokers. It is the true democrat, the only Volapuk, the veritable cosmopolite. Bring together a Hindu and an Englishman; they know not a word of each other's language, but tobacco binds them together, and they sit in such silent converse as smoke alone can afford. Tobacco has played a greater part in the cultivation of man and the progress of civilization than has ever been credited to the divine herb.

W. A. Penn, *The Soverane Herbe: A History of Tobacco*, 1901

CHAPTER FIVE

The All-Conquering Cigarette

The next stage in the progress of smoking was the decline of the cigar and the astonishing rise of the cigarette, which, owing to its combination of elegance with convenience, soon became the fashionable 'smoke', with the result that consumption increased by leaps and bounds, and, since the Great War, has reached quite fantastic heights.

E. C. Corti, *A History of Smoking*, 1930 (trans. Paul England, 1931)

A grown man has no possible excuse for thus imitating the small boy . . . The decadence of Spain began when the Spaniards adopted cigarettes and if this pernicious practice obtains among adult Americans the ruin of the Republic is close at hand . . .

New York Times, 1884

Short, snappy, easily attempted, easily completed or just as easily discarded before completion – the cigarette is the symbol of the machine age . . .

New York Times, 1925

'Will you have some coffee, you fellows? – Waiter, bring coffee, and *fine champagne*, and some cigarettes. No: don't mind the cigarettes; I have some. Basil, I can't allow you to smoke cigars. You must have a cigarette. A cigarette is the perfect type of a perfect pleasure. It is exquisite, and leaves one unsatisfied. What more can one want?'

Oscar Wilde, *The Picture of Dorian Grey*, 1890

At this point, then, a bit of backtracking is required. The cigarette, which took over the smoking world so comprehensively in the twentieth century,*

---

* 'When the twentieth century arrived, about four-fifths of the tobacco smoked in Britain was consumed in pipes and only one-eighth in cigarettes. To-day over four-fifths of the total tobacco consumption in this country is in cigarettes.' Compton Mackenzie, *Sublime Tobacco*, 1957. By 2000, the figure was well over 90 per cent.

didn't appear out of nowhere. For hundreds of years, *papelates*, or paper cigars, had been smoked in Spain – but they spread only very gradually, and despite the best efforts of smoking historians, still somewhat mysteriously. Their first stop, it now seems, was France (where they picked up their new name), then Russia and Turkey; and from there – particularly following the traditional war-related boost, this time in the Crimea – Britain. Even so, cigarettes are barely mentioned in F. W. Fairholt's magisterial *Tobacco: Its History and Associations* (1859), and for decades afterwards were little more than a novelty item.

But in North Carolina the flue-cured Bright tobacco that made possible the triumph of cigarettes was already gaining popularity. This tobacco led to a much gentler smoke, as the Northerners passing through during the Civil War soon recognised. Next, from a small farmstead in the same state came James Buchanan Duke. Realising that the neighbouring Bull Durham brand had cornered the pipe-tobacco market, in the early 1880s Duke took the apparently foolhardy step of putting all his energy into cigarettes. Within 20 years, his annual sales were around $125m a year, his workforce numbered 100,000 and he was controlling almost the whole of the American tobacco industry.

Duke's first breakthrough was to spot the potential of the new Bonsack automatic rolling machine. While others were still arguing that hand-rolling was the essence of the cigarette's appeal, he bought up all the Bonsacks available, also securing a deal whereby he received 25 per cent royalties on every machine bought by anybody else. Now he just needed to create a market for all the cigarettes he could produce so cheaply. He began with aggressive selling – including the introduction of cigarette cards, 'sweeteners' paid to tobacconists and giving out Duke cigarettes to immigrants as they landed. Once this was successful, he moved on to aggressive buying – of nearly all of his competitors.

The result was the American Tobacco Company which made 90 per cent of the country's cigarettes and soon set about undermining those who made the rest. The company was broken up in 1911 by the same kind of government trustbusting that also did for Rockefeller's Standard Oil. (A furious Duke consequently decided to concentrate on the hydroelectric business for which Duke University in Raleigh, North Carolina prefers to remember him today.) The – now much smaller – American Tobacco Company, R. J. Reynolds and Liggett and Myers were among the companies to emerge, and before long their respective brand leaders, Lucky Strikes, Camels and Chesterfields, were slugging it out for supremacy in the States. It was a battle which led to some of the most shameless advertising tricks in history. One famous Lucky Strike slogan, for example, was 'IT'S TOASTED' – in a process that promised to 'remove from Lucky Strike harmful irritants which are present in cigarettes manufactured the old-fashioned way'. Yet, by the definition used in the advert, all other brands of cigarettes were 'toasted' too. (By any normal definition, of course, none was.) Reynolds then hit back for Camels with some pseudo-science of their own ('A harmless restoration of the flow of natural energy') as well as less subtle come-ons: 'So mild . . . you can SMOKE ALL YOU WANT.' The ads mentioned in the Christopher Buckley passages below are not fictional.

The cigarette, however, did not rise unopposed. Although the anti-tobacco movements were much smaller than they had been, on both sides of the Atlantic, the cigarette was greeted with the most hysterical attacks yet. And victories were won. In Britain – where, as you might imagine, the tobacco companies had soon followed Duke's lead – the 1908 Children's Act made it illegal to sell tobacco to anybody under 16. (The relative cheapness of cigarettes and their ease of use had made the new craze highly attractive to children.) More dramatically, between 1895 and 1909 12 American States banned cigarettes entirely – Compton Mackenzie could remember being on a train where the passengers were told to stub out all cigarettes as it crossed into Indiana. (Kansas was the last to repeal such legislation, in 1927.) Most dramatically of all, Lucy Page Gaston, the editor of *Coffin Nails*, stood for the American presidency in 1920 on an anti-smoking ticket, denouncing the eventual winner, Warren Harding, as 'a cigarette-face'. (As pro-smoking writers invariably point out with some glee, Gaston died four years later of throat cancer.)

By then, though, the cigarette was well on the way to its status as the twentieth century's most successful consumer product. The rations for soldiers in the First World War had introduced a new generation to its delights, as well as removing any doubts about its unmanliness. And in the Second World War the British government spent more on tobacco for the troops than on tanks, ships or planes. By 1945, around 80 per cent of British men smoked, with women catching up fast. As this chapter takes the story of the cigarette's golden age into the 1960s, the next will again have to backtrack in order to tell the story of how the dangers were finally discovered. In the meantime, one quick fact relevant to that discovery: whereas fire-cured tobacco is alkaline, flue-cured is acidic. It's this property which makes cigarette smoke, unlike that of cigars and pipes, so easy to inhale.

Some early cigarette smokers

One evening, after it had grown quite dusk, I was leaning over the parapet of the quay, smoking, when a woman came up the steps leading from the river, and sat down near me. In her hair she wore a great bunch of jasmine – a flower which, at night, exhales a most intoxicating perfume. She was dressed simply, almost poorly, in black, as most work-girls are dressed in the evening. Women of the richer class only wear black in the daytime, at night they dress *à la francesa*. When she drew near me, the woman let the mantilla which had covered her head drop on her shoulders, and 'by the dim light falling from the stars' I perceived her to be young, short in stature, well-proportioned, and with very large eyes. I threw my cigar away at once. She appreciated this mark of courtesy, essentially French, and hastened to inform me that she was very fond of the smell of tobacco, and that she even smoked herself, when she could get very mild *papelitos*. I fortunately happened to have some such in my case, and at once offered them to her. She condescended to take one,* and lighted it at a burning string which a child brought us, receiving a copper for its pains. We mingled our smoke, and talked so long, the fair lady and I, that we ended by being almost alone upon the quay.

Prosper Merimée, *Carmen*, 1845 (trans. Lady Mary Loyd, 1902)

I am newly arrived one summer evening, in a certain small town on the Mediterranean. I have had my dinner at the inn, and I and the mosquitoes are coming out into the streets together. It is far from Naples; but a bright brown plump little woman-servant at the inn, is a Neapolitan, and is so vivaciously expert in pantomimic action, that in the single moment of answering my request to have a pair of shoes cleaned which I have left up-stairs, she plies imaginary brushes, and goes completely through the motions of polishing the shoes up, and laying them at my feet. I smile at the brisk little woman in perfect satisfaction with her briskness; and the brisk little woman, amiably pleased with me because I am pleased with her, claps her hands and laughs delightfully. We are in the inn yard. As the little woman's bright eyes sparkle on the cigarette I am smoking I make bold to offer her one; she accepts it none the less merrily, because I touch a most charming little dimple in her fat cheek, with its light paper end. Glancing up at the many green lattices to assure herself that the mistress is not looking on, the little woman then puts her two little

---

* Carmen thus became the first woman in literature to smoke a cigarette.

dimpled arms a-kimbo, and stands on tiptoe to light her cigarette at mine. 'And now, dear little sir,' says she, puffing out smoke in a most innocent and cherubic manner, 'keep quite straight on, take the first to the right, and probably you will see him standing at his door.'

Charles Dickens, *The Uncommercial Traveller*, 1860

Coffin-nails

Smoke cigarettes? Not on your tut-tut. Drop it ... You can't suck coffin-nails and be a ring-champion ... You never heard of a strong arm, a porch-climber, or a bank burglar using a cigarette, did you? They couldn't do it and attend to biz. Why, even drunkards don't use the things. That man Corbett, what licked me, smoked 'em, but then I had the booze ... Who smokes 'em? Dudes and college stiffs – fellows who'd be wiped out by a single jab or a quick undercut. It isn't natural to smoke cigarettes. An American ought to smoke cigars, an Englishman a briar, a Harp a clay pipe and a Dutchy a Meerschaum. It's the Dutchmen, Italians, Russians, Turks and Egyptians who smoke cigarettes and they're no good anyhow.

John L. Sullivan, world heavyweight boxing champion (1882–92), quoted in John Bain Jnr and Carl Werner, editors, *Cigarettes in Fact and Fancy*, 1906

Are cigarettes legitimate articles of commerce? We think they are not because they are wholly noxious and deleterious to health. Their use is always harmful; never beneficial. They possess no virtue, but are inherently bad, and bad only. They find no true commendation for merit or usefulness in any sphere. On the contrary, they are widely condemned as pernicious altogether. Beyond any question, their every tendency is toward the impairment of physical health and mental vigor.

Statement of the Supreme Court of Tennessee, upholding the State's anti-cigarette legislation, 1898

Tobacco using a savage custom

Whatever credit is due for the introduction of the tobacco habit belongs strictly and exclusively to the American savage. It is essentially a savage practice, without a single redeeming feature. The marvel is that it is tolerated in civilized society. To a person who lives habitually in a clean atmosphere, nothing is more surprising than the apathy with which the majority of men and women submit to the wholesale poisoning of the air which they breathe in theaters, lecture halls, even churches, as well as on the street, in sleeping cars, street cars, in hotels, in fact, wherever men congregate in the cities and towns of civilized countries. If some lunatic should take it into his head to carry around a stink pot, promenading up and down all the streets of the town, passing through street cars, churches, hotels, and now and then, on some pretense, getting access to private residences, it would not be long before the public would demand the arrest of such a purveyor of filth as a public nuisance.

The deadly cigarette

The cigarette is a most insidious and potent enemy of health and morality among young men and boys. It undermines both the health and morals in a most certain and effective way. Many a young man finds himself as old at twenty or twenty-five years of age as he ought to be at sixty or seventy. His constitution has been dissipated in smoke at the end of a cigarette or cigar. His lungs, liver, kidneys, and other internal organs are almost as densely saturated with smoke as a ham from a smoke house. The 'bouquet' of such a man has a whiff of perdition in it . . .

Legislation needed

It is clearly the duty of all intelligent men and women to take a strong stand against this evil, and to make earnest efforts to secure such legislation as will prohibit the manufacture, sale, and public use of this most pernicious drug.*

J. H. Kellogg, *The Living Temple*, 1903

---

* This passage was immediately followed by:
TEA AND COFFEE DRINKING. Probably very few of the millions who daily make use of tea and coffee as a beverage are aware of the fact that these common drugs contain from three to six per cent of a deadly poison. The amount of tea and coffee imported annually into the United States alone is more than one billion pounds, or five hundred thousand tons, containing more than fifteen thousand tons of a poison so deadly that twenty grains might produce fatal results if administered to a full-grown man at a single dose, amounting to more than ten billion deadly doses, or six times as much as would be required to kill every man, woman, and child on the face of the earth.

General Lew Wallace,* who died at the early age of seventy-eight, was another victim of the deadly cigarette habit. But for the filthy weed, he might have lived to an even hundred.

The Waterville *Banner of Health*, quoted in Compton Mackenzie, *Sublime Tobacco*, 1957

General Lew Wallace, who posed as a Christian, died at seventy-eight, having prolonged his life beyond the Scriptural three-score and ten by the use of those devilish drugs – cigarettes and coffee. God made seventy the sacred limit of our years, and those who violate it by employing drugs will surely suffer.

The Jericho *Primitive Christian*, quoted in Compton Mackenzie, *Sublime Tobacco*, 1957

A scout does not smoke. Any boy can smoke; it is not such a very wonderful thing to do. But a scout will not do it because he is not such a fool. He knows that when a lad smokes before he is fully grown up it is almost sure to make his heart feeble and the heart is the most important organ in a lad's body. It pumps the blood all over him to form flesh, bone, and muscle. If the heart does not do its work the body cannot grow to be healthy. Any scout knows that smoking spoils his eyesight, and also his sense of smell, which is of greatest importance to him for scouting on active service . . .

No boy ever began smoking because he liked it, but generally because either he feared being chaffed by the other boys as afraid to smoke, or because he thought that by smoking he would look like a great man – when all the time he only looks like a little ass.

So don't funk, but just make up your mind for yourself that you don't mean to smoke till you are grown up: and stick to it. That will show you to be a man much more than any slobbering about with a half smoked cigarette between your lips. The other fellows will in the end respect you much more, and will probably in many cases secretly follow your lead. If they do this you will already have done a good thing in the world, although you are only a boy. From that small start you will most probably go on and do big things as you grow up.

Lieut. Gen. R. S. S. Baden-Powell, *Scouting for Boys*, 1909

If you will study the history of almost any criminal, you will find he

---

* Lew Wallace (1827–1905), US soldier, diplomat and the author of *Ben Hur*.

is an inveterate smoker. Boys, through cigarettes, train with bad company. They go to pool rooms and saloons.

Henry Ford, *The Case against the White Slaver*, 1914

A bloodless boy

A horrible example of cigarette poisoning was published to the world recently in a dispatch from Springfield, Ohio, which says: 'David Hurley, 19 years old, died from the effects of cigarette smoking. The boy smoked five dollars' (£1) worth of cigarettes every week. He had shrivelled up until he looked like an old man. His lungs were in bad shape, and his blood was very thin. The physicians opened the boy's arm a short time after death and found that the main artery did not contain a drop of blood. It had dried up. The boy's father requested that the case be made public so that it would serve as a warning to other boys.' Will not the parents and teachers, as well as the boys, who read this message, take warning? Why should any parent allow a boy to smoke cigarettes and thus commit suicide?

'The cigarette eye'

A New York oculist declares that the cigarette is the greatest enemy to the eyes of young men. He describes a peculiar disease of the eye among smokers, the symptoms of which are dimness and filmlike gatherings over the eye, which appear and disappear at intervals. The best specialists were at a loss for a long time to understand the cause of this trouble, but have at length traced it to the use of the cigarette. It is known as the cigarette eye, and can only be cured by long treatment. A fine young boy of 18 sits in a dark room, his eyes swollen and painful, the cause – cigarette smoking. He has been warned of the danger many times, but would not listen, like thousands of others. This is what he said: 'I can't see now. They told me it would hurt me, but I did not believe it. I never expect to see the beautiful world again, but if I do, I'll never smoke another cigarette.'

Cigarettes and broken health

Physical disorders are the natural consequence of this indulgence. They are varied and numerous. Among them may be named 'smoker's cancer,' 'smoker's heart,' 'heart disease,' and 'paralysis.' Nervousness, dyspepsia, nausea, headaches, bad memory, slowness of thought, poor blood, short breath, pain in the heart, tremor of the hand, and restlessness follow in the footsteps of the smoker. The voice, eyes, and senses of taste and smell are more or less injured. One doctor gives particulars of seventy-two cases of smoker's cancer he had seen in fourteen years, and it is said that the details of the sufferings of patients who have died from this disease are horrible in the extreme.

A *clarion call*

Come now and let us hear the conclusion of the whole matter. If the facts and figures presented, the principles proclaimed, the curse and consequences declared, mean anything, they certainly challenge the co-operation of the church and the home, the school and the state, in the interest of health, happiness and hope, to fight to the death this innocent-looking, blood-sucking, body-breaking, brain-bewildering, heart-hardening, conscience-chloroforming, will-weakening, character-condemning, efficiency-emasculating, and death-dealing parasite – the nasty and noisome cigarette. The expert testimony of the world demands it; the safety of the state requires it; the salvation of the child necessitates it; the success of life advocates it; the future of Christian civilisation calls for it – and, above all, God wills it. Then death to the deadly cigarette! Deliverance to its deluded devotee! Let learning, love, and law combine to crush the viper, curb the passion, and cure the sin of Juvenile Smoking!

Rev. J. Q. A. Henry, DD (of the Christian Temperance Campaign), *The Deadly Cigarette: or, The Perils of Juvenile Smoking*, 1907

Smokers against the cigarette

The President of the United States, Mr. McKinley, smokes so hard that his physicians have limited him to two cigars a day.* Most of France's Presidents have been non-smokers; M. Faure puffed cigarettes, but M. Loubet smokes a pipe, and therefore under his guidance France is likely to experience greater peace and prosperity. The pipe is the emblem of stability and strength, the cigarette of insecurity and weakness.

W. A. Penn, *The Soverane Herbe: A History of Tobacco*, 1901

A good cigar indeed – Havana or Cuban leaf for preference – is an

* McKinley was assassinated in 1901.

inspiration. A meerschaum pipe when 'mellow, rich and ripe' is a treasure; but cigarettes are becoming, if they have not already become, a nuisance.

E. V. Heward, *St. Nicotine, or the Peace Pipe*, 1909

The golden age of the cigarette

[A tobacco industry spokesman of the 1990s talks to his boss]

'In 1910,' Nick said, 'the U.S. was producing ten billion cigarettes a year. By 1930, we were producing one hundred twenty-three billion a year. What happened in between? Three things. World War I, dieting, and talking pictures.'

BR was listening.

'During the war, it was hard for soldiers to carry pipes or cigars on the battlefield, so they were given cigarettes. And they caught on so much that General Pershing sent a cable to Washington in 1917 that said, "Tobacco is as indispensable as the daily ration. We must have thousands of tons of it without delay." ' Nick left out the detail that it was in 1919, just after the war, that the first cases of an up-to-then nearly unheard of illness called lung cancer began to show up. The chairman of a medical school in St. Louis invited his students to watch him do the autopsy on a former doughboy because, he told them, they'd probably never see another case of it again.

'So now the men are smoking cigarettes. In 1925, Liggett and Myers ran the Chesterfield ad showing a woman saying to a man who's lighting up, "Blow some my way." It broke the gender taboo. But it wasn't until a few years later that we *really* gave women a reason to want to smoke. George Washington Hill, who's just inherited the American Tobacco Company from his father, is driving in New York City. He's stopped at a light and he notices a fat woman standing on the corner gobbling chocolate, cramming it down. A taxi pulls up and he sees this elegant woman sitting in the back and what is she doing? She's smoking a cigarette, probably one of Liggett and Myers' Chesterfields. He goes back to the office and orders up an ad campaign and the slogan is born, "Reach for a Lucky instead of a sweet." And suddenly the women are lighting up. And they've been puffing away ever since. As you know, they're about to become our most important customers. By the mid-nineties, for the first time in history, there will be more women smokers than men.'

BR shifted in his chair.

'What else is happening around then? The talkies. Talking pictures – 1927, Al Jolson. Why was this significant? Because now directors had a problem. They had to give actors something to do while they talked. So they put cigarettes in their hands. Audiences see their idols – Cary Grant, Carole Lombard – lighting up. Bette Davis – a chimney. That scene where Paul Henreid lights both cigarettes for them in his mouth at the end of *Now, Voyager*? Pioneered the whole field of cigarette sex. And Bogart. Bogart! Do you remember the first line Lauren Bacall says to him in *To Have and Have Not*, their first picture together?'

BR stared.

'She sort of shimmies in through the doorway, nineteen years old, pure sex, and that voice. She says, 'Anybody got a match?' And Bogie throws the matches at her. And she catches them. The greatest screen romance of the twentieth century, and how does it begin? With a match. Do you know how many times they lit up in that movie? Twenty-one times. They went through two packs in that movie.'

'Now she's hawking nicotine patches,' BR said.

Christopher Buckley, *Thank You For Smoking*, 1995

[Smoking in the 1930s]

Did I mention that we were all smoking away like railway engines? Everyone smoked then, we stumbled about everywhere in clouds of tobacco fumes. I recall with a pang, in this Puritan age, the Watteauesque delicacy of those grey-blue, gauzy billows we breathed out everywhere on the air, suggestive of twilight and misted grass and thickening shadows under great trees – although Alastair's belching pipe was more the Potteries than Versailles.

John Banville, *The Untouchable*, 1997

Above the couch were the originals of two old cigarette magazine ads from the forties and fifties. The first showed an old-fashioned doctor, the kind who used to make house calls and even drive through snow-drifts to deliver babies. He was smilingly offering up a pack of Luckies like it was a pack of lifesaving erythromycin. '20,679* Physicians say

"Luckies are *less irritating*" ' The asterisk indicated that an actual accounting firm had actually counted them. How much easier it had been when medical science was on their side.

The second ad demonstrated how Camels helped you to digest your Thanksgiving dinner, course by course. 'Off to a good start – with hot spiced tomato soup. And then – for digestion's sake – smoke a Camel right after the soup.' You were then supposed to smoke another before your second helping of turkey. Why? Because 'Camels ease tension. Speed up the flow of digestive fluids. Increase alkalinity.' Then it was another before the Waldorf salad. Another after the Waldorf salad. 'This double pause clears the palate – and sets the stage for dessert.' Then one *with* the plum pudding – 'for the final touch of comfort and good cheer.' It amounted to five, and that was just during dinner. Once coffee was served, you were urged to take out that pack and really go to town. 'For digestion's sake.'

Christopher Buckley, *Thank You For Smoking*, 1995

If [a man] is on the dole, and the same assumptions naturally apply whether he is in that position through ill health or ill luck or shiftlessness, both husband and wife assume that he must still have his pocketmoney. Self-respect is involved; 'a man can't be without money in 'is pocket'; he would then feel less than a man, feel 'tied to' his wife and inferior to her, and such a situation is against nature. He must have money for cigarettes and beer, perhaps even for an occasional bet; the amount regularly spent each week, even by men out of work, would seem in many cases excessive to, say, the professional middle-classes. Fifteen cheap cigarettes a day seems normal, and those cost about thirteen shillings a week; for a man out of work and drawing the dole, one pound a week for pocket-money is the figure I most commonly hear nowadays. Such things as cigarettes and beer, it is felt, are part of life; without them, life would not be life; there are rarely any other major interests to make these pleasures less relevant and worth forgoing. It is, I suppose, the sense that such things are part of the minimum staple of life which makes many families, even where the husband is working well and has plenty of money in his pocket, maintain the old arrangement whereby the wife buys 'with the groceries' – that is, out of the housekeeping money – a proportion of the husband's weekly cigarettes.

Richard Hoggart, *The Uses of Literacy*, 1957

When I began that novel about the civil servant I was still interested, but when Sarah left me, I recognized my work for what it was – as unimportant a drug as cigarettes to get one through the weeks and years.

Graham Greene, *The End of the Affair*, 1951

Smoking on television

Smoking on television hasn't always been a sign of villainy, of course. It's still surprising to see Desi Arnaz in 1953, smoking like a fiend in the maternity waiting room, on the famous episode when Lucy gives birth to Little Ricky. You never see the mother, of course, only the expectant father sucking on his cigarette, being brave for his wife but fighting hysterical panic, oblivious to the cigarette he's madly consuming, and we can't stop watching. Cigarettes, it's well known, are magnificent instruments for mitigating anxiety. They are the friend of soldiers, journalists and actors in the wings – people who must wait for fateful events to occur.

It is even more surprising, today, looking at early television, to see the title character of 'Dr Kildare' offering a light to one of his troubled patients. In the very first scene of the premiere show, in 1961, Dr Kildare, played handsomely by Richard Chamberlain, bounds up the hospital stairs and puts quarters in a cigarette machine in the lobby. On the show, cigarettes are practically his signature and convey the pervasive assumption that all good doctors smoke. Offering a light or a cigarette, in the hospital, is a sign of sympathetic attention, a gesture of conviviality and sociality that made Dr Kildare's hospital, before HMO's, a close-knit community.

Richard Klein, 'After the Preaching, the Lure of the Taboo', *New York Times*, 24 August 1997

[An Old Black-and-White Clip from the 'Radioactive Man' TV Show]

RADIOACTIVE MAN: Aaahh . . . These Laramie cigarettes give me the steady nerves I need to combat evil.

FALLOUT BOY: Gee Whillikers, Radioactive Man. Wisht I was old enough to smoke Laramies.

RADIOACTIVE MAN: Sorry, Fallout Boy, not until you're sixteen (*winks at the camera*).

'Three Men and a Comic Book' (episode 7F21, written by Jeff Martin) in Ray Richmond and Antonia Coffman, editors, *The Simpsons: A Complete Guide to Our Favourite Family*, 1997 (created by Matt Groening)

The use of tobacco, which has made its way thanks to the spirit of imitation, as well as to its peculiar effects, has vanquished humanity and will continue to reign until the end of the world.

Louis Lewin, *Phantastica: Narcotic and Stimulating Drugs. Their Use and Abuse*, 1924 (trans. P. H. A. Wirth, 1931)

Although the fight between the smokers and non-smokers still drags on, with varying success, a glance at statistics proves convincingly that the latter are but a feeble and ever-dwindling minority. The hopeless nature of their struggle becomes plain when we remember that all countries, whatever their form of government, now encourage and facilitate the passion for smoking in every conceivable way, merely for the sake of the revenue which it produces . . .

In European countries no serious attempt to prohibit smoking has been made in recent times. Though it is still possible to enforce the drink laws in the United States, by means of a gigantic organization, any proposal to deal in the same way with smoking would call forth such a storm of disapproval as would instantly sweep any government out of office that attempted it, and the same may be confidently affirmed of every country in the world. If we consider how in the past the efforts of the most absolute despots the world has ever seen were powerless to stop the spread of smoking we may rest assured that any such attempts to-day, when the habit has grown to such gigantic dimensions, can result only in a miserable fiasco.

E. C. Corti, *A History of Smoking*, 1930 (trans. Paul England, 1931)

[Smoking] is the most firmly fixed and progressive of recreative habits. Until an equal substitute is provided or some clear proof presented that the use of tobacco is physically dangerous, it will retain its place in the affections of mankind.

Jerome E. Brooks, *The Mighty Leaf: Tobacco through the Centuries*, 1953

CHAPTER SIX

'Has Mankind All These Years Been Nursing a Viper in its Bosom?'

All the alleged harm of cigarettes is due to bad paper, the deadliest thing a smoker can consume.

W. A. Penn, *The Soverane Herbe: A History of Tobacco*, 1901

Notwithstanding the fact that three centuries of experience have shown the comparative harmlessness of tobacco when used in moderation, equally violent diatribes are still being directed against smoking.

Black's Medical Dictionary, 1955

... tobacco is the only legally available consumer product which kills people when it is entirely used as intended.

The Oxford Medical Companion, 1994

When Isaac Adler produced the first full-length book on lung cancer in 1912, he began by apologising for having concentrated on such an obscure and unimportant disease. As we know, it didn't stay that way for long. The question was why such a rapid increase in cases was taking place. In 1761, John Hill, an English doctor, had coupled smoking with cancer of the nasal passages. Thirty years later, in Germany, Samuel T. von Soemmerring did the same for cancer of the lip. And in the 1850s, Etienne-Frédéric Bouisson in Montpellier noticed that 63 of his 68 patients with cancer of the mouth (*cancer des fumeurs* – which must have been a clue) were pipe smokers. Even so, the link between one of the twentieth-century's fastest-growing products and one of its fastest-growing diseases took a surprising length of time to establish, and then to become commonly known.

The first proper studies took place in Nazi Germany where Hitler's hatred of tobacco led to ambitious public-health campaigns against smoking – and to bans on uniformed SS officers, uniformed police officers and anybody under 18 smoking in public. Smoking was also prohibited on city buses and trains, so as to protect the young women who took the tickets. In 1941, at the University of Jena, the Institute for Tobacco Hazards Research was founded by

Karl Astel, whose other interests included 'euthanasia' for the mentally ill, racial hygiene and organising deportations to the death camps. Hitler's telegram to the Institute when it opened read: 'Best of luck in your work to free humanity from one of its most dangerous poisons.'

But by 1941, the two most ground-breaking works had already been published. Fritz Lickint in 1929 produced the first statistical evidence of the connection between lung cancer and cigarettes (which Adler and others had speculated about), but his masterpiece was the 1,100-page *Tabak und Organismus* (Tobacco and the Organism), published 10 years later. In it he blamed tobacco for cancers of lips, tongue, mouth, jaw and lungs. He also named nicotine as addictive, and even coined the phrase 'passive smoking' (*Passivrauchen*), which he saw as a serious threat to non-smokers. In 1939, too, Franz H. Müller, a 25-year-old Cologne doctor of whom there is no trace after the war, wrote in a dissertation, *Tabakmissbrauch und Lungencarcinom*, that 'the extraordinary rise in tobacco use [is] the single most important cause of the rising incidence of lung cancer' – a much more emphatic statement than Richard Doll and Bradford Hill made in their much more famous 'Smoking and Carcinoma of the Lung', in the *British Medical Journal* in September 1950. Nonetheless, their verdict, 'Smoking is a factor, and an important factor, in the production of carcinoma of the lung', was both unambiguous and influential, especially as Ernst Wynder and Evarts Graham had just reached the same conclusion in the United States.

For a while, some writers (most eccentrically H. J. Eysenck) tried to suggest that a link wasn't the same as a causal link. Generally, though, it was bad news for smokers from then on. In 1952, *Reader's Digest* – America's best-selling magazine and a long-time anti-smoking campaigner – took the issue out of the medical journals and placed it before the public with an article entitled 'Cancer by the Carton'. Two years later, Iain Macleod, the British Minister of Health, announced in the House of Commons, 'there is a strong presumption that the relationship [between cigarettes and lung cancer] is causal'. The Medical Research Council's special report of 1957* went beyond presumption – as did the crucial early 1960s reports by the Royal College of Physicians and, in America, by the Surgeon General's Advisory Committee (this last, despite the fact that the tobacco industry won the right to veto any members of the committee whom they felt were biased). And soon, of course, lung cancer was by no means the only disease identified as smoking-related. The evidence may have seemed conclusive – but the tobacco industry was not about to go quietly.

---

* Incidentally, it wasn't until 1957 that the *British Medical Journal* stopped carrying adverts for cigarettes.

Nazi Germany

We also know that the Führer at one point characterized tobacco as 'the wrath of the Red Man against the White Man, vengeance for having been given hard liquor.' Hitler seems to have regretted having allowed his soldiers to smoke: on March 2, 1942, he noted that 'it was a mistake, traceable to the army leadership at the time, to have started giving our soldiers daily rations of tobacco at the beginning of the war.' He added that it was 'not correct to say that a soldier cannot live without smoking,' and vowed to put an end to military tobacco rations once peace was achieved. Hitler himself had smoked some twenty-five to forty cigarettes per day in his Viennese youth, until he realized how much money he was wasting, whereupon he 'tossed his cigarettes into the Danube and never reached for them again.' He also claimed – strange as this sounds today – that Germany might never have achieved its present glory if he had continued to smoke: 'perhaps it was to this, then [that is, his giving up smoking], that we owe the salvation of the German people.'

Robert N. Proctor, *The Nazi War on Cancer**, 1999

[Restrictions on tobacco advertising in Germany, introduced in December 1941]

1. The Content of Tobacco Advertising

Tobacco advertisements should be reserved and tasteful in both images and text. They must not run counter to efforts to maintain and promote public health (*Volksgesundheit*), and must not violate the following principles:

a. Smoking may not be portrayed as health-promoting or as harmless.
b. Images that create the impression that smoking is a sign of masculinity are barred, as are images depicting men engaged in activities attractive to youthful males (athletes or pilots, for example).
c. Advocates of tobacco abstinence or temperance must not be mocked.

* A book, I should acknowledge, that I drew on heavily for the introduction to this chapter.

d. Tobacco advertising cannot be directed at women, and may not involve women in any manner.

e. Tobacco advertising may not be directed at sportsmen or automobile drivers, and may not depict such activities.

f. Attention may not be drawn to the low nicotine content of a tobacco product, if accompanied by a suggestion that the smoker may thereby safely increase his tobacco use.

2. Limits on Advertising Methods

Advertising for tobacco products may not be conducted:

a. In films.

b. Using billboards or posters, especially on gables but also along railway lines, in rural areas, at sports fields and racetracks.

c. On posters in post offices.

d. On billboards in or on public or private transportation, at bus stops or similar facilities.

e. On posters, on walls, fences, at sports arenas or racetracks, or by removable tags on commercial products or adhesive posters on storefronts and doors of shops.

f. By loudspeaker (on top of cars, for example).

g. By mail.

h. By ads in the text sections of journals and newspapers.

Robert N. Proctor, *The Nazi War on Cancer*, 1999

My grandmother's brother, my greatuncle Pepe Castro, grew up hating God, smoking in general and particularly cigars. He hated tobacco so much so that, when he heard or read somewhere that Hitler spurned smoking and smokers alike, he became a Nazi!

G. Cabrera Infante, *Holy Smoke*, 1985

Non-smokers are always inclined to suggest that their noses are in better trim than those of smokers. I do not believe this. Rose and lilac, heliotrope, honeysuckle, carnation and sweet-pea, all smell the sweeter to me because I am a smoker. And what perfume is more potent than that of night-scented Virginia stock and the tobacco-plant of our gardens mingling with the fragrance of a good cigar when in a summer twilight we stroll along a border of flowers in a dusky English garden? The air of life . . .

And as I murmur those words to myself there rises before the mind's eye the spectre of that non-smoking lackey of death in his lavatory-attendant's uniform – Adolf Hitler. I have been fair. I have cited examples of non-smokers to whom the world owes much. I have made it clear I recognize that human greatness may be displayed by one who never smoked so much as half a Woodbine cigarette. I do not propose to attribute the evil that was Hitler to his antipathy against tobacco. Nevertheless, the ineluctable fact remains that the man who brought more misery to the world than any other human being hated smoking as in medieval days the Devil was said to hate holy water. Hitler dreaded the benign influence of tobacco. He must have known intuitively that if he surrendered to that sedative influence his ulcerous mind might be healed, and if once the inner rage that gnawed at him was allayed he must have realized he would be as commonplace as he looked. Yes, I am convinced that Hitler was afraid of tobacco, and murdered it as Macbeth murdered sleep.

Compton Mackenzie, *Sublime Tobacco*, 1957

[After the death of Hitler]

While these last rites and pieties were being observed by guards and sentries, the regents of the Bunker were busy with more practical matters. Having set the bodies alight and paid their last summary respects, they had returned to safety underground, there to contemplate the future. Once again, as after Hitler's first leavetaking, a great cloud seemed to have been lifted from their spirits. The nightmare of ideological repression was over, and if the prospect before them remained dark and dubious, at least they were now free to consider it in a businesslike manner. From this moment nobody seems to have bothered about the past or the two corpses still sizzling in the garden. That episode was over, and in the short space of time remaining they had their own problems to face. As the tragically-minded guard observed, it was sad to see everyone so indifferent to the Fuehrer's body.

The first evidence of the changed atmosphere in the Bunker was noticed by the secretaries, who had been dismissed during the ceremony, but who now returned to their stations. On arrival they learned the details from Guensche and Linge; but it was not from such second-hand information only that they knew that Hitler was dead. Everyone, they observed, was smoking in the Bunker. During Hitler's lifetime that had been absolutely forbidden; but now the headmaster had gone and the boys could break the rules. Under the soothing influence of nicotine, whose absence must have increased the nervous tension of the past week, they were able to consider the administrative problems which the Fuehrer had left them to face.

H. R. Trevor-Roper, *The Last Days of Hitler*, revised edition, 1962

Britain and America

[Sir Richard Doll remembers how the breakthrough was made]

On 1 January 1948, when I began to work with Bradford Hill, there was, if anything, less awareness of the possible ill effects of smoking than there had been 50 years before. For the spread of the cigarette habit, which was as entrenched among male doctors as among the rest of the adult male population (80 per cent of whom smoked) had so dulled the collective sense that tobacco might be a threat to health that the possibility that it might be the culprit was given only scant attention . . .

Consequently, we began our study without any expectation that tobacco was likely to be an important cause of the disease and we included questions about its use primarily because the consumption of tobacco and particularly the consumption of cigarettes had increased at a possibly appropriate interval before the increase in mortality began to be recorded. For my part, I suspected that if we could find a cause it was most likely to have something to do with motor cars and the tarring of roads . . .

Altogether, we had the assistance of four almoners, and data were amassed so quickly that within a year it was obvious to Bradford Hill and me that the lung cancer patients were distinguished from patients in the control groups by the rarity with which they were lifelong non-smokers, a condition that we had defined as never having smoked as much as one cigarette a day (or its equivalent in pipe tobacco or cigars) on average for as long as one year . . .

By the end of 1949 the position was so clear that we had written a paper based on our findings in 709 pairs of lung cancer and control patients drawing the conclusion that (I quote) 'smoking is a factor, and an important factor, in the production of carcinoma of the lung'. When, however, we showed the paper to Sir Harold Himsworth, who had by then succeeded Sir Edward Mellanby as Secretary of the Medical Research Council, he wisely advised us to postpone publication until we had checked that similar results would be reproduced outside London. We consequently withheld publication and started to interview similar groups of patients in some of the principal hospitals in and around Bristol, Cambridge, Leeds and Newcastle. Before we had obtained much more data, however, Wynder and Graham (1950) reported very similar findings in their study of patients in the US, and we consequently published ours a few months later (in September 1950) without waiting for the results of the extended study. The latter were published in 1952, relating to 1,465 pairs of patients and controls and showed essentially identical results in all centres – except that heavy smoking by women had not spread outside London. Our conclusion that 'smoking was an important cause of carcinoma of the lung' was not, of course, based just on the finding that the relative risk in very heavy smokers was some 50 times that in lifelong non-smokers, but on the evidence that we had avoided bias, our inability to envisage any confounding factors that we could not exclude, the progressive increase in risk with the amount smoked, the reduction in risk with time since smoking had been stopped, the temporal relationships between the increase in cigarette consumption and the increase in mortality from lung cancer in Britain and many other countries, the corresponding sex differences in smoking and lung cancer mortality, and, of course, the consistency of the findings with those of the few other reported studies.

By the end of 1950, the results of seven other studies of variable quality were available from Germany, The Netherlands and the USA, and all showed similar results in that lung cancer patients were relatively less often lifelong non-smokers and more often heavy smokers than control patients.

Nevertheless, there was great reluctance on the part of most cancer research workers, physicians and statisticians to accept our conclusion.

Sir Richard Doll, 'The First Reports on Smoking and Lung Cancer' in S. Lock. L. A. Reynolds and E. M. Tansey, editors, *Ashes to Ashes: the History of Smoking and Health*, 1998

The unconvinced

Surely the tobacco addiction of the 20th century is preferable to the alcohol addiction of the 19th as being less disruptive to the physical, moral, and economic health of the community. It might be wiser to concentrate on the question of how smoking can be made even safer than to tamper with a complex mass psychological phenomenon which in this century has found a fairly acceptable outlet. Even if smoking increases the chance of a man developing cancer of the lung from 1 in 10,000 to 1 in 1000, it remains questionable whether community or individual have anything to gain from the abolition of smoking. The chances of drowning increase even more steeply with the acquisition of the ability to swim, and it may after all be better to be a smoker than a swimmer . . .

There will always be cases in which smoking has to be discouraged. But there are many non-smokers to whom the best advice that a doctor can give is that they should get a pipe and dissolve some of their soul- and body-destroying frustrations into blue smoke.

Erich Geiringer, *The Lancet*, 11 October 1952

['Not Proven']

Smoking is said to clear the brain and make concentration easier and this makes a very pleasant contrast with such a drug as opium; in fact it is fairly true to say that, apart from its present-day association with cancer, smoking is not a world-wide habit without good reason. It is on the whole a beneficent weed; it helps suffering humanity at many a crisis; it relieves the monotony of many humble, uneventful lives; it staves off hunger and releases the tension in overstrung nerves; it is one of Nature's gentlest stimulants . . .

If a man is over-excited, tobacco will soothe him; if he is in a depressed mood, smoking can lift him out of it without bad after-effects . . .

Has mankind all these years been nursing a viper in its bosom that distils some poison into the body? Can it be true that tobacco, which has been smoked for centuries, contains a poison that can cause cancer? This is something that will have to be proved to the hilt before man forswears the weed . . .

Having discovered this weed, tobacco, man has certainly contrived to get what he can out of it. He not only smokes it, swallows it, drinks concoctions of it, gargles with it, but licks it in ceremony, chews it or sniffs it up his nose. One question before him now is whether he should do without it. People who are in any way addicted to a drug will rarely give it up, whatever warning may be given. But most smokers are not addicts; the pleasure of smoking is real, and unless the danger of its producing any disease is considerable, the risk may or may not be taken; there is no ruling on the matter. We have had a warning – it might be true – but it seems that the case for cancer of the lung being produced by smoking is Not Proven.

Sidney Russ, CBE, DSC, *Smoking and Its Effects: With Special Reference to Lung Cancer*, 1955 (Russ was Professor Emeritus, University of London, at the time.)

[A prophetic moment]

In 1953 the Hunterian Society held a discussion upon a motion, 'That Tobacco is a Blessing'. Discussion ranged over the good and evil effects of smoking and inevitably lung cancer came into the picture. While to some there is no doubt that smoking and cancer have something causal linking them, this is evidently far from the view of a participator who said: 'If people were to give up smoking because of the fear of dying of cancer of the lung they might as well give up eggs and bacon for breakfast because this increased the coagulability of the blood and so made the partaker more liable to coronary thrombosis.' . . .

A well-known kind of skin cancer occurs in people over-exposed to sun and weather. Are we to label even the elements as causes of cancer? It seems irrational to do so.

Sidney Russ, CBE, DSC, *Smoking and Its Effects: With Special Reference to Lung Cancer*, 1955

The turning-points

Introduction
Several serious diseases, in particular lung cancer, affect smokers more often than non-smokers. Cigarette smokers have the greatest risk of dying from these diseases, and the risk is greater for the heavier smokers. The many deaths caused by these diseases present a challenge to medicine, in so far as they are due to smoking they should be

preventable. This report is intended to give to doctors and others evidence on the hazards of smoking so that they may decide what should be done . . .

Smoking and cancer of the lung

There has been a great increase in deaths from this disease in many countries during the past 45 years. Some of this increase may be due to better diagnosis, but much of it is due to a real increase in incidence. Men are much more often affected than women.

Surveys. Many comparisons have been made in different countries between the smoking habits of patients with lung cancer and those of patients of the same age and sex with other diseases. All have shown that more lung cancer patients are smokers, and more of them heavy smokers than are the controls. The association between smoking and lung cancer has been confirmed by prospective studies in which the smoking habits of large numbers of men have been recorded and their deaths from various diseases observed subsequently. All these studies have shown that death rates from lung cancer increase steeply with increasing consumption of cigarettes. Heavy cigarette smokers may have thirty times the death rate of non-smokers. They have also shown that cigarette smokers are much more affected than pipe or cigar smokers and that those who had given up smoking at the start of the surveys had lower death rates than those who had continued to smoke . . .

Interpretation of the Evidence. The association of lung cancer with cigarette smoking is generally agreed to be true but various possible explanations of this association other than that of cause and effect have to be considered. These are:

  (i) that people who are going to get lung cancer have an increased desire to smoke throughout their adult lives:

  (ii) that smoking produces cancer only in the lungs of people who are in any case going to get cancer somewhere in the body, so that smoking determines only the site of the cancer:

  (iii) that lung cancer affects people who would have died of tuberculosis in former times but have now survived with lungs susceptible to cancer:

  (iv) that smokers inherit their desire to smoke and with it inherit a susceptibility to some other undiscovered agent that causes lung cancer:

(v) that smokers are by their nature more liable to many diseases, including lung cancer, than the 'self-protective' minority of non-smokers:

(vi) that smokers tend to drink more alcohol than non-smokers so that drinking and not smoking may cause lung cancer:

(vii) that motor car exhausts, or –

(viii) that generalised air pollution may render the lungs of smokers more liable to cancer.

None of these explanations fits all the facts as well as the obvious one that smoking is a cause of lung cancer.

Conclusions

The benefits of smoking are almost entirely psychological and social. It may help some people to avoid obesity. There is no reason to suppose that smoking prevents neurosis.

Cigarette smoking is a cause of lung cancer and bronchitis, and probably contributes to the development of coronary heart disease and various other less common diseases. It delays healing of gastric and duodenal ulcers.

The risks of smoking to the individual are calculated from death rates in relation to smoking habits among British doctors.

The chance of dying in the next ten years for a man aged 35 who is a heavy cigarette smoker is 1 in 23 whereas the risk for a non-smoker is only 1 in 90. Only 15 per cent (one in six) of men of this age who are non-smokers but 33 per cent (one in three) of heavy smokers will die before the age of 65. Not all this difference in expectation of life is attributable to smoking.

The number of deaths caused by diseases associated with smoking is large.

Summary at the beginning of *Smoking and Health: A Report of The Royal College of Physicians of London on Smoking in relation to Cancer of the Lung and Other Diseases*, 1962*

The American Surgeon General's report of 1964 was much longer, more technical and – it's generally agreed – more scholarly than its British equivalent. As well as its assertion that nicotine led to 'habituation' rather than 'addiction' (a distinction insisted on by Maurice H. Seevers, one of the two

---

* Ironically, most of the report's 'History of Smoking' section was taken from Compton Mackenzie.

members of the ten-strong advisory committee who'd been put forward by the tobacco manufacturers), its most obviously significant passages included:

Cigarette smoking is causally related to lung cancer in men; the magnitude of the effect of cigarette smoking far outweighs all other factors. The data for women, though less extensive, point in the same direction.

The risk of developing lung cancer increases with duration of smoking and the number of cigarettes smoked per day, and is diminished by discontinuing smoking. In comparison with non-smokers, average male smokers of cigarettes have approximately a 9- to 10-fold risk of developing lung cancer and heavy smokers at least a 20-fold risk.

The risk of developing cancer of the lung for the combined group of pipe smokers, cigar smokers, and pipe and cigar smokers is greater than for non-smokers, but much less than for cigarette smokers.

Cigarette smoking is much more important than occupational exposures in the causation of lung cancer in the general population . . .

On the basis of prolonged study and evaluation of many lines of converging evidence, the Committee makes the following judgment:

Cigarette smoking is a health hazard of sufficient importance in the United States to warrant appropriate remedial action.

Smoking and Health: Report of the Advisory Committee to the Surgeon General of the Public Health Service, 1964

[An eerily accurate glimpse of the smoker's future – apart from always being allowed to smoke in friends' houses]

The aim must be to establish non-smoking as the norm of behaviour, rather than the exception . . .

London is the most smoke-easy city I know. In Moscow, New York, Toronto, Paris, and Stockholm for instance, no smoking at all is allowed on the Underground. This is accepted as normal and makes a tremendous difference, not only to the atmosphere, but to the amount of litter which has to be collected. I think this change in London should be made urgently.

An increasing number of shops are asking customers not to smoke, but in New York, for example, this is a rule in most of the big stores – for fire prevention as well as health reasons. Of course shops are afraid of losing business if they impose restrictions which their competitors ignore, but it might be worth considering whether this could not be dealt with through by-laws, for instance, which could start by banning smoking in food shops. This is done in Sweden.

Nowadays several theatres here ask people not to smoke, and there is no evidence of their suffering any lack of patronage because of this. In Sweden, Finland, France, the Soviet Union, and in parts of North America smoking is absolutely prohibited in both cinemas and theatres. In Italy it is forbidden in theatres but allowed in cinemas. A sensible arrangement exists in some Canadian cinemas, in Toronto, for example, where smoking is allowed only in a special gallery. The seats cost more and the spiralling smoke is an interference to a minimum of other people.

Restrictions on smoking in buses and other forms of public transport are much more severe in most other countries than here. There is, of course, no logic in our restrictions, such as they are. We do not expect people to smoke in church – although we have shown that in the seventeenth century they did. Nor would we expect policemen to smoke on duty. Members of Parliament are not allowed to smoke in the chamber or in the immediate approaches – although there is still a snuff box, permanently supplied, at the entrance to the Commons chamber. There is of course a smoking-room, which is a much less anti-social way of providing for those who must smoke than by making it generally permitted. There must be many public institutions and private undertakings where there would be no great difficulty in extending this idea ... The point is that people should have to take some trouble if they really have to smoke.

Restriction of smoking in places where people congregate for either work or pleasure is important. The discomfort of the non-smoker in a smoke-blue office or railway carriage can be severe. But perhaps even more important is the fact that general tolerance of smoking undermines all the attempts to persuade the young not to smoke ...

The sheer nuisance of the unaesthetic mess which smoking makes has had surprisingly little effect on the habit. Perhaps it is because so many women smoke in this country that they are tolerant of the offensiveness of dirty ashtrays, impregnated curtains, and of fire risks.

But harping on the extra cleanliness of a home where nobody smokes is the least attractive of arguments, conjuring visions of comfortless, sanitary, and unloving women – like Mrs Ogmore-Pritchard in *Under Milk Wood* who wants the sun to wipe his shoes before he comes into her immaculate, cheerless house. This is why the enthusiasts must go carefully. It is useless for a hostess to insist that her tasty cooking will be the better enjoyed by people with clean palates, true though this may be. Making one's guests feel uncomfortable or resented is no part of hospitality and I can see us going on emptying those ashtrays and cleaning up the dog-ends indefinitely. The most one can do is probably not to offer cigarettes, thereby at least suggesting one does not actually expect one's visitors to smoke.

Lena Jeger, 'The Social Implications' in *Common Sense about Smoking*, 1963

The still unconvinced

An alternative hypothesis to that of direct causal relation between smoking and lung cancer has been put forward, postulating that the statistical results obtained may be due to the fact that persons constitutionally predisposed to take up smoking are also constitutionally predisposed to develop cancer. Evidence has been brought forward to show that persons of an extraverted temperament are both more likely to smoke cigarettes, and to develop cancer, than are persons of an introverted temperament. While this evidence is not based on sufficient numbers of cases to establish the point definitively, it must be said that the congruence between several studies which has been a notable point of our survey lends some credence to the hypothesis. A further point in its favour is the established relationship between smoking, cancer proneness, and pyknic (squat, stocky) body build; persons of this body type are known to have predominantly extraverted types of temperament.

The hypothesis that cigarette smoking causes cancer is so appealing because it satisfies simultaneously two sets of relations. In the first place it explains the statistical correlation between smoking and cancer; in the second place it explains the rapid growth in the incidence of lung cancer in recent years, which agrees well with the growth of cigarette consumption. The constitutional hypothesis explains the first of these sets of relations; the second is possibly best explained by reference to the growth in air pollution. Urban air contains the same cyclic hydrocarbons and radioactive isotopes as tobacco smoke, and in addition contains them in much greater profusion. This hypothesis would also serve to explain the close correlation between lung cancer rates and degree of urbanization, a correlation which is not due to differences in smoking habits.

H. J. Eysenck, *Smoking, Health and Personality*, 1965

CIGARETTES, Consumption: The heaviest smokers in the world are the people of the United States, where 529,000 million cigarettes (an average of 3,473 per adult) were consumed at a cost of about $11,500 million (£4,600 *million*) in 1972. The peak consumption in the United Kingdom was 3,090 cigarettes per adult in 1972. The peak volume was 243,100,000 lb. *110,2 million kg* in 1961, compared with 216,200,000 lb. *98,0 million kg* in 1972, when 130,500 million cigarettes were sold.

In the United Kingdom 65 per cent of adult men and 42 per cent of adult women smoke. Nicotine releases acetylcholine in the brain, so reducing tension and increasing resolve. It has thus been described as an anodyne to civilization.

Norris and Ross McWhirter, editors, *The Guinness Book of Records*, 1973

A vivid example of exaggeration was provided by a robust, independent Australian Professor of mathematical statistics, Peter Finch, in an instructive paper republished by FOREST as 'Lies, Damned Lies . . .'. He took the official statistics of annual mortality and contrasted them with the warning that younger smokers (under 45) suffer 15 times the risk of non-smokers of dying of coronary heart disease. It is nicely calculated to bolster the message that SMOKING KILLS. But is it an informative way of presenting a difference in annual risk – on the showing of the anti-smoking lobby themselves – between 7 *per 100,000* for non-smokers and *104 per 100,000* for smokers? True, 104 is roughly 15 times 7. But Professor Finch obligingly re-works the same figures to show that a smoker has 99.9% of the annual chance of the non-smoker of *escaping death from a coronary*. The trick to grasp is that a large increase on a tiny risk may still remain a small risk.

Turning to lung cancer, Professor Finch quotes the standard Doll & Hill figures as showing that heavy smokers face almost 24 times the annual risk faced by non-smokers of dying from that disease. This time the increase is from 7 per 100,000 to 166 per 100,000, which still leaves the smoker with 99.8% of the annual chance enjoyed by non-smokers of *escaping* death from lung cancer.

Ralph Harris and Judith Hatton (both of FOREST, 'Britain's smokers' rights group'), *Murder a Cigarette*, 1998

All the diseases related to smoking that cause large numbers of deaths should by now have been discovered, but further effects like age-related macular degeneration, which was firmly linked to smoking only in 1996, may well remain to be revealed ... That so many diseases – major and minor – should be related to smoking is one of the most remarkable medical research findings of the present century.

Sir Richard Doll, 'Uncovering the Effects of Smoking: Historical Perspective' in *Statistical Methods in Medical Research*, Vol. 7, No. 2: *The Statistics of Smoking*, June 1998

OLIVER Have a cigarette? You don't? I know you don't – you've told me that before. Your disapproval still flashes in neon. Your frown is worthy of the mother-in-law from *Katya Kabanova*. But I have puckish news for you. I read in the paper this morning that if you smoke you're less likely to develop Alzheimer's disease than if you don't. A hit, a veritable hit? Go on, have one, kipper your lungs and keep your brain intact. Isn't life bedizened with jaunty contradictions? Just when you think you've got it straight, along comes the Fool with his pig's bladder and whops you on the nose.

Julian Barnes, *Talking It Over*, 1991

CHAPTER SEVEN

Armageddon Time

It was very difficult when you were asked, as Chairman of a Tobacco Company, to discuss the health question on television. You had not only your own business to consider but the employees throughout the industry, retailers, consumers, farmers growing the leaf, and so on, and you were in much too responsible a position to get up and say: 'I accept that the product which we and all our competitors are putting on the market gives you lung cancer', whatever you might think privately.

Anthony D. McCormick, British American Tobacco, from the minutes of the Southampton research conference, 1962

What happened next, I'm afraid, needs a longer introduction than usual – and also a focus on America, since that's where the most ferocious tobacco battles have been fought in the last 50 years.

So, as the evidence piled up against them, what were the tobacco companies to do? Essentially, their strategy was two-fold: to deny any proven link between their product and disease, while still expressing their strong desire to get to the bottom of the whole business. (O. J. Simpson announcing his hunt for 'the real killer' springs to mind.) It was a strategy put into place almost immediately the first lung-cancer reports appeared – and held on to until long after any chance of convincing people had vanished.

In December 1953 at the Plaza hotel, New York, representatives of American tobacco companies met to form their first ever united front. The result was 'A Frank Statement to Cigarette Smokers' (see below), which foreshadowed their public pronouncements for the next 40 years. It also announced the setting up of the Tobacco Industry Research Committee, later to become the Council for Tobacco Research. Ostensibly, these bodies were part of the companies' plan to dig out the truth from beneath the layers of anti-smoking propaganda. In reality – as leaked memos would eventually reveal – they were at least as much concerned with public relations. Tobacco-friendly doctors were cultivated. Grants were made to scientists who held out against the causal-link theory. Beneficiaries who came up with the wrong answer tended to find themselves in trouble.*

The other important development of the 1950s was the introduction of the filter cigarette – not, the companies were keen to point out, that there was anything wrong with the unfiltered kind. It was just that modern smokers seemed to be demanding less tar and nicotine. Even so, the acceptance of filters was by no means instantaneous. One of the functions of the Marlboro man was to undermine the commonly-held belief that they were for cissies, and in 1960 Pall Mall (selling point: 'You can light either end') overtook the equally unfiltered Camel as America's best-selling cigarette.

Similar tactics were used in Britain – although because the legal system meant less fear of litigation, the Tobacco Research Council may have done more real science than its American counterpart. (This became a problem when documents that British American Tobacco in London had sent to their American subsidiary Brown and Williamson began to show up at US court cases in the 1990s.) In both countries, meanwhile, smoking continued largely unabated.

The quest for the 'safe' cigarette proved trickier. The closest anybody has come so far was probably Dr James Mold, chief doctor for the Liggett group, in the 1970s. Mold discovered that blending tobacco with microscopic amounts of the heavy metal palladium reduced the incidence of tumours on laboratory mice by 95 to 100 per cent. But, as he and his colleagues dreamed of Nobel prizes, the project was cancelled by Liggett, on the traditional tobacco-company grounds that the existence of a 'safe' cigarette might mistakenly imply that other cigarettes are dangerous. (To be fair, the legal implications of announcing the new product to the world as harmless would have been catastrophic if anything went wrong afterwards.)

And, of course, all the time the industry was trying to keep the smoking and health question at the level of 'a controversy', ever more damning reports were being produced. The Surgeon General's report of 1968 called cigarette smoking 'the main cause of lung cancer'; that of 1989 blamed it for one in six American deaths. Legislation was increasing, too – not all of it to the companies' disadvantage. When the US Congress introduced warnings on packs in 1966, for instance, many tobacco lawyers felt these would serve as a useful protection in future trials. (For a long time they did, the defence

---

* This was a pattern repeated across the board in the decades ahead. In the 1980s, a behavioural psychologist called Victor DeNoble was working in the Philip Morris research laboratories in Richmond, Virginia. He discovered that rats that could press a lever to obtain a shot of nicotine developed both an apparent addiction to the drug and a tolerance which meant they needed bigger and bigger doses to achieve the same effect. DeNoble was fired, the rats were killed and within a week the laboratory had become a series of empty rooms.

being along the lines that 'Smoking isn't dangerous – but even if it is, smokers should have known.') The banning of television adverts on both sides of the Atlantic freed up a lot of tobacco money for sponsorship, product placement and magazine blitzes. In America, it also meant that the anti-smoking ads, which had in the late 1960s been entitled to free air-time under the 'fairness doctrine', disappeared as well. By the late 1980s, fewer people were smoking – but the industry was still making serious money, and the most combative anti-tobacco politicians had been seen off, including Jimmy Carter's health secretary, Joseph Califano, and Mrs Thatcher's minister for sport, Richard Tracey. (Even the mildest conspiracy theorists noticed that Carter's support base was in tobacco-growing states and that Thatcher later became a highly-paid consultant for Philip Morris.) Most importantly, despite all the law suits, the industry was still able to boast that it hadn't ever had to pay out a penny in compensation.

The anti-tobacco forces, however, were growing increasingly coherent. For a start, there was the discovery – or invention, according to your point of view – of the dangers of passive smoking. The turning point here was the Surgeon General's report on the subject in 1986 which suggested that environmental tobacco smoke (ETS) killed 3,000 Americans a year. Yet even Richard Kluger in *Ashes to Ashes*, his Pulitzer-prize winning exposé of the tobacco industry, says that, despite the report's claims to the contrary, 'the data were neither abundant nor coherent – and certainly not conclusive', and that some of the key statements were 'misleading, if not disingenuous in the extreme'. Either way, by 1993 the US Environmental Protection Agency (EPA) had decided that ETS was responsible for 52,000 American deaths annually – and the same year classified it as 'a Class-A carcinogen'. (This classification, in turn, was ruled 'misleading' by a federal district court in 1998 – the judge explaining that the EPA had 'cherry-picked' its evidence and then manipulated 'scientific procedure and scientific norms' to reach its conclusions.) Whatever the uncertainties of the issue, passive smoking was used to introduce ever-tighter restrictions on puffing in public places.

Another anti-smoking breakthrough came when the 1988 Surgeon General's report declared that nicotine had properties 'similar to those that determine addiction to drugs such as heroin and cocaine'. This was particularly important because in the right legal hands it could remove a central plank of the tobacco companies' defence in court – and an important reason why juries had always found for them: the idea that the plaintiff's decision to continue smoking had been freely taken. The industry's response was to deny that nicotine was addictive. Famously, in 1994, seven tobacco-company chief executive officers held to this line under oath in the House of Representatives. Which might have been all right – addiction is perhaps a slippery term – except that within a month proof emerged that Big Tobacco was calling nicotine 'addictive' in internal memos as early as 1963, i.e. before the first Surgeon General's report in which they fought to ensure that only the word 'habituation' was used.

The evidence for this, and for much else besides, came in the thousands of Brown and Williamson documents taken by Merrell Williams, who had worked for the company as a paralegal sorting out their archives. The anti-tobacco lawyers to whom Williams gave his booty naturally couldn't believe their luck – the smoking gun at last – and, before long, the documents were being used in court. Williams was then followed by a whistle-blower of much higher rank. Jeffrey Wigand, the sacked head of Brown and Williamson's research department (and later the hero of the film *The Insider*) confirmed the worst. By now the court cases were different, too. Instead of individual plaintiffs asking for compensation, the attorney generals of American States sued the companies for Medicaid expenses; class-actions on behalf of thousands of ill or dead smokers were filed; a coalition had been formed of high-flying anti-tobacco lawyers, who had previous experience of such huge claims as asbestos and Bhopal. The 'Third Wave' of tobacco litigation was under way – and, in 1997, the Big Six tobacco companies, by then spending around $600m a year on legal fees, were ready to make a deal.

But writing about recent tobacco politics is hazardous. Richard Kluger is brilliant on almost all the twentieth-century developments, but his book was published just before the story reached its climax. Peter Pringle's *Dirty Business* (1998) is a painstaking guide to the Comprehensive Tobacco Settlement of June 1997. Unfortunately, the deal then fell through, and is now only an historical footnote. As I write (November 1999), the companies have settled with the States for $206bn, (the anti-tobacco lawyers got around $20bn), but failed to win immunity to prosecution by the federal government, by individuals or from class-actions. Documents are continuing to emerge which show, for example, how much the industry knew all along and how directly it targeted children as replacement smokers. At last, though, Big Tobacco is no longer maintaining its old denials.

Industry reactions, public and private

A Frank Statement to Cigarette Smokers

Recent reports on experiments with mice have given wide publicity to a theory that cigarette smoking is in some way linked with lung cancer in human beings.

Although conducted by doctors of professional standing, these experiments are not regarded as conclusive in the field of cancer research. However, we do not believe that any serious medical research, even though its results are inconclusive should be disregarded or lightly dismissed.

At the same time, we feel it is in the public interest to call attention to the fact that eminent doctors and research scientists have publicly questioned the claimed significance of these experiments.

Distinguished authorities point out:

1. That medical research of recent years indicates many possible causes of lung cancer.
2. That there is no agreement among the authorities regarding what the cause is.
3. That there is no proof that cigarette smoking is one of the causes.
4. That statistics purporting to link cigarette smoking with the disease could apply with equal force to any one of many other aspects of modern life. Indeed the validity of the statistics themselves is questioned by numerous scientists.

We accept an interest in people's health as a basic responsibility, paramount to every other consideration in our business.

We believe the products we make are not injurious to health.

We always have and always will cooperate closely with those whose task it is to safeguard the public health.

For more than 300 years tobacco has given solace, relaxation, and enjoyment to mankind. At one time or another during those years critics have held it responsible for practically every disease of the human body. One by one these charges have been abandoned for lack of evidence.

Regardless of the record of the past, the fact that cigarette smoking today should even be suspected as a cause of a serious disease is a matter of deep concern to us.

Many people have asked us what we are doing to meet the public's concern aroused by the recent reports. Here is the answer:

1. We are pledging aid and assistance to the research effort into all phases of tobacco use and health. This joint financial aid will of course be in addition to what is already being contributed by individual companies.

2. For this purpose we are establishing a joint industry group [which] ... will be known as TOBACCO INDUSTRY RESEARCH COMMITTEE.

3. In charge of the research activities of the Committee will be a scientist of unimpeachable integrity and national repute. In addition there will be an Advisory Board of scientists disinterested in the cigarette industry ...

This statement is being issued because we believe the people are entitled to know where we stand on this matter and what we intend to do about it.

Tobacco industry advert which ran in 448 American newspapers and magazines, January 1954

We will never produce and market a product shown to be the cause of any serious ailment.

From the first draft of 'A Frank Statement to Cigarette Smokers' – left out of final version

Doubt is our product since it is the best means of competing with the 'body of fact' that exists in the mind of the general public. It is also the means of establishing a controversy ... If we are successful in establishing a controversy at the public level, then there is an opportunity to put across the real facts about smoking and health. Doubt is also the limit of our 'product.' Unfortunately, we cannot take a position directly opposing the anti-cigarette forces and say that cigarettes are a contributor to good health. No information that we have supports such a claim.

'Smoking and Health Proposal', Brown and Williamson internal memo, ?1969

Taking all the above into consideration, we believe there is sound evidence to conclude that the statement 'cigarettes cause cancer' is not a statement of fact but merely an hypothesis.

Brown and Williamson public relations document, 1971

At the best, the probabilities are that some combination of constituents of smoke will be found conducive to the onset of cancer or to create an environment in which cancer is more likely to occur.

Internal memo by Addison Yeaman, vice-president and general counsel, Brown and Williamson, 1963

Is there 'mounting evidence' to link cigarette smoking with lung cancer? The 'evidence' is not medical in the usual sense, because clinical and experimental research does not bear out the anti-cigarette theory. There is no scientific cause-and-effect proof. Only statistical studies provide the 'evidence.' The curious thing is that most of what has been written against cigarette smoking in recent years is based on a relatively few statistical reports. The 'mounting evidence' impression is mainly the result of mounting publicity, rather than scientific findings.

Tobacco Industry Research Committee document, 'Cigarette Smoking and Health: What are the Facts?', written after the Royal College of Physicians report was issued in Britain

Addiction

Moreover, nicotine is addictive. We are, then, in the business of selling nicotine, an addictive drug effective in the release of stress mechanisms.

Internal memo by Addison Yeaman, vice-president and general counsel, Brown and Williamson, 1963

I do not believe that nicotine is addictive.

Thomas Sandefur, chairman and chief executive officer of Brown and Williamson testifying before the Health and Environment Subcommittee, House of Representatives, 1994

Q: And so, were you in the presence of Mr Sandefur . . . when he voiced the opinion and belief that nicotine was addictive?
JEFFREY WIGAND: Yes.
Q: And did he express that view on numerous occasions?
JW: Frequently.

Jeffrey Wigand's deposition in Pascagoula, Mississippi, November 1995

Legal tactics

[The] aggressive posture we have regarding depositions and discovery in general continues to make these cases extremely burdensome and expensive for the plaintiffs' lawyers, particularly sole practitioners. The way we won the cases, to paraphrase General Patton, is not by spending all of Reynolds' money, but by making the son-of-a-bitch spend all of his.

R. J. Reynolds legal counsel, Michael Jordan, looks back on early litigation, quoted in Peter Pringle, *Dirty Business: Big Tobacco at the Bar of Justice*, 1998

[Advice to employees of Brown and Williamson and its parent company, British American Tobacco (BAT)]

At the St. Ives Conference, May 8 to 12, 1970, an opening statement was made which included an acknowledgment that tobacco manufacturers are not competent to give authoritative medical opinions and stating that 'causation' is still an open question . . .

In the minutes of this Conference, however, we note a number of statements or expressions which could be most damaging notwithstanding the disclaimer in the opening statement. For example: (i) reference is made on page 6 to the fact that research 'will continue in the search for a safer product'; (ii) on page 14 a product is characterized as 'attractive' because less biologically active; (iii) on page 15 the phrase 'biologically attractive' is used; and (iv) on page 18 reference is made to a 'healthy cigarette' . . .

It is our opinion that statements such as the above constitute a real threat to the continued success in the defense of smoking and health litigation. Of course, we would make every effort to 'explain' such statements if we were confronted with them during a trial, but I seriously doubt that the average juror would follow or accept the subtle distinctions and explanations we would be forced to urge . . .

The testimony of outstanding and independent doctors and scientists of the type who have enabled us to win a number of cancer cases on the causation issue would be nullified or weakened by our own people's statements. Furthermore, after one experience of being disputed by statements of our own employees, it is doubtful that such independent experts would agree to testify again . . .

We, of course, know that the position of BAT, as well as B&W, is that disease causation by smoking is still very much an open question. Cigarettes have not been proved to cause any human disease. Thus, any statement by responsible and informed employees subject to a contrary interpretation could only result from carelessness. Therefore, employees in both companies should be informed of the possible consequences of careless statements on this subject.

Letter from David R. Hardy, outside counsel to the tobacco industry, to DeBaun Bryan, counsel to Brown and Williamson. The letter was written on August 20, 1970 and marked 'CONFIDENTIAL, FOR LEGAL COUNSEL ONLY'

[James Chandler Bowling, Philip Morris's PR chief]

When interviewed on the health issue in 1963 by Thomas Whiteside for *The New Yorker*, Bowling said his company's researchers were hard at the task of modifying the product to make it more 'medically acceptable,' but he spoke of 'the health scare' as if the data were spectral and the charges born of animus. Of the link between smoking and disease, Bowling asserted, 'We believe there is no connection, or we wouldn't be in the business,' and later defended the industry's executives as 'people with a social conscience.' The antismoking case was established, Bowling claimed, 'without a full understanding of the facts. Gosh, we're awed how a story can be told and retold by the anticigarette people, and how little attention is given in the press to claims *for* cigarettes.' As an example of the latter, he cited a remark he had heard recently from a physician that if smoking were suddenly halted, there would be 'more wife-beating and job dissatisfaction than people's natures can tolerate.'

Richard Kluger, *Ashes to Ashes: America's Hundred-Year Cigarette War, the Public Health, and the Unabashed Triumph of Philip Morris*, 1996, 1997

Some women would prefer having smaller babies.

Joseph Cullman, head of Philip Morris on CBS's 'Face the Nation', January 1971

Evidence is now available to indicate that the 14–18-year-old group is an increasing segment of the smoking population. RJR-T must soon establish a successful new brand in this market if our position in the industry is to be maintained over the long term.

R. J. Reynolds document, 'Planning Assumptions and Forecasts for the Period 1976–1986', 15 March 1976

[They said:] 'We don't smoke this shit. We just sell it. We reserve the right to smoke for the young, the poor, the black and the stupid.' . . . They told me on many occasions my job was to get three to four to five thousand kids smoking every day to replace those who quit or die.

Dave Goerlitz, former 'Winston Man', in *Tobacco Wars*, BBC1, 1999

Come to Marlboro Country

As Norman Muse, then a Burnett copywriter for Marlboro and later chairman of the agency's international operations, capsulized it, 'People don't want to be in the city, smelling all that crap.' 'Marlboro Country' transported them past smug suburbia and the cloying sweetness of Norman Rockwell's small towns, out beyond the tidy Arcadia and pastoral prettiness pictured in the Salem and Newport ads, to an immense, indeed limitless, landscape, awesome in its rugged yet serene beauty, where the menaces of nature were ultimately manageable, the mountain streams pure, the chuckwagon fare hearty and unfattening, and the skies were not sooty all day. 'Marlboro Country' was what Bruce Lohof, in a 1969 paean to commercial iconography in the *Journal of Popular Culture*, trenchantly called 'an environmental memoir, reminding Americans of where they had been and inviting them vicariously to return.' Above all, 'Marlboro Country' was unpolluted, free of hazards to one's moral and physical health – precisely the opposite of what science and the government were saying about smoking cigarettes.

Richard Kluger, *Ashes to Ashes: America's Hundred-Year Cigarette War, the Public Health, and the Unabashed Triumph of Philip Morris*, 1996, 1997

Wayne McLaren, who portrayed the rugged 'Marlboro Man' in cigarette ads but became an anti-smoking crusader after developing lung cancer, has died, aged 51 . . . His mother said: 'Some of his last words were: "Take care of the children. Tobacco will kill you, and I am living proof of it".' . . . Mr McLaren, a rodeo rider, actor and Hollywood stuntman . . . was a pack-and-a-half-a-day smoker for about 25 years. In an interview last week, Mr McLaren said his habit had 'caught up with me. I've spent the last month of my life in an incubator and I'm telling you, it's just not worth it.'

The Guardian, 25 July 1992

... the doctors' nickname for this particular operating room was 'Marlboro Country,' this being where they usually did the lung cancer surgery.

Christopher Buckley, *Thank You for Smoking*, 1995

The Marlboro Man and Ronald McDonald, purveyors of cigarettes and hamburgers, have been judged the top two advertising icons of the century – to the fury of health campaigners.

The characters held off strong challenges from the Jolly Green Giant, Michelin Man and Kellogg's Tony the Tiger.

Cars, cigarettes and junk food dominate the lists compiled by the 70-year-old American trade magazine *Advertising Age* of what it regards as the best campaigns, slogans and personalities of 'the advertising century'.

Daily Telegraph, 13 April 1999

———————

The uncertainty of governments

May 10th ... Dr Thorn* came to see me. He had sent me a paper on cigarettes, apparently, and the power and influence of the tobacco lobby in this country. Unfortunately I hadn't had time to read it. He asked me for my reaction to it, so I asked him to summarise it in his own words.

'Those were my own words,' he said, slightly nonplussed.

Bernard came to the rescue, very skilfully. 'The Prime Minister often finds that a brief verbatim summary clarifies the emphasis and focuses on the salient points.'

'Salient points,' I echoed, to encourage Dr Thorn.

So he told me what he had in mind, I was staggered. His idea was for the government to take action to eliminate smoking. He had a five-point plan:

1. A complete ban on all cigarette sponsorship.
2. A complete ban on all cigarette advertising, even at the point of sale.
3. Fifty million pounds to be spent on anti-smoking publicity.

* The Minister of State for Health.

4. A ban on smoking in all public places.
5. Progressive deterrent tax rises over five years until a packet of twenty costs about the same as a bottle of whisky.

It is a drastic scheme. He claims it should reduce smoking by at least eighty per cent. Even ninety per cent, perhaps. He reckons it will drive the tobacco companies out of business.

I had no immediate answer for such radical proposals . . . So I told him that obviously I agreed with him, basically, that smoking ought to be stopped. No question. And I told him that we would definitely stop it in due course, at the appropriate juncture, in the fullness of time . . .

Dr Thorn could see what I was doing, though. 'You mean, forget it?'

I assured him that that wasn't what I meant. And it wasn't! Well, not exactly! But we do have to be realistic. 'After all,' I remarked, 'we weren't born yesterday.'

'No.' He was very tight-lipped. 'And we didn't die yesterday.'

'What do you mean?' I asked.

'Three hundred people did die yesterday, prematurely, as a result of smoking. There are a hundred thousand deaths a year, at least.'

I tried to show Peter just how unrealistic he was being. If I took his proposal to Cabinet, the Treasury and the Chancellor would surely say that smoking brings in four billion pounds a year in revenue, and that we can't possibly manage without it.

Peter insisted that he wasn't unrealistic. 'I know you can't beat the Treasury with financial arguments. But this is a moral argument.'

May 11th Humphrey came to see me this morning. He was very tense. Clearly Bernard has been doing an excellent job of making sure that everyone knows about Dr Thorn's new policies.

'Prime Minister,' he began, 'I just wondered . . . did you have an interesting chat with Dr Thorn?'

'Yes. He has proposed the elimination of smoking.'

Sir Humphrey laughed derisively. 'And how, pray, does he intend to achieve this? A campaign of mass hypnosis, perhaps?'

I remained calm. I leaned back in my chair and smiled confidently at him. 'No. By raising taxes on tobacco sky high, and simultaneously prohibiting all cigarette advertising including at the point of sale.'

Humphrey chuckled confidently, but said nothing.

'Don't you think,' I asked, 'that his position is admirably moral?'

He was as superior as only Humphrey can be. 'Moral perhaps, but extremely silly. No one in their right mind could seriously contemplate such a proposal.'

'I'm contemplating it,' I said.

'Yes, of *course*,' he replied without a moment's hesitation . . . 'Don't misunderstand me, of course it's right to contemplate all proposals that come from your government, but no sane man could ever *support* it.'

'I'm supporting it,' I said.

'And quite right too, Prime Minister, if I may say so.' . . .

I gave him the chance to come over to my side. 'So you'll support it?' I asked.

'Support it?' He was emphatic. 'I support it wholeheartedly! A splended, novel, romantic, well-meaning, imaginative, do-gooding notion.'

As I thought. He is totally against it!

'The only problem is,' he continued, 'that there are powerful arguments against such a policy.'

'And powerful arguments for it,' I replied.

'Oh, *absolutely*! But *against* it,' he persisted, 'there are those who will point out that the tax on tobacco is a major source of revenue to the government.'

'But there are also those who would point out that tobacco is a major cause of death from a number of killer diseases.'

Humphrey nodded earnestly. 'Yes. Indeed. Shocking. If it's true. But of course, no *definite* causal link has ever been proved, has it?'

'The statistics are unarguable,' I said.

He looked amused. 'Statistics? You can prove anything with statistics.'

'Even the truth,' I remarked.

'Ye-es,' he acknowledged with some reluctance. 'But £4 billion revenue per annum is a considerable sum. They would say,' he added hastily, for fear of it being thought that he was taking sides in this dispute. *They* were clearly the Treasury.

I remarked that a hundred thousand unnecessary deaths a year – minimum – is a hideous epidemic. He agreed that it was appalling. So I went for the kill. 'It costs the NHS a fortune to deal with the victims. So the Treasury would be delighted if we discouraged it.'

This was a tactical error. Sir Humphrey swung confidently on to the offensive. 'Now I think you're wrong there, Prime Minister.'

I couldn't see how I could be wrong. 'Smoking-related diseases,' I said, referring to Dr Thorn's paper which I had in front of me, 'cost the NHS £165 million a year.'

But Sir Humphrey had been well briefed too, by the Treasury and by their friends in the tobacco lobby. 'We have gone into that,' he replied. 'It's been shown that, if those extra 100,000 people a year had lived to a ripe old age, they would have cost us even more in pensions and social security than they did in medical treatment. So, financially, it is unquestionably better that they continue to die at about the present rate.'

I was shocked. I've been in politics a long time and not much shocks me any more. But his cynicism is truly appalling.

'Humphrey,' I said, 'when cholera killed 30,000 people in 1833 we got the Public Health Act. When smog killed 2500 people in 1952 we got the Clean Air Act. When a commercial drug kills fifty or sixty people we get it withdrawn from sale, even if it's doing lots of good to many patients. But cigarettes kill 100,000 people a year and what do we get?'

'Four billion pounds a year,' he replied promptly. 'Plus about 25,000 jobs in the tobacco industry, a flourishing cigarette export business which helps the balance of trade. Also, 250,000 jobs indirectly related to tobacco – newsagents, packing, transport . . .'

I interrupted. 'These figures are just guesses.'

'No,' he said, 'they are government statistics.' He saw me smile, and hurriedly continued: 'That is to say, they are facts.'

I couldn't resist it. 'You mean, your statistics are facts, but my facts are just statistics?'

Sir Humphrey decided it was time to tell another little untruth. 'Look, I'm on your side, Prime Minister. I'm only giving you arguments you will encounter.'

I thanked him, and told him that I was glad to know that I should have support such as his. I hoped that would bring the conversation to a close – but no! He was determined to give me *all* the arguments I shall encounter.

'It will also be pointed out that the tobacco industry is a great sponsor of sport. They give much innocent pleasure to millions of people, and you would be taking it all away. After all, where would the BBC sports programmes be if the cigarette companies couldn't advertise on them?' . . .

I reiterated that we were discussing over 100,000 deaths each year. Humphrey agreed immediately.

'Yes, Prime Minister . . . but in a very overpopulated island. And there aren't enough jobs for everyone anyway. The benefits of smoking greatly outweigh the ill-effects: cigarettes pay for *one-third* of the total cost of the National Health Service. We are saving many more lives than we otherwise could because of those smokers who voluntarily lay down their lives for their friends. Smokers are national benefactors.'

'So long as they live,' I reminded him grimly.

'So long as they live.' He nodded. 'And when they die they save the rest of us a lot of money. And anyway, there's always more coming along to replace them. Not that any direct causal link has been proved, as I said before.'

This nonsense about no direct causal link was beginning to irritate me. I reminded Humphrey that the US Surgeon-General says that 'cigarette smoking is the chief avoidable cause of death in our society and the most important public health issue of our time'.

Humphrey dismissed the US Surgeon-General's report with a patronising smile. 'In his society, maybe. But do remember, Prime Minister, that Americans do love overstating everything, bless their warm little hearts.' He begged me to do nothing rash, to be very sure of my ground, and be very careful before I made any move. Of course, that's what he says about virtually everything . . .

[*Meanwhile, an anxious correspondence was taking place between Sir Humphrey Appleby and Sir Frank Gordon, Permanent Secretary of the Treasury. Copies of the letters have been found in both the Cabinet Office files and the Treasury files, all now available to us under the Thirty Year Rule. As the discussion was in writing, both gentlemen were careful to express their enthusiasm for government policy. Their real feelings must be read between the lines – Ed.*]

70 WHITEHALL, LONDON SW1A 2AS

From the Secretary of the Cabinet and Head of the Home Civil Service

May 15th

Dear Frank,

We are, of course, agreed that in an ideal world cigarette smoking would be discouraged. And we agree, obviously, that it is our duty to help the Prime Minister achieve his objectives. Nonetheless, we may have to help him understand that we are not in an ideal world and that he might be wise to reappraise not his objectives but his priorities.

He is unfortunately subject to silly pressure groups and fanatics such as the Royal College of Physicians. These fanatics want the Government to have a policy about smoking.

This is wishful thinking, I regret to say. It is not how the world works. Everyone outside government wants government policies. But none of us in government want them including, I venture to suggest, the Prime Minister when he fully understands the risks and the downside.

If you have a policy someone can hold you to it. And although the anti-smoking lobby see the whole matter in terms of black and white, merely preventing death and so forth, we know that the whole issue is much more complex than this.

As in all government, I'm sure that you agree that there has to be a balance. For instance the Minister of Health may be anti-smoking, but the Minister for Sport needs the tobacco companies.

It would be easier if the government were a team. But as, in fact, it is a loose confederation of warring tribes, it is up to us to find the common ground.

Comments, please.

[The following day a reply was received – Ed.]

H M TREASURY

Permanent Secretary   May 16

Dear Humphrey,

The Minister for Health wishes the smoking problem dealt with by high taxation. The Chancellor, however, will not let me raise taxes too high – he is concerned about his own popularity with the electorate.

I must agree with him, for other reasons. The inflationary effect of such a high rise in cigarette taxes would be considerable.

Nonetheless, it must be admitted that there is a moral principle involved. And we at the Treasury fully understand and applaud the PM's concern. We earnestly believe in the moral principle.

But when four billion pounds of revenue is at stake I think that we have to consider very seriously how far we are entitled to indulge ourselves in the rather selfish luxury of pursuing moral principles.

As you recall, I have been worried about a suggested income tax cut of one and a half billion, and that was in a proposal that may not now happen. A cut of four billion would be a catastrophe!

I suggest we get Noel's opinion and advice. I have copied these letters to him.

Frank

[*The copies of the correspondence were sent to the DHSS for the comments of Sir Noel Whittington, the Permanent Secretary. Two days later this letter was sent to Sir Frank, with a copy to Sir Humphrey – Ed.*]

Department of Health and Social Security

May 18th

Dear Frank,

There are several worrying implications raised by this potential cigarette tax increase:

1. It is not just a matter of revenue loss. There is also the question of scrutiny. If we 'took on' the tobacco companies they would put a host of people on to scrutinising everything we do. They would point out, publicly, any errors of facts, inconsistencies of argument, inaccurate or misleading published figures, and so forth. Of course, it is said that our work should be able to stand up to scrutiny. Quite right

too! Parliamentary scrutiny and press scrutiny are to be applauded. But not professional scrutiny, which could take up far too much government time. It is therefore not in the public interest to provoke it.

2. The tobacco companies might attempt to embarrass us by threatening to drag up all the times we have accepted invitations to lunches and free tickets at Wimbledon, Glyndebourne, etc.

3. Where would the arts be without tobacco sponsorship? They would be at the mercy of the Arts Council!

4. Above all, and here I speak for the DHSS specifically, we must remind the PM that there is a moral issue here: Government must be impartial. It is not proper for us to take sides as between health and cigarettes. This is especially true in the DHSS, which is the Department of Health and Social Security. We have a dual responsibility. What will happen, if we lose the tobacco revenues, to the extra 100,000 people per year who would be alive and drawing pensions?

It is clear that we must, as always, maintain a balance. We want a healthy nation, but we also need a healthy tobacco industry.

We have a duty to be even-handed: tobacco sponsorship may encourage people to smoke, but sponsored sport encourages them to take exercise.

In my view, the DHSS may already go too far on this anti-smoking matter. We already devote one third of an Assistant Secretary's time and half a Principal's time to reducing smoking. Surely this is enough in a free society.

In summation I make two suggestions:

1) that Humphrey Appleby arranges for the PM to meet some of the tobacco people. He would then see what jolly good chaps they are, and how genuinely concerned about health risks. In my view, there cannot be anything seriously wrong with BTG* for instance: they have an ex-Permanent Secretary on their Board. And it has been suggested that they could well need another, in the fullness of time.

2) I think we might raise some questions about our junior Minister, Dr Peter Thorn. He is a highly intelligent, very imaginative Minister. But he is inexperienced, and not at all even-

* British Tobacco Group

handed. Unfortunately, he comes to his post with severe bias: he is a doctor and, as such, he is unable to take the broader view. His sole point is keeping people alive. Seeing patients die must have, regrettably, distorted his judgement. It is understandable, of course, but emotional responses are a great handicap to cool decision-taking.

I look forward to hearing your conclusions. I think it is vital that Sir Humphrey takes some immediate action.
Noel

[*Sir Humphrey considered this correspondence carefully, and made the following note in his private diary – Ed.*]

I shall be meeting the PM after the weekend, and must have a strategy on this tobacco matter.

I believe that the key lies in Noel's comment that we are a free society. Therefore people should be free to make their own decisions. Government should not be a nursemaid. We do not want the Nanny State.

The only drawback to this view is that it is also an argument for legalising the sale of marijuana, heroin, cocaine, arsenic and gelignite . . .

Jonathan Lynn and Antony Jay, 'The Smokescreen' (1986), in *The Complete Yes Prime Minister*, 1989

Passive smoking

[Panama in the 1680s]

Their way of Smoaking when they are in Company together is thus: a Boy lights one end of a Roll and burns it to a Coal, wetting the part next to it to keep it from wasting too fast. The End so lighted he puts into his Mouth, and blows the Smoak through the whole length of the Roll into the Face of every one of the Company or the Council, tho' there be 2 or 300 of them. Then they, sitting in their usual posture upon Forms, make, with their Hands held hollow together, a kind of Funnel round their Mouths and Noses. Into this they receive the Smoak as 'tis blown upon them, snuffing it up greedily and strongly as long as ever they are able to hold their Breath, and seeming to bless themselves, as it were, with the Refreshment it gives them.

Lionel Wafer, *A New Voyage and Description of the Isthmus of America*, 1699

It is estimated by Doll in the *Journal of Cancer Research*, September, 1953, that people who do not smoke show a smaller percentage of deaths from lung cancer than do the smokers. If the estimate is valid, it has a twofold interest; on the one hand it suggests that the higher lung cancer death rate among the smokers has something to do with smoking, and on the other hand reminds us that if people who do not smoke yet die of lung cancer, then tobacco smoke cannot very well here be the causative agent, unless we invoke as an agent the tobacco smoke that the non-smoker perforce breathes; this would indeed be stretching the long arm of causation.

Sidney Russ, *Smoking and Its Effects: With Special Reference to Lung Cancer*, 1955

Passive smoking can provoke tears or can be otherwise disagreeable, but it has no influence on health [because] the doses are so small.

Ernest Wynder, co-author of the 1950 American report linking smoking and lung cancer, at an international cancer conference, 1975

[1986: The American Surgeon General, Dr C. Everett Koop, produces his report on passive smoking]

. . . That same year, the *American Review of Respiratory Diseases* summed up the evidence this way: '[T]he existing data on passive smoking and lung cancer do not meet the strict criteria for causality of this association,' adding that to reach that point 'may be exceedingly difficult, if not impossible,' due to methodological problems like measuring dosages and determining who was truly a nonsmoker. Even one of the soundest and most astute of the public-health investigators with an antismoking bent, economist Kenneth E. Warner of the University of Michigan, noted in his 1986 booklet, *Selling Smoke: Cigarette Advertising and Public Health*, that although a majority of the twenty or so studies done since 1980 had found a statistically significant elevated risk of lung cancer from ETS,* 'the likelihood that a lifelong nonsmoker will contract lung cancer is so small that a doubling of that risk remains relatively small.' What made even that small risk

---

* Environmental tobacco smoke.

significant, Warner did not fail to note, was that ETS exposure was so widespread, indeed nearly universal, that a substantial death toll 'may be found in the aggregate.' . . .

In short, the precise magnitude of the danger posed by other people's cigarette smoke was both uncertain and beside the point by the mid-1980s, so far as most in the public-health community were concerned. Their watchwords were preventive medicine, and linking ETS with direct smoking in order to alarm and mobilize the public against the still widely practiced habit served to counter the unstinting drumbeat of denial, distortion, and disinformation sounded by the tobacco industry in order to stay in business. As epidemiologist Lester Breslow, former dean of the UCLA School of Public Health, remarked, it is hard to awaken the people to a public-health peril, but once the arousal has begun, 'it builds to a mighty wave, gathering force from almost any supporting evidence.' Koop had won the people's attention on the smoking menace as no individual before him had, but 'the turning point' he had spoken of was not to be found in the scientific evidence about ETS but in the public perception of what by any rigorous standard was a complex risk measurement. To Congressman Charles Whitley, retiring that year after five terms in the House representing North Carolina's tobacco-rich Third District, the 1986 Surgeon General's report and Koop's dissemination of it were 'a very deliberate attempt to turn nonsmokers into antismokers' and thus the document was 'a political, not a health, report.' In truth, it was both, as purveyed by America's foremost public-health protector – and some felt that it was about time to put aside the velvet gloves in battling the tobacco interests.

Richard Kluger, *Ashes to Ashes: America's Hundred-Year Cigarette War, the Public Health, and the Unabashed Triumph of Philip Morris*, 1996, 1997

As a result of the identification of the risks of passive smoking, the non-smoker came to be empowered – on the basis of both scientific and moral claims – to act as an agent of enforcement. Individuals who a decade ago would not have dreamed of asking a smoker to stop became emboldened in a new cultural environment. The non-smoker was 'deputized' as an agent of the State. Further, it seems increasingly clear that smokers themselves came to view violation of these new norms as inviting personal humiliation and embarrassment, if not hostility. In short, smokers came to internalize a new set of ethics about public smoking, just as non-smokers developed new and heightened sensitivities to smoke. Peer pressure and social conformity – critical aspects of the popularity of the cigarette in the twentieth-century – were now effectively employed to limit smoking.

Allan M. Brandt, 'Blow Some My Way: Passive Smoking, Risk and American Culture' in S. Lock, L. A. Reynolds and E. M. Tansey, editors, *Ashes to Ashes: The History of Smoking and Health*, 1998

Showdowns

Note: The Buckley and Grisham novels are both from the mid-1990s, when the tobacco companies were still denying all.

[A tobacco spokesman on the Oprah Winfrey show]

Nick just had time for a quick jog along Lake Michigan.

If you represented death, you had to look your best. One of the first smokesmen to get the axe was Tom Bailey. Poor Tom. Nice guy, didn't even smoke, until he'd boasted about that one time too many to a reporter, who put it in her lead. JJ had called him in on the carpet, handed him a pack of cigarettes, told him that as of now he was a smoker. So Tom had started to smoke. But he had not kept up at the gym. A couple of months later JJ saw him on C-SPAN wheezing and pale and flabby, and that was the beginning of the end for Tom. So Nick kept up: jogging, weights, and every now and then a tanning salon where he would lie inside a machine that looked like it had been designed to toast gigantic grilled-cheese sandwiches.

'*You* look good,' Oprah said backstage before the show. She was very cheery and chatty. 'You look like a lifeguard.'

'Not as good as you.' Nick was pleased to see that she had put back on some of those seventy-five pounds that she'd lost. As long as there were overweight women in the world, there was hope for the cigarette industry.

'We tried to get the surgeon general to come on, but she said she wouldn't come on with a death merchant.' Oprah laughed. 'That's what she called you. A death merchant.'

'It's a living.' Nick grinned.

'I can't understand what that woman is saying half the time with that accent of hers.' Oprah looked at him. 'Why *do* you do this? You're young, good-looking, white. Weren't you . . . you look familiar, somehow.'

'I'm on cable a lot.'

'Well why *do* you do this?'

'It's a challenge,' Nick said. 'It's the hardest job there is.'

She didn't seem to buy that. Better get on her good side before the show. 'You really want to know?'

'Yeah.'

Nick whispered, 'Population control.'

She made a face. 'You're bad. I wish you'd say that on the show.' She left him in the care of the makeup woman.

Nick studied the sheet listing the other panelists, and he was not happy about it. There had been changes since Friday.

It showed: the head of Mothers Against Smoking – swell – an 'advertising specialist' from New York, the head of the National Teachers' Association, one of Craighead's deputies from the Office of Substance Abuse Prevention. It irked Nick to be up against someone's deputy. What was Craighead doing today that was more important than trying to scrape a few inches of hide off the chief spokesman for the tobacco industry? Dispensing taxpayers' dollars to dweebish do-gooders? There was not much preshow banter between them as they sat in their makeup chairs.

They were taken onstage to be miked. Nick found himself being ushered to a chair next to another guest, a bald teenage kid. Who, Nick wondered, was he?

'Hello,' Nick said.

'Hello,' said the kid, friendly enough.

Now why would a bald teenage kid – bald, with no eyebrows – be on this particular panel? A technician wearing large earphones called out, 'One minute!' Nick waved over a supervising producer, who rushed over to inform him that it was too late to go to the bathroom. A lot of first-timers were stricken with nervous bladders at the last minute and ended up sitting through the entire hour in damp underwear.

'I, uh,' Nick said. 'I'm fine.' He whispered, '*Who's the kid?*'

'Robin Williger,' the producer whispered back.

'Why is he on?'

'He's got cancer.'

'Tell Oprah I need to speak to her *right now.*'

'Too late.'

Nick pinched the little alligator clip on his lapel mike and unclamped it from his Hermès necktie, the orange one with the giraffe motif. 'Then she's doing this show without me.'

The producer bolted. Oprah came hurrying, her admirable bosom jiggling under blue silk.

'What's the problem?'

Nick said, 'I don't like surprises.'

'He was a last-minute substitution.'

'For who? Anne Frank? Well, he can substitute for me.'

'Nick,' she hissed, 'you know we can't do the show without you!'

'Yes, I do.'

'Fifteen seconds!' a technician shouted.

'What do you want me to do? Kick him off the set?'

'Not my problem.'

But she did nothing. Nick's instinct told him to get out of there. Quick! But there she was, this black woman, commanding him to sit there and finish his supper and he couldn't move.

She wheeled around with her wireless hand mike and bared her gleaming pearlies at the camera with the little red light.

Get up! Flee!

Too late! They were live! Maybe he could just slip quietly away.

Headline: CIGARETTE FLACK FLEES CANCER KID.

To complete the humiliation, he would trip on an electrical cable and bring a klieg light crashing down. The audience would laugh as he lay there, dazed on the studio floor. They would laugh across America, all the housewives hooting, pointing at him. BR would not laugh.

Cancer Kid would not laugh. No, only the merest, thinnest smile of triumph would play over his lips, tinged with sadness at the tragedy that was so personally his. Nick felt the hot trickle of sweat above his hairline, little beads of molten lava, nothing between them and his eyebrows but smooth, tanning-saloned forehead. And didn't *that* always look good on TV, having to mop your forehead while you sat next to some dying National Merit Scholar – surely he was one, oh yes, surely he was the president of the student council and debating society and ran the soup kitchen in his spare time when he wasn't tutoring young inner-city kids. His only imperfection had been to smoke that one cigarette – yes, just one, that was all, one; proof that nicotine can be fatal in even minute doses – and it had been forced on him, against his better instincts, by the tobacco companies, and by those . . . fucking . . . saxophone-playing camels with the phallic noses; and by him, by Nick Naylor, senior vice president for communications, Academy of Tobacco Studies, Merchant of Death.

And he could not move. She had epoxied him to his seat. The perfidious bitch had outmaneuvered him!

In such moments – not that he had experienced this extreme before – he imagined himself at the controls of a plane. Pilots always managed to remain so calm, even when all their engines were on fire and the landing gear was stuck and the Arabic-looking passenger in 17B had just pulled the pin on his grenade.

He sucked in a lungful of air and let it out slowly, slowly, slowly. That's it. Breathing exercise. He remembered it from Lamaze classes. Still, his heart was going kaboom-kaboom ka-boom in his chest. Would the necktie microphone pick that up? How suave that would be, having his thumping heartbeat broadcast into everyone's living room.

Maybe he should offer some small sign of comradeship to Cancer Kid. He needed an opening line. *So, how long do they give you?*

Oprah was doing her introduction.

'Last year, RJR Nabisco, the company that makes Camel cigarettes, launched a new seventy-five-million-dollar ad campaign. The star of the campaign is Old Joe, a camel. But this is no ordinary ruminant quadruped.' Shots of Old Joe were shown: playing the sax, playing bass, hanging out at the beach, checking out the chicks, being cool, the old coffin nail hanging jauntily from his mouth, or foreskin, depending on your phallic suggestibility. 'He's become very popular, especially among children. According to a recent poll, over ninety percent of six-year olds . . . *six*-year-olds, not only recognized Old Joe, but knew what he stood for. He is almost as well-known as Mickey Mouse.

'Before Old Joe began showing up on billboards and magazine pages everywhere, Camel's share of the illegal children's cigarette market was less than one percent. It is now . . . thirty-two percent – thirty-two point eight percent, to be precise. That amounts to four hundred seventy-six million dollars a year in revenues.

'The surgeon general of the United States has called on RJR to withdraw this ad campaign. Even *Advertising Age,* the top advertising industry trade magazine, has come out against the Old Joe campaign. But the company refuses to withdraw them.

'Then last Friday she called for a *total* ban on advertising for cigarettes. Magazines, billboards, everything. This is bound to be controversial. A lot of money is at stake.

'I want you to meet Sue Maclean, head of the National Organization of Mothers Against Smoking. Sue began organizing NOMAS after her daughter fell asleep in bed while smoking and burned down her dormitory at college. Fortunately, no one was hurt. Sue tells me that her daughter quit smoking right after that.'

Laughter in the studio. Heartwarming.

'Her daughter is now a mother herself, and a very active member of NOMAS.'

The audience cooed.

Nick, synapses overheating, tried to coordinate his facial features into an appropriate expression, something between waiting for a bus that was very late and being lowered headfirst into a tank full of electric eels.

'Frances Gyverson is executive director of the National Teachers' Association in Washington. She is in charge of the NTA's health issues program, which instructs teachers in how to relay the dangers of smoking to their students.

'Ron Goode is deputy director of the Office of Substance Abuse Prevention at the Department of Health and Human Services in Washington, D.C. OSAP is the command center in the nation's war against cigarettes, so that would make you, what, Ron, a colonel?'

'Just a footsoldier, Oprah.'

Where, Nick wondered, was *this* gorgeous self-effacement coming from? Goode was one of the more pompous, self-important assholes in the entire federal government.

Oprah smiled. A warm and fuzzy murmur went through the studio audience. *He has so much power, and yet look at him, he's so humble!*

She turned toward Cancer Kid.

'Robin Williger is a high school senior from Racine, Wisconsin. He likes studying history and he is on the swimming team.' Momentarily, Nick's heart leapt. Perhaps it had all been a dream. Perhaps he didn't have cancer. Weren't swimmers always shaving their heads for speed? And didn't the weird ones also shave their eyebrows?

'He was looking forward to continuing his education at college. But then something happened. Recently, Robin was diagnosed with cancer, a very tough kind of cancer. He is currently undergoing chemotherapy treatment. We wish him all the luck in the world.' The audience and other guests burst into applause. Nick joined in, wanly.

'The reason we asked him to be on this show with us is that he started smoking Camel cigarettes when he was fifteen. Because, he told me, he wanted to be quote cool like Old Joe. He also tells me he's quit smoking Camels since learning about the cancer. And that he no longer thinks smoking is quote cool.' Thunderous applause.

Nick yearned for a cyanide capsule. But now Oprah turned to face Nick.

'Nick Naylor is a vice president of the Academy of Tobacco Studies. You might think with a name like that that they're some sort of scientific institution. But they are the tobacco industry's main lobby in Washington, D.C., and Mr. Naylor is their chief spokesman. Thank you for coming, Mr. Naylor.'

'Pleasure,' Nick croaked, though what he was experiencing was far from pleasure. The audience glared hatefully at him. So this is how the Nazis felt on opening day at the Nuremberg trials. And Nick unable to avail himself of their defense. No, it fell to him to declare with a straight face that ze Führer had never invaded Poland. *Vere are ze data?*

'Who'd like to start?' Oprah said.

Nick raised his hand. Oprah and his fellow panelists looked at him uncertainly. 'Is it all right,' he said, 'if I smoke?'

The audience gasped. Even Oprah was taken aback.

'You want to *smoke?*'

'Well, it's traditional at firing squads to offer the condemned a last cigarette.'

There was a stunned silence for a few seconds, and then someone in the audience laughed. Then other people laughed. Pretty soon the whole audience was laughing.

'I'm sorry, but I don't think that's funny,' Mrs. Maclean said.

'No,' said the National Teachers' Association lady. 'I don't either. I think it's in extremely poor taste.'

'I have to agree,' Goode said. 'I don't see the humor in it. And I suspect Mr. Williger doesn't either.' But Cancer Kid was laughing. God *bless* him, he was laughing! Nick was seized with love. He wanted to adopt this young man, take him back to Washington, cure him of his cancer, give him a high-paying job, a car – a luxury car – a house, a pool, a big one so he could keep up with his swimming. Nick would buy him a wig, too, and get him eyebrow hair transplants. Anything he wanted. He felt so badly about the cancer. Maybe, with radiation . . .

Forget the kid! He's history! Press the attack! Attack! Attack!

'Oh why don't you leave him alone,' Nick wheeled on Goode. 'And stop trying to tell him how he ought to feel.' He turned to Oprah. 'If I may say so, Oprah, that is typical of the attitude of the federal government. "We know how you should feel." It's this same attitude that brought us Prohibition, Vietnam, and fifty years of living on the brink of nuclear destruction.' Where was *this* going? And how had nuclear deterrence gotten in? *Never mind! Attack!* 'If Mr. Goode wants to score cheap points off this young man's suffering just so he can get his budget increased so he can tell more people what to do, well I just think that's really, really sad. But for a member of the federal government to come on this show and lecture about cancer, when that same government for nearly fifty years has been producing atomic bombs, twenty-five thousand of them, as long as we're throwing numbers around, Mis-ter Sta-tistics, bombs capable of giving every single person on this planet, man, woman, and child, cancers so awful, so ghastly and untreatable, so, so, so *incurable*, that medical science doesn't even have a name for them yet . . . is' – *Quick, get to the point! What is the point?* – ' . . . is just beneath contempt. And frankly, Oprah, I'd like to know how a man like . . . *this* comes to occupy a position of such power within the federal bureaucracy. The answer is – he doesn't *have* to get elected. Oh no. *He* doesn't have to participate in democracy. He's *above* all that. Elections? Consent of the governed? Pah! Of the very people who pay his salary? Oh no. Not for Ron Goode. *He* just wants to cash in on people like poor Robin Williger. Well, let me tell you something, Oprah, and let me share something with the fine, concerned people in the audience today. It's not pleasant, but you, and they, need to hear it. The Ron Goodes of this world *want* the Robin Willigers to die. Awful, but true. I'm sorry, but it's a fact. And do you know why? I'll tell you why. So that their . . . *budgets*' – he spat out the distasteful word – 'will go up. This is nothing less than trafficking in human misery, and you, sir, ought to be *ashamed* of yourself.'

Ron Goode never recovered. For the next hour, he could only scream at Nick, in violation of every McLuhanesque injunction against putting out heat in a cool medium. Even Oprah strained to calm him down.

For his part, Nick assumed a serene mask of righteous serenity and merely nodded or shook his head, more in sadness than in anger, as if to say that his outburst only validated everything he had said. 'All well and fine, Ron, but you haven't answered the question,' or, 'Come on, Ron, why don't you stop pretending you didn't hear me,' or, 'And what about all those people you irradiated during those nuclear test blasts in New Mexico? Want to talk about *their* cancers?'

During one of the commercials Ron Goode had to be physically restrained by a technician.

Christopher Buckley, *Thank You for Smoking*, 1995

[Tobacco in the dock]

After a very long coffee break at three, Wendall Rohr was given his first crack at Jankle. He started with a vicious question, and matters went from bad to worse.

'Isn't it true, Mr Jankle, that your company spends hundreds of millions trying to convince people to smoke, yet when they get sick from your cigarettes your company won't pay a dime to help them?'

'Is that a question?'

'Of course it is. Now answer it!'

'No. That's not true.'

'Good. When was the last time Pynex paid a penny of one of your smoker's medical bills?'

Jankle shrugged and mumbled something.

'I'm sorry, Mr Jankle. I didn't catch that. The question is, when was the last time – '

'I heard the question.'

'Then answer it. Just give us one example where Pynex offered to help with the medical bills of someone who smoked your products.'

'I can't recall one.'

'So your company refuses to stand behind its products?'

'We certainly do not.'

'Good. Give the jury just one example of Pynex standing behind its cigarettes.'

'Our products are not defective.'

'They don't cause sickness and death?' Rohr asked incredulously, arms flopping wildly at the air.

'No. They don't.'

'Now lemme get this straight. You're telling this jury that your cigarettes do not cause sickness and death?'

'Only if they are abused.'

Rohr laughed as he spat out the word 'abused' in thorough disgust. 'Are your cigarettes supposed to be lit with some type of lighter?'

'Of course.'

'And is the smoke produced by the tobacco and the paper supposed to be sucked through the end opposite the end that is lit?'

'Yes.'

'And is this smoke supposed to enter the mouth?'

'Yes.'

'And is it supposed to be inhaled into the respiratory tract?'

'Depends on the choice of the smoker.'

'Do you inhale, Mr Jankle?'

'Yes.'

'Are you familiar with studies showing ninety-eight percent of all cigarette smokers inhale?'

'Yes.'

'So it's accurate to say that you know the smoke from your cigarettes will be inhaled?'

'I suppose so.'

'Is it your opinion that people who inhale the smoke are actually abusing the product?'

'No.'

'So tell us, please, Mr Jankle, how does one abuse a cigarette?'

'By smoking too much.'

'And how much is too much?'

'I guess it depends on each individual.'

'I'm not talking to each individual smoker, Mr. Jankle. I'm talking to you, the CEO of Pynex, one of the largest cigarette producers in the world. And I'm asking you, in your opinion, how much is too much?'

'I'd say more than two packs a day.'

'More than forty cigarettes a day?'

'Yes.'

'I see. And what study do you base this on?'

'None. It's just my opinion.'

'Below forty, and smoking is not unhealthy. Above forty, and the product is being abused. Is this your testimony?'

'It's my opinion.' Jankle was starting to squirm and cast his eyes at Cable, who was angry and looking away. The abuse theory was a new one, a creation of Jankle's. He insisted on using it.

Rohr lowered his voice and studied his notes. He took his time for the setup because he didn't want to spoil the kill. 'Would you describe for the jury the steps you've taken as CEO to warn the public that smoking more than forty cigarettes a day is dangerous?'

Jankle had a quick retort, but he thought the better of it. His mouth opened, then he hung in mid-thought for a long, painful pause. After the damage was done, he gathered himself and said, 'I think you misunderstand me.'

Rohr wasn't about to let him explain. 'I'm sure I do. I don't believe I've ever seen a warning on any of your products to the effect that more than two packs a day is abusive and dangerous. Why not?'

'We're not required to.'

'Required by whom?'

'The government.'

'So if the government doesn't make you warn folks that your products can be abused, then you're certainly not going to do it voluntarily, are you?'

'We follow the law.'

'Did the law require Pynex to spend four hundred million dollars last year in advertising?'

'No.'

'But you did, didn't you?'

'Something like that.'

'And if you wanted to warn smokers of potential dangers you could certainly do it, couldn't you?'

'I suppose.'

Rohr switched quickly to butter and sugar, two products Jankle had mentioned as being potentially dangerous. Rohr took great delight in pointing out the differences between them and cigarettes, and made Jankle look silly.

He saved the best for last. During a short recess, the video monitors were once again rolled into place. When the jury returned, the lights were dimmed and there was Jankle on-screen, right hand raised while being asked to tell the truth and nothing but the truth. The occasion was a hearing before a congressional subcommittee. Standing next to Jankle were Vandemeer and the other two CEO's of the Big Four, all summoned against their will to give testimony to a bunch of politicians. They looked like four Mafia dons about to tell Congress there was no such thing as organized crime. The questioning was brutal.

The tape was heavily edited. One by one, they were asked point-blank if nicotine was addictive, and each emphatically said no. Jankle went last, and by the time he made his angry denial, the jury, just like the subcommittee, knew he was lying.

John Grisham, *The Runaway Jury*, 1996

———————————

[A tobacco spokesman and his boss]

'Let's be professional about this. I'm not packing a heavy agenda. I'm putting it to you straight, guy-to-guy: how are we *doing* out there? I get this sense of . . . defeatism from your shop. All I see is white flags.'

Nick strained to cool his rapidly boiling blood. 'White *flags*?'

'Yeah, like that stupid proposal you floated last month suggesting we admit that there's a health problem. What was *that* all about, for Chrissake?'

'Actually,' Nick said, 'I still think it was a pretty bold proposal. Let's face it, BR, no one appears to be buying into our contention that smoking isn't bad for you. So why *not* come out and say, "All right, in some cases, sure, smoking's bad for you. So's driving a car for some people. Or drinking, or flying in airplanes, or crossing the street, or eating too much dairy product. But it's a legitimate, pleasurable activity that, done moderately, probably isn't that much more dangerous than . . . I don't know . . . life itself." I think a lot of people would think, "Hey, they're not such liars after all." '

'Stupidest idea I ever heard,' BR said with asperity. 'Stupid *and* expensive. I had to have every copy of that memo burned. Can you imagine what would happen if it turned up in one of these goddamn liability trials? An internal document admitting that we know smoking is bad for you? Jesus Christ on a toasted bagel – do you have any *idea* what a disaster that would be?'

'Okay,' Nick shrugged, 'let's go on pretending there's no proof that it's bad for you. Since that's working so well . . .'

'See what I mean,' BR shook his head, 'defeatism.'
Christopher Buckley, *Thank You for Smoking*, 1995

Cigarette Smoking: Health Issues for Smokers

Cigarette Smoking and Disease in Smokers: There is an overwhelming medical and scientific consensus that cigarette smoking causes lung cancer, heart disease, emphysema and other serious diseases in smokers. Smokers are far more likely to develop serious diseases, like lung cancer, than non-smokers. There is no 'safe' cigarette. These are and have been the messages of public health authorities worldwide. Smokers and potential smokers should rely on these messages in making all smoking-related decisions.

Cigarette Smoking and Addiction: Cigarette smoking is addictive, as that term is most commonly used today. It can be very difficult to quit smoking, but this should not deter smokers who want to quit from trying to do so.
Click here for information about quitting smoking.

Additional information from public health authorities on cigarette smoking and addiction is available on this page. Here are a few examples:

- 'The determination that cigarettes and other forms of tobacco are addicting is based on standard criteria used to define drugs as addicting.' *(US Surgeon General)*
- 'The World Health Organization has classified smoking as an addiction.' *(World Health Organization)*
- ' . . . the nicotine in cigarettes and smokeless tobacco causes and sustains addiction.' *(US Food and Drug Administration)*

The Philip Morris website (www.philipmorris.com), October 1999

PART TWO

Smoking Themes

CHAPTER EIGHT

Women and Smoking

Moreover, which is a great iniquity, and against all humanity, the husband shall not be ashamed to reduce thereby his delicate, wholesome, and clean complexioned wife to that extremity, that either she must also corrupt her sweet breath therewith, or else resolve to live in a perpetual stinking torment.

James I, *A Counterblaste to Tobacco*, 1604

AUGGIE: Any time. And congratulations to you and your wife. Just remember, though, in the immortal words of Rudyard Kipling: 'A woman is only a woman, but a cigar is a smoke.'
YOUNG MAN: *(Confused)* What does that mean?
AUGGIE: Damned if I know. But it has a nice ring to it, don't it?

'Smoke' in *Smoke and Blue in the Face: Two Films by Paul Auster*, 1995

This is the only chapter in Part Two that needs an introduction and, at the by-now traditional risk of oversimplifying, I'll keep it as brief as possible. Essentially, for most of tobacco history, smoking was regarded primarily as a male pursuit and one of which women disapproved. Many women, of course, did smoke, but – depending largely on whether they were posh or not – they were usually seen as either racy or vulgar.

The gender divide in Britain, apparently rather narrow in the first days of tobacco (see *Stow's Annales* below), was at its widest in the nineteenth century. Queen Victoria's opposition to the habit was total, and only unrespectable women – Grace Poole in *Jane Eyre*, Mrs Brown in *Dombey and Son* – can be found puffing in the novels of the time. Also, bachelors were often expected to give up when they got married (the context from which the famous Kipling line misquoted above by Auggie derives its meaning), while married men who persisted are regularly shown in comic writing as receiving more than their fair share of wifely nagging.

So, not until the twentieth century did women – certainly in Britain and America – take whole-heartedly to the habit. This was partly because of the general move to equality – many 'new women' of the 1890s, and earlier, took smoking as a provocative badge of honour, as did the cosmopolitan likes of Dorothy Parker in the 1920s; partly because of the rise of the cigarette – even today, you'll notice, there aren't many pipe-smoking women about. From the 1920s, too, women were targeted by a tobacco industry keen to double its customer-base at a stroke. At first, the industry stressed the slimming qualities of cigarettes – most famously with the slogan 'Reach for a Lucky instead of a sweet' as mentioned in Chapter Five. (Vigorous objections from the sweet-manufacturers of America meant that this was later changed to 'Reach for a Lucky instead'.) Later on, there were brands specifically aimed at women. American Tobacco's Silva Thins introduced in 1967 ('Cigarettes are like girls – the best ones are rich and thin') perhaps misread the mood of the times. Far more successful was the response from Philip Morris in the shape of Virginia Slims. Their ads used simulated photos of Victorian women wearing, say, a constricting swimming costume and thinking aloud: 'Just you wait. Someday we'll be able to wear any bathing suit we want. Someday we'll be able to vote. Someday we'll be able to smoke like a man. Someday we'll even have our own cigarette.' The clincher was a picture of an independent Sixties chick smoking a Virginia Slim, and the words: 'You've come a long way, baby'.*

The early days

PIERO: Faith, mad niece, I wonder when thou wilt marry.
ROSALINE: Faith, kind uncle, when men abandon jealousy, forsake taking of tobacco, and cease to wear their beards so rudely long. O, to have a husband with a mouth continually smoking, with a bush of furze on the ridge of his chin, ready still to slop into his foaming chaps; ah, 'tis more than most intolerable.

John Marston, *Antonio and Mellida*, c. 1600

WIFE: Fie, this stinking tobacco kills me; would there were none in England! – Now, I pray, gentlemen, what good does this stinking

---

* The advertising agency responsible was very uneasy about the word 'baby', fearing it was patronising – but Philip Morris insisted and, apparently, were proved right.

tobacco do you? Nothing, I warrant you; make chimneys o' your faces!

Francis Beaumont, *The Knight of the Burning Pestle, c.* 1607

> Himself all day in taverns he bestows,
> And comes to bed at night in shoes and hose;
> And there he lies as cleanly as a hog,
> Perfum'd as sweet as any stinking dog,
> With filthy leaves he smokes his head withal,
> Such weeds as Indians do tobacco call . . .
> I think a thousand times I do complain,
> And tell my husband that he should refrain
> This making of a chimney of his nose;
> He had a breath as sweet as any rose,
> Before he used this same scurvy trick,
> But now if I do kiss him I am sick,
> With this same fough; beshrew your heart say I,
> Tobacco stinks, you poison me, I die.

Samuel Rowlands (?1570–?1630), *The Fifth Gossip's Complaint*

I burned my pipe yesternight, and 'twas never used since, if you will 'tis at your service gallants, and tobacco too, 'tis right pudding I can tell you; a Lady or two took a pipe full or two at my hands, and praised it for the Heavens . . .

Thomas Dekker, *Satiromastix,* 1601

URSULA: I can but hold life and soul together with this (here's to you, Nightingale) and a whiff of tobacco at most. Where's my pipe now? Not filled? Thou arrant incubee!

Ben Jonson, *Bartholomew Fair,* 1614

[England, 1614]

Tobacco . . . at this day, commonly used by most men, and many women.

Stow's Annales, continued by E. Howes, 1615

[In 1789]

A comfortable well clad old woman rode up the field with a pipe of Tobacco in her Mouth, the Puffs from which softened the keenness of the air and must make her journey over the mountains delectable.

Lady Eleanor Butler's journal in G. H. Bell, editor, *The Hamwood Papers of the Ladies of Llangollen*, 1930

The smoking sex war

Pernicious weed! Whose scent the fair annoys,
Unfriendly to society's chief joys,
Thy worst effect is banishing for hours
The sex whose presence civilizes ours.
Thou art indeed the drug a gardener wants
To poison vermin that infest his plants;
But are we so to wit and beauty blind
As to despise the glory of our kind,
And show the softest minds and fairest forms
As little mercy, as he, grubs and worms?

William Cowper, *Conversation*, 1782

I shall half wish you unmarried (don't show this to Mrs C.) for one evening only, to have the pleasure of smoking with you and drinking egg-hot in some little smoky room in a pot-house, for I know not yet how I shall like you in a decent room and looking quite happy. My best love and respects to Sara notwithstanding.

Charles Lamb, a Letter to Coleridge, 14 June 1796

And here, were I allowed to occupy the reader with extraneous matters, I could give a very curious and touching picture of the Swigby *ménage*. Mrs S., I am very sorry to say, quarrelled with her husband on the third day after their marriage, – and for what, pr'ythee? Why, because, he would smoke, and no gentleman ought to smoke. Swigby, therefore, patiently resigned his pipe, and with it one of the quietest, happiest, kindest companions of his solitude. He was a different man after this; his pipe was as a limb of his body. Having on Tuesday conquered the pipe, Mrs Swigby, on Thursday did battle with her husband's rum-and-water, a drink of an odious smell, as she very properly observed; and the smell was doubly odious, now that the tobacco smoke no longer perfumed the parlour-breeze, and counter-acted the odours of the juice of West India sugar-canes. On Thursday, then, Mr Swigby and rum held out pretty bravely. Mrs S. attacked the punch with some sharp-shooting, and fierce charges of vulgarity; to which S. replied, by opening the battery of oaths (chiefly directed to his own eyes, however), and loud protestations that he would never surrender. In three days more, however, the rum-and-water was gone. Mr Swigby, defeated and prostrate, had given up that stronghold; his young wife and sister were triumphant; and his poor mother, who occupied her son's house, and had till now taken her place at the head of his table, saw that her empire was for ever lost, and was preparing suddenly to succumb to the imperious claims of the mistress of the mansion.

William Makepeace Thackeray, *A Shabby Genteel Story*, 1840

I am not, in the first place, what is called a ladies' man, having contracted an irrepressible habit of smoking after dinner, which has obliged me to give up a great deal of the dear creatures' society; nor can I go much to country-houses for the same reason. Say what they will, ladies do not like you to smoke in their bedrooms; their silly little noses scent out the odour upon the chintz weeks after you have left them . . .

What is this smoking that it should be considered a crime? I believe in my heart that women are jealous of it, as a rival. They speak of it as of some secret, awful vice that seizes upon a man, and makes him a Pariah from genteel society. I would lay a guinea that many a lady who has just been kind enough to read the above lines, lays down the book, after this confession of mine that I am a smoker, and says, 'Oh, the vulgar wretch!' and passes on to something else.

The fact is, that the cigar *is* a rival to the ladies, and their conqueror, too.

William Makepeace Thackeray, *Fitzboodle Papers*, 1842–3

The Betrothed

'You must choose between me and your cigar.'
  – *Breach of Promise Case, circa 1885*

Open the old cigar-box, get me a Cuba stout,
For things are running crossways, and Maggie and I are out.

We quarrelled about Havanas – we fought o'er a good cheroot,
And *I* know she is exacting, and she says I am a brute.

Open the old cigar-box – let me consider a space;
In the soft blue veil of the vapour musing on Maggie's face.

Maggie is pretty to look at – Maggie's a loving lass,
But the prettiest cheeks must wrinkle, the truest of loves must pass.

There's peace in a Larranaga, there's calm in a Henry Clay;
But the best cigar in an hour is finished and thrown away –

Thrown away for another as perfect and ripe and brown –
But I could not throw away Maggie for fear o' the talk o' the town!

Maggie, my wife at fifty – grey and dour and old –
With never another Maggie to purchase for love or gold!

And the light of Days that have Been the dark of the Days that Are,
And Love's torch stinking and stale, like the butt of a dead cigar –

The butt of a dead cigar you are bound to keep in your pocket –
With never a new one to light tho' it's charred and black to the
                                                        socket!

Open the old cigar-box – let me consider a while.
Here is a mild Manila – there is a wifely smile.

Which is the better portion – bondage bought with a ring,
Or a harem of dusky beauties, fifty tied in a string?

Counsellors cunning and silent – comforters true and tried,
And never a one of the fifty to sneer at a rival bride?

Thought in the early morning, solace in time of woes,
Peace in the hush of the twilight, balm ere my eyelids close,

This will the fifty give me, asking nought in return,
With only a *Suttee's* passion – to do their duty and burn.

This will the fifty give me. When they are spent and dead,
Five times other fifties shall be my servants instead.

The furrows of far-off Java, the isles of the Spanish Main,
When they hear my harem is empty will send me my brides again.

I will take no heed to their raiment, nor food for their mouths withal,
So long as the gulls are nesting, so long as the showers fall.

I will scent 'em with best vanilla, with tea will I temper their hides,
And the Moor and the Mormon shall envy who read of the tale of
my brides.

For Maggie has written a letter to give me my choice between
The wee little whimpering Love and the great god Nick o' Teen.

And I have been servant of Love for barely a twelvemonth clear,
But I have been Priest of Cabanas a matter of seven year;

And the gloom of my bachelor days is flecked with the cheery light
Of stumps that I burned to Friendship and Pleasure and Work and
Fight.

And I turn my eyes to the future that Maggie and I must prove,
But the only light on the marshes is the Will-o'-the-Wisp of Love.

Will it see me safe through my journey or leave me bogged in the
mire?
Since a puff of tobacco can cloud it, shall I follow the fitful fire?

Open the old cigar-box – let me consider anew –
Old friends, and who is Maggie that I should abandon *you*?

A million surplus Maggies are willing to bear the yoke;
And a woman is only a woman, but a good Cigar is a Smoke.

Light me another Cuba – I hold to my first-sworn vows.
If Maggie will have no rival, I'll have no Maggie for Spouse!

Rudyard Kipling, 1888

Matrimony and smoking compared

The circumstances in which I gave up smoking were these.

I was a mere bachelor, drifting toward what I now see to be a tragic middle age. I had become so accustomed to smoke issuing from my mouth that I felt incomplete without it; indeed the time came when I could refrain from smoking if doing nothing else, but hardly during the hours of toil. To lay aside my pipe was to find myself soon afterwards wandering restlessly round my table. No blind beggar was ever more abjectly led by his dog, or more loth to cut the string . . .

I should like to say that I left off smoking because I considered it a mean form of slavery, to be condemned for moral as well as physical reasons; but though I see the folly of smoking clearly now, I was blind to it for some months after I had smoked my last pipe. I gave up my most delightful solace, as I regarded it, for no other reason than that the lady who was willing to fling herself away on me said that I must choose between it and her. This deferred our marriage for six months.

I have now come, as those who read will see, to look upon smoking with my wife's eyes. My old bachelor friends complain because I do not allow smoking in the house, but I am always ready to explain my position, and I have not an atom of pity for them. If I cannot smoke here neither shall they. When I visit them in the old Inn they take a poor revenge by blowing rings of smoke almost in my face. This ambition to blow rings is the most ignoble known to man. Once I was member of a club for smokers, where we practised blowing rings. The most successful got a box of cigars as a prize at the end of the year. Those were days. Often I think wistfully of them. We met in a cosy room off the Strand. How well I can picture it still; time-tables lying everywhere, with which we could light our pipes. Some smoked clays, but for the Arcadia Mixture give me a briar. My briar was the sweetest ever known. It is strange now to recall a time when a pipe seemed to be my best friend.

My present state is so happy that I can only look back with wonder at my hesitation to enter upon it . . .

Two cigars a day at ninepence apiece come to £27 7s. 6d. yearly, and four ounces of tobacco a week at nine shillings a pound come to £5 17s. yearly. That makes £33 4s. 6d. When we calculate the yearly expense of tobacco in this way we are naturally taken aback, and our extravagance shocks us the more after we have considered how much more satisfactorily the money might have been spent. With £33 4s. 6d. you can buy new Oriental rugs for the drawing-room, as well as a spring bonnet and a nice dress. These are things that give permanent pleasure, whereas you have no interest in a cigar after flinging away the stump. Judging by myself, I should say that it is want of thought rather than selfishness that makes heavy smokers of so many bachelors. Once a man marries his eyes are opened to many things that he was quite unaware of previously, among them being the delight of adding an article of furniture to the drawing-room every month and having a bed-room in pink and gold, the door of which is always kept locked. If men would only consider that every cigar they smoke would buy part of a new piano-stool in terra-cotta plush, and that for every pound tin of tobacco purchased away goes a vase for growing dead geraniums in, they would surely hesitate. They do not consider, however, until they marry, and then they are forced to it. For my own part, I fail to see why bachelors should be allowed to smoke as much as they like when we are debarred from it.

The very smell of tobacco is abominable, for one cannot get it out of the curtains, and there is little pleasure in existence unless the curtains are all right. As for a cigar after dinner, it only makes you dull and sleepy and disinclined for ladies' society. A far more delightful way of spending the evening is to go straight from dinner to the drawing-room and have a little music. It calms the mind to listen to your wife's niece singing 'Oh, that we two were maying.' Even if you are not musical as is the case with me, there is a great deal in the drawing-room to refresh you. There are the Japanese fans on the wall, which are things of beauty, though your artistic taste may not be sufficiently educated to let you know it except by hearsay; and it is pleasant to feel that they were bought with money which, in the foolish old days, would have been squandered on a box of cigars. In like manner every pretty trifle in the room reminds you how much wiser you are now than you used to be. It is even gratifying to stand in summer at the drawing-room window and watch the very cabbies passing with cigars in their mouths. At the same time, if I had the making of the laws I would prohibit people's smoking in the street. If they are married men, they are smoking drawing-room fire-screens and mantelpiece borders for the pink and gold room. If they are bachelors, it is a scandal that bachelors should get the best of everything . . .

Occasionally I feel a little depressed after dinner still, without being able to say why, and if my wife has left me I wander about the room restlessly, like one who misses something. Usually, however, she takes me with her to the drawing-room, and reads aloud her delightfully long home letters or plays soft music to me. If the music be sweet and sad it takes me away to a stair in an Inn, which I climb gaily and shake open a heavy door on the top floor, and turn up the gas. It is a little room I am in once again, and very dusty. A pile of papers and magazines stands as high as a table in the corner furthest from the door. The cane-chair shows the exact shape of Marriot's back. What is left (after lighting the fire) of a framed picture lies on the hearthrug. Gilray walks in uninvited. He has left word that his visitors are to be sent on to me. The room fills. My hand feels, along the mantelpiece for a brown jar. The jar is between my knees, I fill my pipe . . .

J. M. Barrie, *My Lady Nicotine*, 1890

Women join in

BENNET: . . . I have put the newspapers and telegrams on the sideboard, sir.

CARR: Is there anything of interest?

BENNET: There is a revolution in Russia, sir.

CARR: Really? What sort of revolution?

BENNET: A social revolution, sir.

CARR: A *social* revolution? Unaccompanied women smoking at the Opera, that sort of thing?

Tom Stoppard, *Travesties*, 1974

And now, sir, I will describe, modestly, tamely, literally, the visit to the small select circle which I promised should make your hair stand on end. In our hotel were Lady A and Lady B, mother and daughter, who came to the Peschière shortly before we left it, and who have a deep admiration for your humble servant the inimitable B. They are both very clever. Lady B, extremely well-informed in languages, living and dead; books, and gossip; very pretty, with two little children, and not yet five and twenty. Lady A, plump, fresh and rosy; matronly, but full of spirits and good looks. Nothing would serve them but we *must* dine with them; and accordingly, on Friday at six, we went down to their room. I knew them to be rather odd ... Consequently I was not surprised at such sparkles in the conversation (from the young lady) as, 'Oh God, what a sermon we had here, last Sunday!' 'And did you ever read such infernal trash as Mrs Gore's?' – and the like. Still, but for Kate and Georgy* (who were decidedly in the way, as we agreed afterwards), I should have thought it all very funny; and as it was, I threw the ball back again, was mighty free and easy, made some rather broad jokes, and was highly applauded. 'You smoke, don't you?' said the young lady, in a pause of this kind of conversation. 'Yes,' I said, 'I generally take a cigar after dinner when I am alone.' 'I'll give you a good 'un,' said she, 'when we go upstairs.' Well, sir, in due course we went upstairs, and there we were joined by an American lady residing in the same hotel, who looked like what we call in old England 'a reg'lar Bunter' – fluffy face (rouged); considerable development of figure; one groggy eye; blue satin dress made low with short sleeves, and shoes of the same. Also a daughter; face likewise fluffy; figure likewise developed; dress likewise low, with short sleeves and shoes of the same; and one eye not yet actually groggy, but going to be. American lady married at sixteen; American daughter sixteen now, often mistaken for sisters, etc., etc., etc. When that was over, Lady B brought out a cigar-box, and gave me a cigar, made of negrohead she said, which would quell an elephant in six whiffs. The box was full of cigarettes – good large ones, made of pretty strong tobacco; I always smoke them here, and used to smoke them at Genoa, and I knew them well. When I lighted my cigar, Lady B lighted hers, at mine; leaned against the mantelpiece, in conversation with me; put out her stomach, folded her arms, and with her pretty face cocked up sideways and her cigarette smoking away like a Manchester cotton mill, laughed, and talked, and smoked, in the most gentlemanly manner I ever beheld. Lady A immediately lighted her cigar; American lady immediately lighted hers; and in five minutes the room was a cloud of smoke, with us four in the centre pulling away bravely, while American lady related stories of her 'Hookah' upstairs, and described different kinds of pipes. But even this was not all. For presently two

---

* 'Kate and Georgy' are the wife of Dickens and her sister, Georgina Hogarth.

Frenchmen came in, with whom, and the American lady, Lady B sat down to whist. The Frenchmen smoked, of course (they were really modest gentlemen and seemed dismayed), and Lady B played for the next hour or two with a cigar continually in her mouth – never out of it. She certainly smoked six or eight. Lady A gave in soon – I think she only did it out of vanity. American lady had been smoking all the morning. I took no more; and Lady B and the Frenchmen had it all to themselves.

Conceive this in a great hotel, with not only their own servants, but half a dozen waiters coming constantly in and out! I showed no atom of surprise; but I never *was* so surprised, so ridiculously taken aback, in my life; for in all my experience of 'ladies' of one kind and another, I never saw a woman – not a basket woman or a gipsy – smoke, before!

Charles Dickens in a letter from Geneva in 1846, quoted in John Forster, *Life of Charles Dickens*, 1872

[A mother on her daughter]

'And now she's all for this horse-riding. She saw the count through the window on horseback once, and kept on and on at me, "I want to ride and that's all about it." I did all I could to stop her but no – "I want to!" Madcap! We didn't ride when I was a girl. That's not how we were brought up at all. But nowadays – oh, horror! – ladies have actually begun to smoke! There's a young widow living over the way there – she sits on the balcony all day smoking cigarettes. People walk by, drive past, and she doesn't care a bit. Why, in my young days if a gentleman so much as smelled of tobacco in the drawing-room – '

Ivan Goncharov, *The Same Old Story*, 1847 (trans. Ivy Litvinova)

More and worse, some of the *ladies* of this refined and fashion-forming metropolis [New York] are aping the silly ways of some pseudo-accomplished foreigners, in smoking Tobacco through a weaker and more *feminine* article, which has been most delicately denominated *cigarette*.

R. T. Trall, *Tobacco: Its History, Nature and Effects*, 1849

By the mere effect of her love Madame Bovary's manners changed. Her looks grew bolder, her speech more free; she even committed the impropriety of walking out with Monsieur Rodolphe, a cigarette in her mouth, 'as if to defy the people.'

Gustave Flaubert, *Madame Bovary*, 1857 (trans. Eleanor Marx-Aveling)

If all women sought comfort in a cigarette, how great a relief would that be from those variations on the theme of bickering and fault-finding to which the best of them are at times addicted.

William G. Hutchinson, Introduction to *Lyra Nicotiana: Poems and Verses Concerning Tobacco*, 1898

> Maidens now are not particular,
> And for ways lascivious burn,
> Zola, cigarettes, auricular
> Practices they used to spurn,
> Cinerary acts and urn;
> And, though lashed with songs and sermons,
> Hanker for their unwashed Germans
> And to French professors turn.
>
> Women too will not put stitches
> In their henpecked husbands' socks,
> Have the whip-hand, wear the breeches,
> Dabble in the sea of Stocks
> To be wrecked upon its rocks,
> Dare to ask improper questions,
> And regardless of digestions
> Drink like men in blooming frocks.

Frederick William Orde Ward, *Sixes and Sevens*, 1894

LORD GORING: I am glad you have called. I am going to give you some good advice.

MRS CHEVELEY: Oh! pray don't. One should never give a woman anything that she can't wear in the evening.

LORD GORING: I see you are quite as wilful as you used to be.

MRS CHEVELEY: Far more! I have greatly improved. I have had more experience.

LORD GORING: Too much experience is a dangerous thing. Pray have a cigarette. Half the pretty women in London smoke cigarettes. Personally I prefer the other half.

MRS CHEVELEY: Thanks. I never smoke. My dressmaker wouldn't like it, and a woman's first duty in life is to her dressmaker, isn't it?

Oscar Wilde, *An Ideal Husband*, 1895

[Gil has smelled smoke in his house, and so thinks his wife
has a lover . . .]

(*Gil, beside himself, draws Suzanne towards him in passionate embrace, but suddenly he pushes her from him and starts up stupefied.*)

GIL: Ah! That awful smell! Even in her clothes!

SUZANNE (*Startled by Gil's outburst, and rising in confusion*): Ah! He has noticed the scent!

GIL: Ah! (*Watching her with increasing agitation*)
She is confused . . .
Suspicion no longer,
But certainty!

SUZANNE (*In despair*): Heavens!
Is my fault so very serious?

GIL: Suzanne! No quibbling! (*Seizing her hand*)
You're hiding something?

SUZANNE (*Staggered*): I?

GIL: Yes! You have a secret! Confess!

SUZANNE (*Trembling*): Well, – er . . .

GIL: Out with it!

SUZANNE: Suppose it were true?

GIL (*Starting back, aghast*): Suzanne!

SUZANNE: If something that I could not help . . .

GIL: Suzanne!

SUZANNE: A failing . . . a whim – that would not be denied . . .

GIL: Suzanne!

SUZANNE: While you were at your club . . .
I was passing the time . . .

GIL: You mean the worst?

SUZANNE: Can't you be like other husbands.
And wink at my secret failing . . .

GIL: I? (*In a paroxysm of fury*)
I'll make short work of it!

SUZANNE (*Half tauntingly*): You'll have to find it out first!
I shall take good care you don't.

GIL (*Exploding*): Wanton! I'll appeal to your mother,
That pattern of dignified austerity
Who has never countenanced such infamy!
SUZANNE: Why, she's just as bad!
GIL (*Exasperated beyond bearing*): This is the climax! No more of it!
  (*With a mixture of scorn and reproach.*)
How can you say these horrible things
With such an air of innocence?
Prattling as if they were nothing,
You . . . wickedness incarnate!
SUZANNE (*Hurt and in tears*): How can you be so cruel about a trifle?
GIL: Trifle! Abandoned creature!
SUZANNE: Lots of women do the same!
GIL: This beats everything!
Hang it, I won't stand this,
I'll be fooled no more! (*Breaks down*)

[And later . . .]

SUZANNE: I can breathe again! He has gone . . .
Heavens! How he scared me . . .
With that umbrella! (*Reflecting*)
His brain must be softening!
Goodness knows what nonsense it's stuffed with.
But now I have the respite
I yearn for
And am free to enjoy
My heart's delight! (*She fishes out the hidden cigarette, re-lights it, settles herself jauntily in an easy chair, and smokes placidly and contentedly.*)
What joy to watch with half-closed eyes
The gossamer mist
Rising in azure rings,
And circling into nothingness,
Like some bewitching phantom
That disappears into cloudless skies!
(*Suzanne smokes on in a brown study. During this the lamplight fails and grows dim. GIL suddenly appears at the window, umbrella in hand.*)
GIL: I've caught you this time!

[155]

SUZANNE: (*Suzanne jumps up terrified, and hides behind her the hand holding her cigarette.*) Oh! Gil!

GIL (*Rushing into the room*): Where is the villain?

SUZANNE: What villain? (*Here the lamp goes out altogether.*)

GIL: The man you've concealed in my absence! (*Snatching at Suzanne's hidden hand he burns himself.*)

Damnation! I've burnt myself!

Faithless woman! What have you got there?

SUZANNE (*Nervously holding out her cigarette*): My cigarette . . . (*At this moment moonlight floods the room.*)

GIL (*Dumbfounded*): You were the smoker?

SUZANNE (*Flopping on to her knees*): Forgive me!

GIL (*Ditto*): Sweet angel!

It is you who must forgive;

I was . . . so . . . (*Shamefaced*) jealous!

SUZANNE (*Sitting on the ground, with a satirical laugh*): Jealous! Of my smoking, Ha, ha!

Let us forgive each other!

I'll give up smoking,

If you really wish it . . .

Only for love of you!

GIL: No! We'll smoke together!

SUZANNE (*With a cry of joy*): Ah! (*Giving him a cigarette.*) Take one!

GIL (*Taking one, and offering her the box*): And one for you?

SUZANNE (*Showing her lighted cigarette, which she puts to her lips*): Another time! (*She lights his cigarette from hers, lips to lips.*)

GIL: You little minx! (THEY *get up.*)

SUZANNE: Dearest, will you really smoke?

GIL: I'll do my best to learn!

SUZANNE: You'll never be jealous again?

GIL: No, love, I'll just smoke.

BOTH:

All life ends in smoke

That scatters with the wind,

Excepting only true love,

Which burns without end.

(*Cigarette in mouth, and holding hands, they dance around like children.*)

Ermanno Wolf-Ferrari's opera *Suzanne's Secret*, 1909 (trans. Claude Aveling, 1939).

Cousin Nancy

Miss Nancy Ellicott
Strode across the hills and broke them,
Rode across the hills and broke them –
The barren New England hills –
Riding to hounds
Over the cow-pasture.

Miss Nancy Ellicott smoked
And danced all the modern dances;
And her aunts were not quite sure how they felt about it,
But they knew that it was modern.

Upon the glazen shelves kept watch
Matthew and Waldo, guardians of the faith,
The army of unalterable law.

T. S. Eliot, 1915

Great has always been my interest in the youth of the age, especially the young women, and how very important it is that they should be kept unpolluted. The future of the human race depends upon what kind of mothers they are to be.

The question is as important today as it was in the day of Solomon: – 'Who can find a virtuous woman, or wife?' And equally true: – 'Her price is far above rubies' or she would be a prize far above rubies. She is admitted to sisterhood with angels. A lamp is lit in woman's eye: –

'That souls else lost, on earth, remember angels by.
Soft, as the memory of buried love,
Pure, as the Prayer which childhood wafts above – was she.'

The watch-men on the walls of our high civilization send not forth the serious warning, that young women are on the down grade . . .

And evidently they go from bad to worse. Young women nowadays, are anxious to imitate the young men in their worst. Such as kicking Football, Boxing, Drinking Cocktail, Betting and the lowest, filthiest of all – SMOKING.

Is it possible that HIGH EDUCATION and the VOTE are going to destroy our womanhood? . . .

The Mother and Cigarette Smoking

In the year 1929, a young mother in Cardiff gave birth to her first born child.

When allowed to see him, she was shocked at his horrid appearance. So unlike ordinary human babies.

With a breaking heart she asked,

'What is the matter with my baby, Doctor?'

The Doctor said with a moistened eye,

'Sorry to tell you, Mam, that it is the effect of your cigarette smoking.'

Rev. T. D. Gwernogle Evans MH, Neath, *Smoking: A Message of Love to the Daughters of Wales*, 1934

The stationmaster came into the tent, crab-like and obsequious.

'Well, my good man?' said the Doctor.

'The young lady I have been telling that no other tunes can we play whatever with the lady smoking at her cigarette look you.'

'God bless my soul. Why not?'

'The other tunes are all holy tunes look you. Blasphemy it would be to play the songs of Sion while the lady at a cigarette smokes whatever. *Men of Harlech* is good music look you.'

'This is most unfortunate. I can hardly ask Mrs Beste-Chetwynde to stop smoking. Frankly I regard this as impertinence.'

'But no man can you ask against his Maker to blaspheme whatever unless him to pay more you were. Three pounds for the music is good and one for blasphemy look you.'

Evelyn Waugh, *Decline and Fall*, 1928

British, French, and German women smoked in public for some years before their American sisters dared to do so. Still, in the States, only radical or careless or defiant women smoked openly. (It was by an ordinance of 1908, very largely ignored by the authorities, illegal for them to use tobacco publicly in New York City.) Demireps were far too careful of their reputations to be seen in the open with the tainted cigarette. And it was to be some time before nervous males would wish to appear on the street with a female companion smoking the disreputable 'thing'. These harassed gentlemen were willing to concede that women were wonderful and that they were people and that it was true they now had the vote, but public smoking was carrying their independence too far.

A factual anecdote of the postwar period, in the early twenties, is illuminating. When the most conspicuous figure in the American tobacco trade was being interviewed by an intelligent reporter he was asked his opinion of a subject then under wide discussion: Should women smoke cigarettes? Leaning forward for emphasis and pointing a quivering finger, the celebrity among manufacturers began belligerently, 'If I ever caught a daughter of mine . . .' At this breathless juncture a convenient vice-president (probably the one in charge of sales) tapped him warningly on the shoulder. 'Sir,' he said urgently, 'you wished to be reminded not to talk on that subject for publication.' Equally pertinent is the experience of the noted opera singer, Madam Schumann-Heink, believed to be the first woman of note to provide a public testimonial for a cigarette. As a result of her favorable comment a number of colleges in the West canceled her pending engagements. Thereafter she not only refrained from praising cigarettes, but denounced the use of tobacco . . .

There were frequent cases, in the 1920's, of women dismissed from employment, expelled from institutions of learning or otherwise penalized for daring to smoke.

Jerome E. Brooks, *The Mighty Leaf: Tobacco through the Centuries*, 1953

Ironically, while nowadays in progressive countries women, along with men, are being persuaded to stop smoking, in some backward countries they are being ordered, unlike men, to stop. One day in March 1979 a thousand women held a meeting at Teheran University, smoking cigarettes all through it, in protest at the Khomeini regime's threat to forbid them.

V. G. Kiernan, *Tobacco: A History*, 1991

Antismoking legislation, at this moment in history, intersects the struggle for women's liberation – as it always has. The degree to which women have the right to smoke in society is an unmistakable indicator of the general equality they have achieved, a test of their full membership in civil society. Antismoking legislation is one of the subterranean forms in which that war for women's liberation is still raging . . .

Recently a commission of the European Economic Community sur-
veyed the practice of smoking cigarettes among the citizens of its
twelve member countries. The survey reveals that the country with
the highest percentage of women smokers is Denmark; the country
with the lowest is Portugal. The statistics are not an aberration:
Denmark is followed by Holland and Great Britain; Greece and Portugal are at the other end of the scale. Question: In which of these
countries would you rather have your daughter grow up, if you hoped
she would be liberated, independent, and self-sufficient? Paradoxically,
it is in nations in which smoking is most expensive that one finds the
highest percentage of women smokers: in Denmark, 45 percent of
the women smoke; in Holland, 37; and in Great Britain, 32. Sociocul-
tural variables seem preponderant with respect to economic factors.
'Is the cigarette a symbol of the equality between man and woman?'
ask the experts of the European Community.

Richard Klein, *Cigarettes Are Sublime*, 1993

————————

No Smoking

Lent is the time for cutting out what's bad.

I'll give up going to bed with men who smoke –
for that and other seasons of the year.

Is it the taste? That's not too bad as long
as I don't put my tongue into their mouths.
The tiredness of their skin? Their blood-shot eyes?
Is it the smell of fag-ash in my hair
next day? Not really. That can be washed out,

Post-coital light-up is what worries me.
We've had each other, then the smoking man
turns desperately seeking something else,
scouring the bedside cupboard, pockets, drawers,
he sighs on finding what he really wants,
then's silently unfaithful with his fag.

Some keep their little weapons to themselves.
The worst kind start a sort of troilism.
I don't feel easy with a naked flame

too near my vulnerable naked flesh –
you, me, a cigarette, a smoky kiss –
out of the corner of one eye I see
a toppling inch of ash above a stub
while lover-boy is fiddling with my tits –
foreplay designed to set the bed on fire.

Fiona Pitt-Kethley, 1989

CHAPTER NINE

Smokers v. Non-Smokers

Forces arrayed against smoking have little feeling for the historical irony of their position. They are unable to see that their movement belongs to the permanent, parallel alliance between smoking tobacco and antitabagism, which has persisted throughout the history of tobacco's universalization. It is as if not only the censors but also the censored, not only antismokers but smokers, require each other's permanent hostility as the condition of their continuing existence.

Richard Klein, *Cigarettes are Sublime*, 1993

———————

[A seventeenth-century father-in-law]

A Citizen settled his whole Estate,
In Marriage, upon his only Son,
And for a season friendly with him livd:
At length, his Sons Wife proves with-Child, and thus
Spoke to her Husband, I am Breeding, my Dear,
And can't endure to see your Father spaul,
And smoke stinking Tobacco, in my Hall:
As you love me, and this your Child, unborn,
Laying her Hand upon her pregnant Womb,
Let it be so no more. Away he goes,
And tells his Father this Complaint of's Wife,
And prays him for the future, to look out
Some other place, wherein to Spit and Smoke.
This to the Old Man was a Thunder-clap,
But he was forc'd to yield to those hard Terms,
For they must needs go whom the Devil drives.

Walter Pope, 'The Two Citizens and Ungrateful Son' in *Moral and Political Fables*, 1698

[The Berlin Revolution, 1848]

The Revolution of February in Paris, and the rising in Vienna on March 13, 1848, found an echo in Berlin, where the inhabitants were still groaning under the prohibition of smoking in the street, strictly enforced by the police and the army. The cigar, as distinguished from the traditional Conservative, Philistine pipe, that might be smoked only at home, was still regarded as an unseemly novelty, a mark of Liberal audacity, the democratic badge of the agitator and stump orator; it was therefore persistently persecuted. Now, when the Revolution broke out, in March 1848, and the people gathered before the royal palace, cries were raised for the repeal of the ban on smoking, as well as for more important concessions – such as lighter taxation, freedom of the Press, and so on . . .

Werner von Siemens tells us in his memoirs that he was present when, on March 19, 1848, the revolted townspeople brought the bodies of those who had been killed on the barricades to the Schlossplatz, to show them to the King and Queen. In the midst of the confusion, when some were wanting to storm the palace, now that the troops had been withdrawn from the city, young Prince Lichnowsky jumped on a table, and addressed the crowd in a loud voice. He said that his Majesty had graciously and kindly put an end to the fighting by withdrawing all the troops and trusting himself to the citizens. All their demands were granted, and they had only to go home quietly. When people asked whether everything had really been granted he answered, 'Yes, everything, gentlemen.'

'Smoking too?' said another voice.

'Yes, smoking too,' was the answer.

'In the Tiergarten too?' was asked again.

'Yes, gentlemen, you may smoke in the Tiergarten too.'

That clinched the matter. 'Well, then, we may go home,' was heard on all sides, and in a few minutes the joyous crowd left the square . . .

By order of the King, on March 25, 1848, the following notice appeared: 'The prohibition of smoking, when there is no risk of fire, in the streets and suburbs of the capital is repealed.' . . .

Smoking was free; but this liberty did not appeal to all. Formerly the police headquarters were deluged with petitions for free smoking, now they received angry letters from non-smokers, asking to have the old rule restored. A certain C. Schartmann, 'in the interests of public decency and morality and the common good,' approached the Prussian Minister of the Interior on December 22, 1851, with the request that 'he would check the consumption of tobacco, which has increased so enormously since 1848, and especially stop the cultivation of tobacco, or at least reduce it to its former limits, and restore the prohibition in Berlin, as it was in 1848'.

It was monstrous that a bad habit should be allowed in public, and that those who had not been enslaved by it should have to tolerate it . . .

Another 'private person' was of the same opinion, and declared that the unhappy Revolution of 1848, with all its sad consequences, disobedience, unbelief, and lawlessness, had also brought with it the 'unfortunate' liberty of the smoking habit, which offended all decency. 'Non-smokers,' so the writer ended his epistle,

> hope that you, the Chief of Police, will restore the rule forbidding smoking, and the non-smoking public will give you their silent but heartfelt thanks for being able to breathe pure fresh air again.

Many non-smokers even now are heartily in agreement with this appeal. The history of smoking in Berlin only shows how hard – nay, impossible – it is for a man in authority to satisfy the contradictory demands of the populace.

E. C. Corti, *A History of Smoking*, 1930 (trans. Paul England, 1931)

[Prince Albert and Napoleon III]

The Emperor thaws more and more. This evening after dinner I withdrew with him to his sitting-room for half an hour before rejoining his guests, in order that he might smoke his cigarette, in which occupation, to his amazement, I could not keep him company.

Letter from Prince Albert to Queen Victoria, 5 September 1854

[Engels in Worthing]

Here we are . . . in as primitive a place as the British seaside will admit of – the first lodgings we took we had to leave because the old Madame objected to smoking!

Letter to Laura Marx in August 1884

LUCY, *sitting by the window, with* GATEWOOD *partly in shot beside her, looks pale and uncomfortable. She raises a handkerchief to her face, then turns away and looks out of the window.*

HATFIELD *watches her covertly, with a worried frown. Smoke drifts from* BOONE'S *stogie and* HATFIELD *raises his handkerchief to try and blow it away.* [LUCY *coughs,] and* HATFIELD *looks coldly at* DOC BOONE.)

HATFIELD: Put out that cigar.

(DOC BOONE *has the stogie stuck in the corner of his mouth. He puffs on it absently. Then he turns somewhat nervously in* HATFIELD'S *direction* [*as* LUCY *can be heard stifling another cough*].

HATFIELD *stares at him firmly.*)

HATFIELD: You're annoying this lady.

(DOC BOONE *looks across towards* LUCY. *He does not like* HATFIELD'S *tone, but he is a kindly soul and he takes the cigar-butt out of his mouth, at the same time nodding towards her with great dignity.*)

DOC BOONE: Excuse me, madam.

(LUCY *smiles at him graciously.*

DOC BOONE *tosses the butt out of the window.*)

DOC BOONE: Being so partial to the weed myself, I forget it disagrees with others.

(LUCY *smiles, then lowers her eyes and looks away out of the window again.*

HATFIELD *fixes a cold eye on* DOC BOONE.)

HATFIELD: A gentleman doesn't smoke in the presence of a lady.

(DOC BOONE *leans back and folds his hands over his plump belly, addressing no one in particular in an amiable tone.*)

DOC BOONE: Three weeks ago I took a bullet out of a man who was shot by a gentleman. The bullet was . . .

(HATFIELD'S *eyes blaze as he stares at* BOONE, *half-rising in anger.*)

DOC BOONE (*off*): . . . in his *back.*

John Ford and Dudley Nichols, *Stagecoach*, 1939

Many a non-smoker when questioned about his indifference to her gracious influence has heaved a pensive sigh and lamented Dame Nature's ill-usage in denying him the taste for the nicotian incense. Consolation comes not to him when told that the good genius has knit together a brotherhood who, regaled with her balmy breath, realize the touch of nature which makes the whole world kin; that on her approach petty vexations vanish into space, and fancy, untrammelled, roves in Parnassian bowers, or sees in the vapour rising from the bowl nebulous forms resembling those in the far-off starry sky.

E. V. Heward, *St Nicotine, or The Peace Pipe*, 1909

[Proust and Joyce]

In 1922, both writers were at a black-tie dinner given at the Ritz for Stravinsky, Diaghilev and members of the Russian Ballet, in order to celebrate the first night of Stravinsky's *Le Renard*. Joyce arrived late and without a dinner jacket, Proust kept his fur coat on throughout the evening and what happened once they were introduced was later reported by Joyce to a friend:

> Our talk consisted solely of the word 'Non.' Proust asked me if I knew the duc de so-and-so. I said, 'Non.' Our hostess asked Proust if he had read such and such a piece of *Ulysses*. Proust said, 'Non.' And so on.

After dinner, Proust got into his taxi with his hosts, Violet and Sydney Schiff, and without asking, Joyce followed them in. His first gesture was to open the window and his second to light a cigarette, both of which were life-threatening acts as far as Proust was concerned. During the journey, Joyce watched Proust without saying a word, while Proust talked continuously and failed to address a word to Joyce. When they arrived at Proust's flat at the Rue Hamelin, Proust took Sydney Schiff aside and said: 'Please ask Monsieur Joyce to let my taxi drive him home.' The taxi did so. The two men were never to meet again.

Alain de Botton, *How Proust Can Change Your Life*, 1997

[An American woman in London]

The hotel guests fit perfectly into the atmosphere and *décor* – having, most of them, a flinty cast of face ... The clergymen are the mildest feature of the landscape. They run to silver hair, and scan Henry and me wistfully over their copies of the *Church Times*. The clergymen's wives, on the other hand, are no more wistful than Gibraltar. Their hostility arises, I think, from my having automatically lit a cigarette in the dining-room after dinner last night. Before I had even laid down the match, a Prime Ministerial man came thudding up, in the nearest thing to a hurry he could muster, and asked me not to smoke. By a perceptible effort, he stopped himself from adding, 'There are ladies present.' I doused the fatal instrument with lightning promptitude, but it was a good seven minutes before the last indignant handkerchief had folded its wings and gone back to its reticule and the last manufactured cough died protestingly away.

Margaret Halsey, *With Malice Toward Some*, 1938

'I have to know something about you,' the small voice said very firmly. 'This is a very delicate matter, very personal. I couldn't talk to just anybody.'

'If it's that delicate,' I said, 'maybe you need a lady detective.'

'Goodness, I didn't know there were any.' Pause. 'But I don't think a lady detective would do at all. You see, Orrin was living in a very tough neighbourhood, Mr Marlowe. At least I thought it was tough. The manager of the rooming house is a most unpleasant person. He smelled of liquor. Do you drink, Mr Marlowe?'

'Well, now that you mention it – '

'I don't think I'd care to employ a detective that uses liquor in any form. I don't even approve of tobacco.'

'Would it be all right if I peeled an orange?'

Raymond Chandler, *The Little Sister*, 1949

Hubby Malcolm Wilding wears a World War Two gas mask at home because he can't stand wife Liz's smoking.

Mal, 46, wears it in the lounge when they watch telly, at the dinner table between mouthfuls and even in BED if Liz insists on a last ciggie before sleep.

Mal bought the mask from an army surplus store after trying in vain to get Liz, 43, to kick her 40-a-day habit.

Mal – married 27 years – said: 'I've tried everything to make her give up. I'm hoping to embarrass her so much and make her so sick of the sight of the mask she'll chuck the fags.

'Her smoking does have a big effect on our lives.

'If I'm watching my favourite wildlife programmes the smoke is sometimes so thick I can hardly see the TV. I get angry and my mask steams up. When she has friends round, all smoking together, I put the mask on and sit with them but it doesn't embarrass Liz.' . . .

Liz said: 'I have smoked since I was a teenager but I started smoking heavily a few years ago and I'm addicted now. I can't stop.

'When he first walked in the house in his mask he looked like Darth Vader. I fell about laughing because he looked such a prat.

'He thought it would make me feel guilty about smoking but it didn't work. I'm not that soft.'

Andrew Parker, Story headlined 'Cig Heil' in *The Sun*, 28 October 1997

Penny gave up smoking nine months ago. Her husband, also a smoker, has cut down to five a day in the flat, out of consideration for her, but she and the children dislike the smell of smoke and argue that it's a health problem as well as a human one. They have no garden or balcony. What should Penny do?

I'm afraid that for Penny, as Elvis used to say, if she's looking for trouble, she's come to the right place. I'm a fanatical anti-anti-smoker, and feel that her demands are quite preposterous, particularly in view of the fact that her poor husband is already smoking barely any cigarettes at all.

Like all born-again non-smokers, Penny wants to control the world and bring everyone round to her views. It happens with born-again Christians, who are frightful bores, and it happens in the world of cigarettes, too. 'Oh, the smell!' say the anti-smoking brigade, holding their noses, without realising that there are numerous anti-odour sprays around that would fix that immediately. Indeed, even a lighted candle will burn up any few fumes that there are, in the same way as lighting a match in the loo burns up unwanted pongs. Or, 'Oh, but passive smoking kills!' they cry, without looking at the evidence properly and finding that, if it's examined properly, it's shot full of holes. What anti-smoking is all about is control, and the smoker knows this and, rightly, gets angry.

Virginia Ironside, 'Dilemmas' in *The Independent*, 1 January 1998

We tried to be nice to you nonsmokers. We tried. You wanted your own sections in restaurants; we gave that to you. But that's not enough for you, is it? Because every smoker here knows that when you sit in the 'Smoking Area,' the legal little area where you're allowed to smoke, and you screw that baby onto your lips and you light it up – and you taste your first few relaxing sucks – 'Ahh . . . Ahh . . .' – what do

you hear coming from that nonsmoking section? Those little pussy-coughs: 'Ahem... Ahem... AHEM... ACHH!... ACHH!... AHHCHCHCH!... THE SMELL OF YOUR CIGARETTE IS KILLING ME!'
... You wanted the airplanes? We gave you the whole goddamned plane. Are you happy now? I'd like an explanation about that one, folks, because I'll guarantee you that if the plane is going down the first announcement you're going to hear is: 'Folks, this is your captain speaking. Light 'em up because we're goin' down. Okay? I've got a carton of Camel unfiltereds. I'll see ya on the ground. Take it easy.' Actually, it's more like this (*through a voice box*): '*This is your captain speaking. Smoke 'em if you got 'em.*'

And you're always doing your nonsmoking math, aren't you? Always figuring out the future. 'Okay. I'm thirty-four. If I quit smoking now, I'll live to be... about seventy... Okay, I'm thirty-seven... if I quit now I'll live to be...' Forget it. Forget it all. Stop trying to seal your fate. You quit. And then you start jogging and stairing and lifting and eating high fiber and drinking carrot juice and planning for the future. HEY! Two words: Jim Fixx. Remember Jim Fixx? The jogging guru? Wrote a jogging book, did a jogging video and dropped dead of a massive heart attack. When? When he was jogging, that's when. What do you want to bet it was two smokers who found the body the next morning? (*Inhaling, staring at the ground*) 'Hey. That's Jim Fixx, isn't it? What a tragedy. C'mon. Let's go buy some cigarettes.'...

C'mon. Light up. LIGHT UP! (*Tosses a handful*) GIVE IN! (*Tosses remainder of pack*) Stop fighting the urge. Give in. Enjoy. Relax. (*Tosses empty pack*)

(*Mimicking audience*) 'Oh, please, Mr. Leary. Please don't make us smoke. Please? Smoking takes ten years off your life.' Well, it's the ten worst years, isn't it? It's the ones at the end! It's the wheelchair-kidney-dialysis-adult-diaper years. I don't want them.

Denis Leary, *No Cure for Cancer* (based on his live show), 1992

The intrinsic or constitutional factors which lead people to smoke, and to smoke very heavily, were studied by comparing small numbers of heavy smokers and non-smokers in one American study. The heavy smokers were of a restless, ardent, energetic personality, the non-smokers steadier, more dependable, quieter. In another recent American study cigarette smokers were found to have changed jobs more often, moved more often, entered hospital more often, and participated in sports more often than non-smokers; on a psychological test, their responses were more neurotic than those of non-smokers. In a British survey of 2,360 men selected according to their age, social class and smoking habits, cigarette smokers were found to be more extraverted than non-smokers, while pipe smokers were the most introverted group. It was suggested that these findings indicated genotypic differences between non-smokers, cigarette smokers and pipe smokers. That differences in smoking habits may be in part due to a hereditary disposition is supported by four studies which have shown that identical twins are more significantly concordant in smoking habits than non-identical twins – a contrast which is not due to greater similarity of environment of the former for it is discernible when the identical twins have been brought up apart.

Smoking and Health: A Report of the Royal College of Physicians of London on Smoking in relation to Cancer of the Lung and Other Diseases, 1962

I have never seen a single neurosis or psychosis which could definitely be attributed in any way to tobacco. On the other hand one is more justified in looking with suspicion at the abstainer . . . most of the fanatic opponents of tobacco I have known were all bad neurotics.

A. A. Brill, 'Tobacco and the Individual' in *International Journal of Psychoanalysis,* 1922

And on the railways . . .

To-day . . . non-smoking compartments are as few and far between as the smoking compartments of once upon a time. The notification of a sanctuary for non-smokers is so inconspicuous that the smoker often gets into one inadvertently, and only realizes his mistake when he puts a cigarette between his lips and finds his lighter burning blue under the baleful eyes of his fellow-travellers. Most smokers have been caught this way, and I am sure all of them will agree with me that nothing is so lowering to the spirits as the enforced companionship of a bunch of non-smokers when travelling through flat country on a wet afternoon at autumn's end, nothing so poignant as the sight of an occasional bonfire of dead leaves in the back garden to remind them of the smokelessness of the staid compartment in which they are temporarily immured.

Compton Mackenzie, *Sublime Tobacco*, 1957

Wednesday April 22nd My father gave me a lift to the station. He also gave me a bit of advice about the journey; he said I was not to buy a pork pie from the buffet car.

I stood in the train with my head out of the window and my father stood on the platform. He kept looking at his watch. I couldn't think of anything to say and neither could he. In the end I said, 'Don't forget to feed the dog, will you?' My father gave a nasty laugh, then the train started to move so I waved and went to look for a non-smoking seat. All the filthy smokers were crammed together choking and coughing. They were a rough-looking, noisy lot so I hurried through their small carriage holding my breath. The non-smoking carriages seemed to have a quieter type of person in them.

Sue Townsend, *The Secret Diary of Adrian Mole Aged 13¾*, 1982

Ugh. 'Smoking Carriage' turned out to be Monstrous Pigsty where smokers were huddled, miserable and defiant. Realize it is no longer possible for smokers to live in dignity, instead being forced to sulk in the slimy underbelly of existence. Would not have been in least surprised if carriage had mysteriously been shunted off into siding never to be seen again. Maybe privatized rail firms will start running Smoking Trains and villagers will shake their fists and throw stones at them as they pass, terrifying their children with tales of fire-breathing freaks within.

Helen Fielding, *Bridget Jones's Diary*, 1996

[The Trans-Siberian Railway]

Each train car carries two middle-aged ladies whose job, as far as I could tell, is to walk up and down the corridor making sure no one smokes. You can drink on the train, you can puke on the train, you can yell and quarrel and party all night, you can cook tripe on alcohol stoves and make fetid picnics of smoked fish and goat cheese, but you can't smoke. In order to smoke, you have to stand between the cars and risk getting shoved under the wheels by all the people from the adjoining compartments who are standing between the cars, too, because everyone smokes in Russia.

And this is the first-class section of the train.

P.J. O'Rourke, *Eat the Rich*, 1998

CHAPTER TEN

The True Smoker; or, The Hopeless Addict

PATSY *enters. She flies down the stairs, swearing as she goes. She is fumbling in her bag for her fags.*

PATSY: Light, light, light, light!

She grabs the packet and takes four or five of them and smokes them as a bunch. EDINA *lights one, too, blowing extra smoke in* PATSY'S *direction.*

EDINA: Oh dear, Pats, honestly. Not another no-smoking cab, Pats?

They must see you coming these days.

PATSY: Bloody bastard asthmatic cab-driver.

EDINA: Well, I hope you refused to pay him this time.

Saffy tuts.

PATSY: It was one of your account cabs, Eds. I think you should get him fired.

SAFFRON: Oh, so not only do you want the man to die of passive smoking, but you also want to deny him a living of any kind?

EDINA: (*Mockingly.*) Passive smoking? I suppose we're shortening your life, are we, darling?

PATSY: If only.

EDINA: For your information, you have to be taking great big lung bucketfuls to make any difference.

PATSY: Not little wasp breaths.

EDINA: No. And excuse me if I sue and I die prematurely of passive boredom, or dull-as-dishwater-daughter induced stress. All right?

PATSY: Whole bloody hour it took me. I nearly didn't make it.

EDINA: God! Well, why didn't you use those nicotine patches I gave you for emergencies, darling?

PATSY: I did. (*She opens her shirt to reveal patches stuck on every available piece of skin.*) They're all dead now. Can you get the ones off my back.

EDINA: (*Preparing to take one off.*) Ready?

PATSY: Yeah, yeah.

EDINA: Go. (*Removes first patch.*)

PATSY: (*Groaning.*) Uh!

EDINA: Ready?

PATSY: Okay. Oh!

EDINA: Actually, most of these ones seem all right, darling. In fact, they're leeching something off your skin rather than the other way round.

SAFFRON: She's probably recharging them.

Jennifer Saunders, 'Poor' in *Absolutely Fabulous 2*, 1994

In this year also William Bredon, parson or vicar of Thornton in Buckinghamshire, was living, a profound divine, but absolutely the most polite person for nativities in that age, strictly adhering to Ptolemy, which he well understood; he had a hand in composing Sir Christopher Heydon's defence of judicial astrology, being that time his chaplain; he was so given over to tobacco and drink, that when he had no tobacco, he would cut the bell-ropes and smoke them.

William Lilly (astrologer, 1602–81), *Memoirs*, 1774

Even starker mutations were seen in the moral void produced by Macquarie Harbor. A group of prisoners were being led in single file through the forest when, without provocation or warning, one of them crushed the skull of the prisoner in front of him with his ax. Later he explained that there was no tobacco to be had in the settlement; that he had been a smoker all his life and would rather die than go without it; so, in the torment of nicotine withdrawal, he had killed the man in order to be hanged himself. At least he could get a twist of nigger-head shag in Hobart before he died.

Robert Hughes, *The Fatal Shore: A History of the Transportation of Convicts to Australia, 1787–1868*, 1987

'But his left-handedness?'

'You were yourself struck by the nature of the injury as recorded by the surgeon at the inquest. The blow was struck from immediately behind, and yet was upon the left side. Now, how can that be unless it were by a left-handed man? He had stood behind that tree during the interview between the father and son. He had even smoked there. I found the ash of a cigar, which my special knowledge of tobacco ashes enabled me to pronounce as an Indian cigar. I have, as you know, devoted some attention to this, and written a little monograph on the ashes of 140 different varieties of pipe, cigar, and cigarette tobacco. Having found the ash, I then looked round and discovered the stump among the moss where he had tossed it. It was an Indian cigar, of the variety which are rolled in Rotterdam.'

'And the cigar-holder?'

'I could see that the end had not been in his mouth. Therefore he used a holder. The tip had been cut off, not bitten off, but the cut was not a clean one, so I deduced a blunt penknife.'

'Holmes,' I said, 'you have drawn a net round this man from which he cannot escape . . .

Arthur Conan Doyle, 'The Boscombe Valley Mystery' in *The Adventures of Sherlock Holmes*, 1892

[On being warned by his doctor that death was certain if he didn't give up cigars]

But I thought it over & resumed [smoking]. I don't care for death & I do care for smoking.

Mark Twain, Letter to Margery H. Clinton, 27 August 1909

> Tobacco is a dirty weed: I like it.
> It satisfies no normal need: I like it.
> It makes you thin, it makes you lean,
> It takes the hair right off your bean;
> It's the worst darn stuff I've ever seen: I like it.

Graham Hemminger, 'Tobacco', in *Penn State Froth*, November 1915

'I don't understand it,' Hans Castorp said. 'I never can understand how anybody can *not* smoke – it deprives a man of the best part of life, so to speak – or at least of a first-class pleasure. When I wake in the morning, I feel glad at the thought of being able to smoke all day, and when I eat, I look forward to smoking afterwards; I might almost say I only eat for the sake of being able to smoke – though of course that is more or less of an exaggeration. But a day without tobacco would be flat, stale, and unprofitable, as far as I am concerned. If I had to say to myself to-morrow: "No smoke to-day" – I believe I shouldn't find the courage to get up – on my honour, I'd stop in bed.

But when a man has a good cigar in his mouth – of course it mustn't
have a side draught or not draw well, that is extremely irritating –
but with a good cigar in his mouth a man is perfectly safe, nothing
can touch him – literally. It's just like lying on the beach: when you
lie on the beach, why, you lie on the beach, don't you? – you don't
require anything else, in the line of work or amusement either. – People
smoke all over the world, thank goodness; there is nowhere one could
get to, so far as I know, where the habit hasn't penetrated. Even polar
expeditions fit themselves out with supplies of tobacco to help them
carry on. I've always felt a thrill of sympathy when I read that. You
can be very miserable: I might be feeling perfectly wretched, for
instance; but I could always stand it if I had my smoke.'

    Thomas Mann, *The Magic Mountain*, 1924 (trans. H. T. Lowe-Porter, 1928)

Three hundred yards from the gate a narrow track, sifted over with
brown oak leaves from last autumn, curved around a granite boulder
and disappeared. I followed it around and bumped along the stones
of the outcrop for fifty or sixty feet, then swung the car around a tree
and set it pointing back the way it had come. I cut the lights and
switched off the motor and sat there waiting.

  Half an hour passed. Without tobacco it seemed a long time.

    Raymond Chandler, *The Lady in the Lake*, 1943

Right now I'd give the other leg for a cigarette.

    William Bendix in Alfred Hitchcock's *Lifeboat*, 1944

I must confess though that I'm convinced that smoking is not at all
like writing. Cigars in particular are like movies: an art that is an
industry, an industry to make art. Like movies cigars are the stuff
dreams are made of. My idea of happiness is to sit alone in the lobby
of any old hotel after a late dinner, when the lights go out at the
entrance and only the desk and the doorman are visible from my
comfortable armchair. I then smoke my long black cigar in peace, in
the dark: once a primeval bonfire in a clear of the forest, now a
civilized ember glowing in the night like a beacon to the soul.

    G. Cabrera Infante, *Holy Smoke*, 1985

It was impossible to dislike John Braine, and almost as difficult not
so much to take him seriously as to be quite sure how serious he was

being about this or that. He was a heavy smoker who had a small sticker made to put on his cigarette packets with the legend, CIGARETTES ARE GOOD FOR YOU – SMOKE MORE, LIVE LONGER.

Kingsley Amis, *Memoirs*, 1991

Once upon a sunbeam, Oliver, despite vociferous New Year's Resolutions to the contrary, finds himself yet again at one of those slovenly events attended by lumpen frolickers bearing miniature beer-kegs under their arms, where all the girls ferociously inhale Silk Cut as if beneficial to health (I speak as no priggish reformee – but if you're going to smoke, *smoke*), and where you fear that at any moment you will be seized from behind by some chintzy pair of hands seeking to enlist you in that never-fail lithium-inducer, the drabble-tailed conga. It was – you've guessed! – a party.

Julian Barnes, *Talking It Over*, 1991

[Two writers playing tennis]

Richard was enjoying his breather – and *breather* was definitely the word he wanted. 'You haven't got a backhand. It's just a wound in your side. It's just an absence. Like an amputee's memory of a vanished limb. You haven't got a forehand either. Or a volley. Or an overhead. *That's* the trouble with your game. You haven't got any shots. You're a dog on the court. Yeah. A little Welsh retriever.'

He put a cigarette in his mouth and, as a matter of silent routine, offered one to Gwyn, who said,

'Just couldn't concentrate. No thanks.'

Richard looked at him.

'I packed it in.'

'You *what*?'

'I stopped. Three days ago. Cold. That's it. You just make the life choice.'

Richard lit up and inhaled needfully. He gazed at his cigarette. He didn't really want to smoke it. He wanted to eat it. This move of Gwyn's was a heavy blow. Almost the only thing he still liked about Gwyn was that Gwyn still smoked.

Of course, Gwyn never smoked seriously. Just a pack a day. Not like Richard with his carton-eons, his suede lungs, his kippered wisteria . . .

'You bastard,' said Richard. 'I thought we were in this together.'

'Three days ago. Hark at you gasping away. Couple of years I'll be having you six-love, six-love.'

'What's it like?'

Richard had *imagined* giving up smoking; and he naturally assumed that man knew no hotter hell. Nowadays he had long quit thinking about quitting. Before the children were born he sometimes thought that he might very well give up smoking when he became a father. But the boys seemed to have immortalized his bond with cigarettes. This bond with cigarettes – this living relationship with death. Paradoxically, he no longer wanted to give up smoking: what he wanted to do was take up smoking. Not so much to fill the little gaps between cigarettes with cigarettes (there wouldn't be time, anyway) or to smoke two cigarettes at once. It was more that he felt the desire to smoke a cigarette even when he was smoking a cigarette. The need was and wasn't being met.

'Actually it's a funny thing,' said Gwyn. 'I gave up three days ago, right? And guess what?'

Richard said longsufferingly, 'You haven't wanted one since.'

'Exactly.'

Martin Amis, *The Information*, 1995

I once burnt the back of my hand trying to put a cigarette in my mouth when there was already one there.

Allen Carr, *Easy Way to Stop Smoking*, 1995

I've been smoking 30 years now. And there's nothing wrong with my lung.

Freddie Starr in *The Sun*, 9 August 1997

. . . only a fool expects smoking and drinking to bring happiness, just as only a dolt expects money to do so. Like money, booze and fags *are* happiness, and people cannot be expected to pursue happiness in moderation. This distillation of ancient wisdom requires constant reassertion as the bores and prohibitionists and workhouse masters close in.

Christopher Hitchens, 'Booze and Fags' in *For the Sake of Argument*, 1993

The idea that one could smoke just enough to enjoy smoking cigarettes contradicts the actual nature of the experience and the habit. Pope

John Paul II is reputed, perhaps apocryphally, to smoke only three cigarettes a day, one after every meal – but only a saint can exercise such control over a practice that seems to have to be compulsively excessive or not at all.

Richard Klein, *Cigarettes are Sublime*, 1993

There is also ample evidence on the strength of tobacco dependence from those who have contracted smoking-related diseases. Among those surviving surgery for lung cancer, about 50% resume smoking. In smokers suffering heart attacks, 70% take up smoking again within a year (40% whilst still in hospital) and among those undergoing a laryngectomy, 40% try smoking again.

John Stapleton. 'Cigarette Smoking Prevalence, Cessation and Relapse' in *Statistical Methods in Medical Research*, Vol. 7, No. 2, June 1998

There's a guy, he's English (I don't think we should hold that against him), but apparently he has this life's dream – and I say apparently because he's flying over here with his own money in a couple of weeks to have a Senate hearing and this is what he wants to do: he wants to make the warnings on cigarette packs bigger. He wants the whole front of the pack to be the warning. Like the problem is we haven't noticed yet, right? Like he's gonna get his way and smokers around the world are gonna be going, 'Yeah, Bill, I've got some cigarettes – *(Noticing warning on pack)* Hey! Wait a minute. Jesus Christ. These things are bad for you! Shit, I thought they were good for you. I thought they had vitamin C in 'em and stuff.' *(Slams pack loudly onto stool)* You dolt! ... It doesn't matter how big the warnings are or how much they cost. Keep raising the prices. We'll break into your houses to buy the cigarettes, okay? We're addicted. It's a drug.

Denis Leary, *No Cure for Cancer* (based on his live show), 1992

Four famous examples

[Franz Liszt]

Sometime in the early part of the year the young composer Ludwig Meinardus (1827–96) presented himself at the Altenburg. 'Since I know you *à peu près* from your C major Sonata,' said Liszt jocularly, 'you must smoke – for every good musician is a smoker.'

In mid-October the violinist Joseph Joachim (1831–1907) came to Weimar as leader of Liszt's orchestra. The two had met at Vienna in 1846, when, in a private performance at Liszt's hotel, the talented youngster had played the Mendelssohn Concerto, Liszt accompanying at the piano. 'To this day,' remarked Joachim's biographer half a century later, 'Joachim cherishes the memory of Liszt's wonderful playing, particularly of the manner in which he accompanied the finale of the concerto, all the time holding a lighted cigar between the first and middle fingers of his right hand.'

Adrian Williams, *Portrait of Liszt: by Himself and His Contemporaries*, 1990

[Sigmund Freud]

. . . something may be said here about Freud's smoking habits. He was always a heavy smoker – 20 cigars a day were his usual allowance – and he tolerated abstinence from it with the greatest difficulty. In the correspondence there are many references to this attempt to diminish or even abolish the habit, mainly on Fliess's advice. But it was one respect in which even Fliess's influence was ineffective. Freud soon flatly refused to take his advice: 'I am not following your interdict from smoking; do you think then it is so very lucky to have a long miserable life?'

Ernest Jones, *The Life and Work of Sigmund Freud*, 1953–7

[Albert Einstein]

Among the dozens of refugees now living in Princeton, Einstein made close friends with historian Erich Kahler and his wife, Alice, who were from Germany. They had been encouraged to settle in Princeton by another German refugee, novelist Thomas Mann, a mutual friend. Einstein first met the couple at a poetry reading in their Princeton home. A neighbor, Charles Bell, who was there, described him, said Alice Kahler, as ' "the idol of my science-loving youth, with parchment face and a corona of hair, a resigned and sphinx-like wisdom, between a Saint Bernard and an angel, as if he had lived the whole rise from brute to human, and was himself the record of the trial and achievement." This is a bit exaggerated,' she added, with a laugh. 'But Einstein was the most charming friend you can imagine if he was in the mood.' . . .

Alice Kahler was aware of Einstein's addiction to tobacco, which his doctor had forbidden him to use. 'He loved to smoke,' she said, 'but his secretary, Helen Dukas, and daughter [*sic*], Margot, were adamant about doctor's orders. When he got tobacco as a gift he sent it with a little note to my husband, and when he came to our home he asked Erich, "Give me a little of the stuff so I can at least smell it." His desire was so great that he would pick up cigarette butts from the street – which was nearly tragic.'

Denis Brian, *Einstein: A Life*, 1996

[Luis Buñuel]

To continue this panegyric on earthly delights, let me just say that it's impossible to drink without smoking. I began to smoke when I was sixteen and have never stopped. My limit is a pack a day. I've smoked absolutely everything but am particularly fond of Spanish and French cigarettes (Gitanes and Celtiques especially) because of their black tobacco.

If alcohol is queen, then tobacco is her consort. It's a fond companion for all occasions, a loyal friend through fair weather and foul. People smoke to celebrate a happy moment, or to hide a bitter regret. Whether you're alone or with friends, it's a joy for all the senses. What lovelier sight is there than that double row of white cigarettes, lined up like soldiers on parade and wrapped in silver paper? If I were blindfolded and a lighted cigarette placed between my lips, I'd refuse to smoke it. I love to touch the pack in my pocket, open it, savor the feel of the cigarette between my fingers, the paper on my lips, the taste of tobacco on my tongue. I love to watch the flame spurt up, love to watch it come closer and closer, filling me with its warmth.

I once had a friend from my student days called Dorronsoro, who was from the Basque country and, as a Spanish Republican, was exiled to Mexico. When I visited him in the hospital, he had tubes everywhere, as well as an oxygen mask, which he'd take off from time to time for a quick puff on a cigarette. He smoked until the last hours of his life, ever faithful to the pleasure that killed him.

Finally, dear readers, allow me to end these ramblings on tobacco and alcohol, delicious fathers of abiding friendships and fertile reveries, with some advice: Don't drink and don't smoke. It's bad for your health.

It goes without saying that alcohol and tobacco are excellent accompaniments to lovemaking – the alcohol first, then the cigarettes. No, you're not about to hear any extraordinary erotic secrets. Men of my generation, particularly if they're Spanish, suffer from a hereditary timidity where sex and women are concerned. Our sexual desire has to be seen as the product of centuries of repressive and emasculating Catholicism, whose many taboos – no sexual relations outside of marriage (not to mention within), no pictures or words that might suggest the sexual act, no matter how obliquely – have turned normal desire into something exceptionally violent. As you can imagine, when this desire manages to overcome the obstacles, the gratification is incomparable, since it's always colored by the sweet secret sense of sin.

With rare exceptions, we Spaniards knew of only two ways to make love – in a brothel or in marriage. When I went to France for the first time in 1925, I was shocked, in fact disgusted, by the men and women I saw kissing in public, or living together without the sanction of marriage. Such customs were unimaginable to me; they seemed obscene. Much of this has changed, of course, over the years; lately, my own sexual desire has waned and finally disappeared, even in dreams. And I'm delighted; it's as if I've finally been relieved of a tyrannical burden. If the devil were to offer me a resurgence of what is commonly called virility, I'd decline. 'Just keep my liver and lungs in good working order,' I'd reply, 'so I can go on drinking and smoking!'

Luis Buñuel, *My Last Breath*, 1982 (trans. Abigail Israel, 1983)

A pipe for the hour of work; a cigarette for the hour of conception; a cigar for the hour of vacuity.

George Gissing (1857–1903), *Commonplace Book*, 1962

As for myself, could I be granted a perfect end to this transitory life I would choose to leave it like the father of George Blake the novelist. When he was in his hundredth year he was sitting at sunset by a window that looked over the Clyde. He lit his pipe, and as he blew out the first fragrant puff of smoke his spirit followed it.

Compton Mackenzie, *Sublime Tobacco*, 1957

[Our most destructive habits] commonly begin as pleasures of which we have no need and end as necessities in which we have no pleasure. Nonetheless we tend to resent the suggestion that anyone should try and change them, even on the disarming grounds that they do so for our own good.

Thomas McKeown, *The Role of Medicine: Dream, Mirage or Nemesis?*, 1976

CHAPTER ELEVEN

Writing and Smoking

'*Das Kapital*,' he said to me once, 'will not even pay for the cigars I smoked writing it.'

> Karl Marx's son-in-law, Paul Lafargue, in *Reminiscences of Marx and Engels*

———

[William Faulkner]

INTERVIEWER: Then what would be the best environment for a writer?

FAULKNER: ... The only environment the artist needs is whatever peace, whatever solitude, and whatever pleasure he can get at not too high a cost. All the wrong environment will do is run his blood-pressure up; he will spend more time being frustrated or outraged. My own experience has been that the tools I need for my trade are paper, tobacco, food, and a little whisky.

INTERVIEWER: Bourbon, you mean?

FAULKNER: No, I ain't that particular. Between scotch and nothing, I'll take scotch.

> *Writers at Work: The Paris Review Interviews*, 1958 (the interview took place in early 1956)

[Martin Amis]

INTERVIEWER: Do you have any superstitions about writing?

AMIS: It's amazing – I do sometimes feel tempted by computers until I realize what an amazing pleasure a new Biro is.

INTERVIEWER: A new Biro?

AMIS: A Biro, you know – a ballpoint. The pleasure you get from a new Biro that works. So you have the childish pleasure of paper and pen.

INTERVIEWER: New supplies.

AMIS: New supplies. Superstitions ... I think someone must have told me at some point that I write a lot better if I'm smoking. I'm sure if I stopped smoking, I would start writing sentences like: 'It was bitterly cold,' or 'It was bakingly hot.'

The Paris Review No. 146, 1998

Nobody has yet been able to demonstrate to me how I can join words into whole sentences on a blank page without a cigarette burning away between my lips.

Dennis Potter in *The Sunday Times*, 30 October 1977

It is supposed that tobacco cheers one up, clears the thoughts, and attracts one merely like any other habit – without at all producing the deadening of conscience produced by wine. But you need only observe attentively the conditions under which a special desire to smoke arises, and you will be convinced that stupefying with tobacco acts on the conscience as wine does, and that people consciously have recourse to this method of stupefaction just when they require it for that purpose . . .

That man-cook who murdered his mistress said that when he entered the bedroom and had gashed her throat with his knife and she had fallen with a rattle in her throat and the blood had gushed out in a torrent – he lost his courage. 'I could not finish her off,' he said, 'but I went back from the bedroom to the sitting-room and sat down there and smoked a cigarette.' Only after stupefying himself with tobacco was he able to return to the bedroom, finish cutting the old lady's throat, and begin examining her things.

Evidently the desire to smoke at that moment was evoked in him, not by a wish to clear his thoughts or be merry, but by the need to stifle something that prevented him from completing what he had planned to do.

Any smoker may detect in himself the same definite desire to stupefy himself with tobacco at certain specially difficult moments . . .

Why do gamblers almost all smoke? Why among women do those who lead a regular life smoke least? Why do prostitutes and madmen *all* smoke? Habit is habit, but evidently smoking stands in some definite connexion with the craving to stifle conscience, and achieves the end required of it . . .

It is usually said (and I used to say) that smoking facilitates mental work. And that is undoubtedly true if one considers only the quantity of one's mental output . . .

When a man works he is always conscious of two beings in himself: the one works, the other appraises the work. The stricter the appraisement the slower and the better is the work; and vice versa, when the appraiser is under the influence of something that stupefies him, more work gets done, but its quality is poorer.

'If I do not smoke I cannot write. I cannot get on; I begin and cannot continue,' is what is usually said, and what I used to say. What does it really mean? It means either that you have nothing to write, or that what you wish to write has not yet matured in your consciousness but is only beginning dimly to present itself to you, and the appraising critic within, when not stupefied with tobacco, tells you so.

Leo Tolstoy, *Why Do Men Stupefy Themselves?*, 1890 (trans. Aylmer Maude, 1937)

[Wodehouse replies to Tolstoy]

... day by day in every way we smokers are being harder pressed. Like the troops of Midian, the enemy prowl and prowl around. First it was James the Second [*sic*], then Tolstoy, then all these doctors, and now – of all people – Miss Gloria Swanson, the idol of the silent screen, who not only has become a non-smoker herself but claims to have converted a San Francisco business man, a Massachusetts dress designer, a lady explorer, a television script-writer and a Chicago dentist.

'The joys of not smoking,' she says 'are so much greater than the joys of smoking,' omitting, however, to mention what the former are. From the fact that she states that her disciples send her flowers, I should imagine that she belongs to the school of thought which holds that abstention from tobacco heightens the sense of smell. I don't want my sense of smell heightened. When I lived in New York, I often found myself wishing that I didn't smell the place as well as I did.

But I have no quarrel with Miss Swanson. We Wodehouses do not war upon the weaker sex. As far as Miss Swanson is concerned, an indulgent 'There, there, foolish little woman' about covers my attitude. The bird I am resolved to expose before the bar of world opinion is the late Count Leo N. Tolstoy.

For one reason and another I have not read Tolstoy in the original Russian, and it is possible that a faulty translation may have misled me, but what he is recorded as saying in his Essays, Letters and

Miscellanies is that an excellent substitute for smoking may be found in twirling the fingers, and there rises before one's mental eye the picture of some big public dinner (decorations will be worn) at the moment when the toast of the Queen is being drunk.

'The Queen!'

'The Queen, God bless her!'

And then—

'Gentlemen, you may twirl your fingers.'

It wouldn't work. There would be a sense of something missing. And I don't see that it would be much better if you adopted Tolstoy's other suggestion – viz. playing on the dudka. But then what can you expect of a man who not only grew a long white beard but said that the reason we smoke is that we want to deaden our conscience, instancing the case of a Russian murderer of Czarist times who half-way through the assassination of his employer found himself losing the old pep?

'I could not finish the job,' he is quoted as saying, 'so I went from the bedroom into the dining-room, sat down there and smoked a cigarette.'

'Only when he had stupefied himself with tobacco,' says Tolstoy, 'did he feel sufficiently fortified to return to the bedroom and complete his crime.'

Stupefied with tobacco! On a single gasper! They must have been turning out powerful stuff in Russia under the old régime.

And, of course, our own manufacturers are turning out good and powerful stuff today, so let us avail ourselves of it. Smoke up, my hearties. Never mind Tolstoy. Ignore G. Swanson ... Think what it would mean if for want of our support the tobacco firms had to go out of business. There would be no more of those photographs of authors smoking pipes, and if authors were not photographed smoking pipes, how would we be able to know that they were manly and in the robust tradition of English literature?

P. G. Wodehouse, 'Healthward Ho!' in *Over Seventy: an Autobiography with Digressions*, 1957

Like many of my idle day-dreaming egotistical tribe, I am a heavy pipe-smoker, having long found it necessary to stupefy myself with tobacco in order not to feel too acutely the pangs of injured vanity, the shame of poverty and obscurity, and the constant prickings of a

Nonconformist conscience. However, I will not apologize for my pipe, for man, being terribly burdened with a consciousness, must dope himself in one way or another, and if he is not smoking or drinking he is making illicit love or denouncing something or somebody, delivering a message to all thinking men, passing unnecessary laws, drugging himself with a sense of power; so that it seems to me that my way of escaping the tedium of being conscious or the pain of thought is perhaps the least guilty, for smoky and blackened though I may be, I am at least amiable, puffing away.

J. B. Priestley, 'A New Tobacco' in *The Balconinny*, 1929

It will not, I trust, be supposed by any reader that I have intended in this so-called autobiography to give a record of my inner life. No man ever did so truly, – and no man ever will. Rousseau probably attempted it, but who doubts but that Rousseau has confessed in much the thoughts and convictions rather than the facts of his life? If the rustle of a woman's petticoat has ever stirred my blood; if a cup of wine has been a joy to me; if I have thought tobacco at midnight in pleasant company to be one of the elements of an earthly paradise; if now and again I have somewhat recklessly fluttered a £5 note over a card-table; – of what matter is that to any reader? I have betrayed no woman. Wine has brought me to no sorrow. It has been the companionship of smoking that I have loved, rather than the habit. I have never desired to win money, and I have lost none. To enjoy the excitement of pleasure, but to be free from its vices and ill effects, – to have the sweet, and leave the bitter untasted, – that has been my study. The preachers tell us that this is impossible. It seems to me that hitherto I have succeeded fairly well. I will not say that I have never scorched a finger, – but I carry no ugly wounds.

Anthony Trollope, *Autobiography*, 1883 (published the year after he died)

La Pipe

Je suis la pipe d'un auteur;
On voit, à contempler ma mine
D'Abyssinienne ou de Cafrine,
Que mon maître est un grand fumeur.

Quand il est comblé de douleur,
Je fume comme la chaumine

Où se prépare la cuisine
Pour le retour du laboureur.

J'enlace et je berce son âme
Dans le réseau mobile et bleu
Qui monte de ma bouche en feu,

Et je roule un puissant dictame
Qui charme son cœur et guérit
De ses fatigues son esprit.

Charles Baudelaire, *Fleurs du Mal*, 1857

The Author's Pipe

I am an author's pipe. To see me
And my outlandish shape to heed,
You'd know my master was a dreamy
Inveterate smoker of the weed.

When he is loaded down with care,
I like a stove will smoke and burn
Wherein the supper they prepare
Against the labourer's return.

I nurse his spirit with my charm
Swaying it in a soft, uncertain,
And vaguely-moving azure curtain.

I roll a potent cloud of balm
To lull his spirit into rest
And cure the sorrows in his breast.

trans. Roy Campbell, 1952

Tennyson

We have had Alfred Tennyson here; very droll, and very wayward:
and much sitting up of nights till two and three in the morning with
pipes in our mouths: at which good hour we would get Alfred to give
us some of his magic music, which he does between growling and

smoking; and so to bed. All this has not cured my Influenza as you may imagine: but these hours shall be remembered long after the Influenza is forgotten.

Edward Fitzgerald, Letter to Bernard Barton, April 1838, in *Letters of Edward Fitzgerald*, 1894

My dear Mrs Gladstone
On Monday then – if all be well. As you are good enough to say that you will manage anything rather than lose my visit – will you manage that I may have my pipe in my own room whenever I like?
    Yours ever
    A. Tennyson

The full text of a letter accepting an invitation to the Gladstones*, 25 October 1876

One woman with whom Tennyson got on well immediately was Mrs Carlyle, and it is suggestive that he spent an evening with her later in the same week he met Mrs Norton, almost as if to cleanse his memory of the Rogers party. Jane Carlyle was at home alone, dozing in front of the fire as she waited for her husband to come back from dinner, when to her surprise she heard a carriage draw up in the quiet street. Tennyson had brought Moxon to call; Jane could only be sensible of her husband's 'misfortune in having missed the man he likes best'. She noticed how embarrassed Tennyson was 'with women alone – for he entertains at one and the same moment a feeling of almost adoration for them and an ineffable contempt! adoration I suppose for what they *might be* – contempt for what they *are*!' To make him forget her 'womanness', she did as Carlyle had so often done, getting out pipes and tobacco with brandy and water 'with a deluge of *tea* over and above'. To her delight he smoked on 'for *three* mortal hours! – talking like an angel – only exactly as if he were talking with a clever *man* – which – being a thing I am not used to – men always adapting their conversation to what they *take to be* a woman's taste – strained me to a terrible pitch of intellectuality'. When Carlyle arrived home at midnight he found her alone, reliving the evening 'in an atmosphere of tobacco so thick that you might have cut it with a knife'.

Robert Bernard Martin, *Tennyson: the Unquiet Heart*, 1980

---

* Gladstone hated smoking.

Thomas Carlyle

[In 1872]

William Maccall, who had first come to see Carlyle twenty-four years before, records a conversation about tobacco, which followed Carlyle's enquiry as to the literary work in which he was engaged. Maccall told him he was now writing for the *Tobacco Plant* on appropriate topics, and added, alluding to his own lack of prosperity: 'My life has begun in smoke, and seems destined to end in smoke.'

Thereupon Carlyle, who had been a smoker from the age of eleven, began to praise tobacco, 'one of the divinest benefits that had ever come to the human race, arriving as compensation and consolation at a time when social, political, religious anarchy and every imaginable plague made the earth unspeakably miserable.' He declared that he could never think of 'this miraculous blessing from the Gods without being overwhelmed by a tenderness for which he could find no adequate expression.'

David Alec Wilson and David Wilson MacArthur, *Carlyle in Old Age (1865–1881)*, 1934

Had they sent me ¼lb of good tobacco, the addition to my happiness had probably been suitabler and greater!

Carlyle on being awarded the Prussian Order of Merit – in a letter to his brother John, 14 February 1874

T. S. Eliot and Groucho Marx

25 January 1963

Dear Mr Eliot:

I read in the current Time Magazine that you are ill. I just want you to know that I am rooting for your quick recovery. First because of your contributions to literature and, then, the fact that under the most trying conditions you never stopped smoking cigars.

Hurry up and get well.

Regards,

Groucho Marx

23 February 1963

Dear Groucho Marx,

It seems more of an impertinence to address Groucho Marx as 'Dear Mr. Marx' than it would be to address any other celebrity by his first name. It is out of respect, my dear Groucho, that I address you as I do. I should only be too happy to have a letter from Groucho Marx beginning 'Dear T. S. E.' However, this is to thank you for your letter and to say that I am convalescing as fast as the awful winter weather permits, that my wife and I hope to get to Bermuda later next month for warmth and fresh air and to be back in London in time to greet you in the spring. So come, let us say, about the beginning of May.

Will Mrs. Groucho be with you? (We think we saw you both in Jamaica early in 1961, about to embark in that glass-bottomed boat from which we had just escaped.) You ought to bring a secretary, a public relations official and a couple of private detectives, to protect you from the London press; but however numerous your engagements, we hope you will give us the honour of taking a meal with us.

Yours very sincerely,
T. S. Eliot

P. S. Your portrait is framed on my office mantelpiece, but I have to point you out to my visitors as nobody recognises you without the cigar and rolling eyes. I shall try to provide a cigar worthy of you.

To Gummo Marx

June 1964

Dear Gummo:

Last night Eden and I had dinner wth my celebrated pen pal, T. S. Eliot. It was a memorable evening.

The poet met us at the door with Mrs Eliot, a good-looking, middle-aged blonde whose eyes seemed to fill up with adoration every time she looked at her husband. He, by the way, is tall, lean and rather stooped over; but whether this is from age, illness or both, I don't know.

At any rate, your correspondent arrived at the Eliots' fully prepared for a literary evening. During the week I had read 'Murder in the Cathedral' twice; 'The Waste Land' three times, and just in case of a conversational bottleneck, I brushed up on 'King Lear.'

Well, sir, as cocktails were served, there was a momentary lull – the kind that is more or less inevitable when strangers meet for the first time. So, apropos of practically nothing (and 'not with a bang but a whimper') I tossed in a quotation from 'The Waste Land.' That, I thought, will show him I've read a thing or two besides my press notices from vaudeville.

Eliot smiled faintly – as though to say he was thoroughly familiar with his poems and didn't need me to recite them. So I took a whack at 'King Lear.' I said the king was an incredibly foolish old man, which God knows he *was*; and that if he'd been *my* father I would have run away from home at the age of eight – instead of waiting until I was ten.

That, too, failed to bowl over the poet. He seemed more interested in discussing 'Animal Crackers' and 'A Night at the Opera.' He quoted a joke – one of mine – that I had long since forgotten. Now it was my turn to smile faintly. I was not going to let anyone – not even the British poet from St Louis – spoil my Literary Evening. I pointed out that King Lear's opening speech was the height of idiocy. Imagine (I said) a father asking his three children: Which of you kids loves me the most? And then disowning the youngest – the sweet, honest Cordelia – because, unlike her wicked sister [*sic*], she couldn't bring herself to gush out insincere flattery. And Cordelia, mind you, had been her father's favorite!

The Eliots listened politely. Mrs Eliot then defended Shakespeare; and Eden, too, I regret to say, was on King Lear's side, even though I am the one who supports her. (In all fairness to my wife, I must say that, having played the Princess in a high school production of 'The Swan,' she has retained a rather warm feeling for all royalty.)

As for Eliot, he asked if I remembered the courtroom scene in 'Duck Soup.' Fortunately I'd forgotten every word. It was obviously the end of the Literary Evening, but very pleasant none the less. I discovered that Eliot and I had three things in common: (1) an affection for good cigars and (2) cats; and (3) a weakness for making puns – a weakness that for many years I have tried to overcome. T. S., on the other hand, is an unashamed – even proud – punster. For example, there's his Gus, the Theater Cat, whose 'real name was Asparagus.'

Speaking of asparagus, the dinner included good, solid English beef, very well prepared. And, although they had a semi-butler serving, Eliot insisted on pouring the wine himself. It was an excellent wine and no maitre d' could have served it more graciously. He is a dear man and a charming host.

When I told him that my daughter Melinda was studying his poetry at Beverly High, he said he regretted that, because he had no wish to become compulsory reading.

We didn't stay late, for we both felt that he wasn't up to a long evening of conversation – especially mine.

Did I tell you we called him Tom? – possibly because that's his name. I, of course, asked him to call me Tom too, but only because I loathe the name Julius.

Yours,
Tom Marx

The Groucho Letters: Letters from and to Groucho Marx, 1967

The summer of 1972 was, then, a busy one. Warner Brothers sent me to the Cannes film festival to promote Kubrick's film. This was *hors de concours*, since only a film not previously shown could compete for the prizes, but Cannes, with the entire cinema world present, was the place for the, so to speak, ultimate press conference. For me the high point of the visit was a meeting with Groucho Marx. A luncheon was given for him, but the guests were mostly intellectual Parisians, the majority monoglot, who were more concerned with the structuralist and semiotic content of *A Night at the Opera* than with the rollicking fun that had never aroused their laughter. Groucho was shy and bewildered, though Mordecai Richler and Louis Malle eased him into reminiscence of the old vaudeville days with hookers at two bucks a throw. I asked Malle if he was acquainted with the work of Messrs Gilbert and Sullivan, and then Groucho's blue eyes opened wide and he sang:

> Taken from the county jail
> By a set of curious chances,
> Liberated then on bail
> On my own recognizances . . .

From then on things went well. Groucho had come with the notorious girl who was to claim, four years later, the bulk of his estate. She kept saying 'Aw, cut it out, Grouch,' whenever he sang bawdily: this was to show that she was in charge. It was clear that Groucho's great days had been the penurious ones on tour in the sticks: the films were no more than inadequate spin-offs. He quoted T. S. Eliot ('Aw, cut it out, Grouch'). His French and German were rusty but adequate: after all, the Marx family was from Alsace-Lorraine. He gave me a Romeo and Juliet cigar which I kept till it fell to pieces. He was spontaneously witty, but not above filing away the occasional unpurposed crack. It was on this occasion that a lady was mentioned who had ten children because she loved her husband. 'I love my cigar,' Groucho said, 'but I take it out sometimes.'

Anthony Burgess, *You've Had Your Time: Being the Second Part of the Confessions of Anthony Burgess*, 1990

Finally in this chapter, a real literary curiosity. In the 1880s, A. Arthur Reade tried – unsuccessfully as it turned out – to settle once and for all the question of whether alcohol and tobacco helped or hindered the creative process, by writing to the leading intellectuals of the day to ask about their experiences. He received replies from an impressive roster of the famous, whose answers were published in *Studies and Stimulants: or the Use of Intoxicants and Narcotics in Relation to Intellectual Life, as Illustrated by Personal Communications on the Subject from Men of Letters and Science* (1883). Isaac ('Eizak') Pitman wrote back in the reformed spelling of which he was a champion ('ei hav a ferm konvikshon that they ekserseiz a dedli influens on the hiuman rase'); a New York Professor of Medicine proclaimed the advantages of opium over alcohol; and some other notable contributions were as follows – with Mark Twain predictably stealing the show:

Mr Wilkie Collins

When I am ill (I am suffering from gout at this very moment) tobacco is the best friend that my irritable nerves possess. When I am well, but exhausted for the time by a hard day's work, tobacco nerves and composes me. There is my evidence in two words. When a man allows himself to become a glutton in the matter of smoking tobacco, he suffers for it; and if he becomes a glutton in the matter of eating meat, he just as certainly suffers in another way. When I read learned attacks on the practice of smoking, I feel indebted to the writer – he adds largely to the relish of my cigar.

Wilkie Collins
February 10, 1882

Mr Ivan Tourguéneff

In answer to your enquiry I have to state that I have no personal experience of the influence of tobacco and alcohol on the mind, as I do not smoke or use alcoholic drinks. My observations on other people lead me to the conclusion that tobacco is generally a bad thing, and that alcohol taken in very small quantities can produce a good effect in some cases of constitutional debility.

Iv. Tourguéneff
March 14, 1882

Professor Darwin

I drink a glass of wine daily, and believe I should be better without any, though all doctors urge me to drink wine, as I suffer much from giddiness. I have taken snuff all my life, and regret that I ever acquired the habit, which I have often tried to leave off, and have succeeded for a time. I feel sure that it is a great stimulus and aid in my work. I also daily smoke two little paper cigarettes of Turkish tobacco. This is not a stimulus, but rests me after I have been compelled to talk, with tired memory, more than anything else. I am 73 years old.

Ch. Darwin
February 9, 1882

Professor Edison

I think chewing tobacco acts as a good stimulant upon anyone engaged in laborious brain work. Smoking, although pleasant, is too violent in its action; and the same remark applies to alcoholic liquors. I am inclined to think that it is better for intellectual workers to perform their labours at night, as after a very long experience of night work, I find my brain is in better condition at that time, especially for experimental work, and when so engaged I almost invariably chew tobacco as a stimulant.

Thos. A. Edison
April 4, 1882

(For) Mr John Ruskin

You are evidently unaware that Mr Ruskin entirely abhors the practice of smoking, in which he has never indulged. His dislike of it is mainly based upon his belief (no doubt a true one) that a cigar or pipe will very often make a man content to be idle for any length of time, who would not otherwise be so. The excessive use of tobacco amongst all classes abroad, both in France and Italy, and the consequent spitting everywhere and upon everything, has not tended to lessen his antipathy. I have heard him allow, however, that there is reason in the soldiers and the sailors pipe, as being some protection against the ill effects of exposure, etc. As to the effect of tobacco on the brain, I know that he considers it anything but beneficial.

Feb. 12, 1882

Mark Twain

I have not had a large experience in the matter of alcoholic drinks. I find that about two glasses of champagne are an admirable stimulant to the tongue, and is, perhaps, the happiest inspiration for an after dinner speech which can be found; but, as far as my experience goes, wine is a clog to the pen, not an inspiration. I have never seen the time when I could write to my satisfaction after drinking even one glass of wine.

As regards smoking, my testimony is of the opposite character. I am forty-six years old, and I have smoked immoderately during thirty-eight years, with the exception of a few intervals, which I will speak of presently. During the first seven years of my life I had no health – I may almost say that I lived on allopathic medicine, but since that period I have hardly known what sickness is. My health has been excellent, and remains so. As I have already said, I began to smoke immoderately when I was eight years old; that is, I began with one hundred cigars a month, and by the time I was twenty I had increased my allowance to two hundred a month. Before I was thirty, I had increased it to three hundred a month. I think I do not smoke more than that now; I am quite sure I never smoke less. Once, when I was fifteen, I ceased from smoking for three months, but I do not remember whether the effect resulting was good or evil. I repeated this experiment when I was twenty-two; again I do not remember what the result was. I repeated the experiment once more, when I was thirty-four, and ceased from smoking during a year and a half. My health did not improve, because it was not possible to improve health which was already perfect. As I never permitted myself to regret this abstinence, I experienced no sort of inconvenience from it. I wrote nothing but occasional magazine articles during pastime, and as I never wrote one except under strong impulse, I observed no lapse of facility. But by and by I sat down with a contract behind me to write a book of five or six hundred pages – the book called 'Roughing it' – and then I found myself most seriously obstructed. I was three weeks writing six chapters. Then I gave up the fight, resumed my three hundred cigars, burned the six chapters, and wrote the book in three months, without any bother or difficulty. I find cigar smoking to be the best of all inspirations for the pen, and, in my particular case, no sort of detriment to the health. During eight months of the year I am at home, and that period is my holiday. In it I do nothing but very occasional miscellaneous work; therefore, three hundred cigars a month is a sufficient amount to keep my constitution on a firm basis. During the family's summer vacation, which we spend elsewhere, I work five hours every day, and five days in every week, and allow no interruption under any pretext. I allow myself the fullest possible marvel of inspiration; consequently, I ordinarily smoke fifteen cigars during my five hours' labours, and if my interest reaches the enthusiastic point, I smoke more. I smoke with all my might, and allow no intervals.

Mark Twain
March 14, 1882

CHAPTER TWELVE

Smoking, Prison and Prison Camps

'Did you know,' said Joe, 'there's a book called *Crime and Punishment* – it's about a geezer that kills an 'ore with an 'atchet.'

'It's by a Russian called Dostoyevsky,' said I. 'Did you read it?'

'No,' said Joe, 'can't say as I did. But I 'eard a bloke tell it once. You know the way you tell a film. It was double good. But the best book I ever saw in the nick was the Bible. When I was in Brixton on remand, I 'ad one in the flowery. Smashing thin paper for rolling dog-ends in. I must 'ave smoked my way through the book of Genesis, before I went to court.'

Brendan Behan, *The Borstal Boy*, 1957

─────────

'Right, young Godber. True, very true. Hang about. I'm not saying don't put down for educational classes. Education, that's different. Current affairs, pottery, archaeology. I'll be putting down for some. Can't beat it. An hour every night in a warm classroom. With a bit of luck you might get a female teacher. Then, with a bit more luck, she might drop the chalk and wallop! There you are, a quick flash of a nylon-clad thigh. Oh yes, I've nothing against educational classes.'

By now we'd finished our meal. Young Lenny Godber took a packet of cigarettes out of his pocket and offered the packet to me and Heslop. We quickly took one each and put it in our pockets.

'Why'd you do that?' he asked.

'We're not being impolite, Lenny, my son. It's just that Heslop and me have been inside before, an' you see, inside, snout is like gold. You was mad to give us a fag.'

'But you took them.'

'Ah, yes, you gotta learn the hard way, haven't you? Learn not to be lavish, you're not Paul Getty! Should have just lit one and shared it.' And I lean over and takes his fag and has a puff before passing it to Heslop.

From Dick Clement and Ian La Frenais, 'New Faces, Old Hands' in *Three Helpings of Porridge*, 1984

To return to Dartmoor, where the 'rag' was proceeding merrily. The men in the punishment cells were released, for the tough-guy jailors in chokey considered discretion the better part of valour and put up no resistance. Yet these men are hand-picked for their supposed ability to rough-house. Yes, when the odds are six to one in their favour, they are able and willing to 'man-handle' half-starved convicts, but when the shoe is on the other foot they go down on their knees and beg for mercy, as happened in the punishment cells on that January 24th, although this was not related in the Report.

Some records were burnt; the mess was raided; cigarettes and tobacco were distributed to the convicts.

Throughout the Report no reference is made to the prohibition of smoking as a contributory factor to the ragged nerves of men in gaol.

It is obvious that, with the wretched conditions of Dartmoor, a small allowance of tobacco would do more to help and steady a man doing a long sentence than all the prison visitors in England.

In gaol, tobacco is the currency of currencies, and its power is illimitable. It is no exaggeration to say that for tobacco one can have one's enemy maimed or can buy sexually the body of a fellow convict; between the two the whole gamut of prison life runs, and tobacco rules the range . . .

By depriving the convict of tobacco the prison administration has caused physical distress, moral degeneracy, and has created a graft which enables all sorts of corruptions to flourish.

Tobacco, to most of the inhabitants of an industrial State, is almost as much an essential part of their existence as oxygen. Almost everybody in England now smokes almost every day of his life. Tobacco is now an integral part of every adult's life. Suddenly, the sedative is taken away. I may be a non-smoker, but I could recognise the agony caused to men by the lack of tobacco.

Not only are men deprived of tobacco, but they are severely punished for being in possession of it . . .

To many jailors the finding of tobacco in men's possession becomes a keen sport. Every form of cunning is employed to entrap men;

frequent searches are made, which include a strict examination of every orifice in the body. Five times within a short period was I subjected to these obscene searches.

Informers are suborned to watch, and even to smell the breaths of their comrades. At least a quarter of disciplinary activity in prison is concerned with suppressing the use of tobacco among the inmates.

The devices employed on both sides are legion, and are both grim and humorous. One bright lad who had the job of cleaning the adjudication room kept pounds of tobacco sewn up in the governor's leather chair! Another, who was prison watchmaker, hid his tobacco in the big main clock, and fixed the clock so that it needed frequent attention.

One of the best 'snout' stories concerns Yankee Klynes, who always managed to have a good deal of tobacco. He was a straightforward fellow, and always under suspicion.

Klynes was head market gardener, and one of his duties was to turn over hundreds of tons of potatoes – a long and tedious job. Klynes gave a large piece of 'snout' to a notorious nark, swore him to secrecy, and told him that there was a great deal of tobacco hidden beneath the spuds, and threatened to break his neck if anything untoward eventuated.

At once the nark ran to the deputy-chief jailor and told him breathlessly of the immense store of tobacco to be found amongst the spuds.

That afternoon, Klynes and the men working with him were kept locked up in their cells while four brawny jailors worked for hours in a vain attempt to find the non-existent tobacco. The net result was that four jailors got sweaty, Klynes got his spuds turned, and one informer was in future considered by the deputy-chief to be unreliable.

Wilfred Macartney, *Walls Have Mouths: A Record of Ten Years' Penal Servitude*, 1936*

For those in jail, like Bonaventure Nyibizi, a staffer at the Kigali mission of the United States Agency for International Development, the expectation of death was even greater. 'They were killing prisoners every night, and on October 26, I was going to be killed,' he told me. 'But I had cigarettes. The guy came and said, "I'm going to kill you," and I gave him a cigarette, so he said, "Well, we're killing people for nothing and I'm not going to kill you tonight." People were dying every day from torture. They were taken out, and when they came back, they were beaten, bayoneted, and they were dying. I slept with

* The book helped to change the rules on tobacco in British prisons.

dead people several nights. I think the initial plan was to kill everybody in prison, but the Red Cross started registering people, so it became difficult. The regime wanted to keep a good international image.'

Philip Gourevitch, *We Wish to Inform You That Tomorrow We Will Be Killed with Our Families: Stories from Rwanda*, 1998

Long afterwards, Emalia people would call the Schindler camp a paradise. Since they were by then widely scattered, it cannot have been a description they decided on after the fact. The term must have had some currency while they were in Emalia. It was of course only a relative paradise, a heaven by contrast to Plaszów. What it inspired in its people was a sense of almost surreal deliverance, something preposterous which they didn't want to look at too closely for fear it would evaporate . . .

A girl named Lusia, for example. Her husband had recently been picked out from the mass of prisoners on the Appellplatz at Plaszów and shipped off with others to Mauthausen. With what would turn out to be mere realism, she grieved like a widow. Grieving, she'd been marched to Emalia. She worked at carrying dipped enamelware to the furnaces. You were permitted to heat up water on the warm surfaces of machinery, and the floor was warm. For her, hot water was Emalia's first beneficence.

She saw Oskar at first only as a large shape moving down an aisle of metal presses or traversing a catwalk. It was somehow not a threatening shape. She sensed that if she were noticed the nature of the place – the lack of beatings, the food, the absence of guards in the camp – might somehow reverse itself. She wanted only to work her shift unobtrusively and return down the barbed-wire tunnel to her hut in the compound.

After a while she found herself giving an answering nod of the head to Oskar and even telling him that, Yes thank you, Herr Direktor, she was quite well. Once he gave her some cigarettes, better than gold both as a comfort and as a means of trading with the Polish workers.

Thomas Keneally, *Schindler's Ark*, 1982

At once he noticed that his team-mate Tsezar was smoking, and smoking a cigarette, not a pipe. That meant he might be able to cadge a smoke. But he didn't ask straight away, he stood quite close up to Tsezar and, half turning, looked past him.

He looked past him and seemed indifferent, but he noticed that after each puff (Tsezar inhaled at rare intervals thoughtfully) a thin ring of glowing ash crept down the cigarette, reducing its length as it moved stealthily to the cigarette-holder.

Fetiukov, that jackal, had come up closer too and now stood opposite Tsezar, watching his mouth with blazing eyes.

Shukhov had finished his last pinch of tobacco and saw no prospects of acquiring any more before evening. Every nerve in his body was taut, all his longing was concentrated in that fag-end – which meant more to him now, it seemed, than freedom itself: but he would never lower himself like that Fetiukov, he would never look at a man's mouth . . .

'Tsezar Markovich,' slobbered Fetiukov, unable to restrain himself. 'Give us a drag.'

His face twitched with greedy desire.

Tsezar slightly raised the lids that drooped low over his black eyes and looked at Fetiukov. It was because he didn't want to be interrupted while smoking and asked for a drag that he had taken up a pipe. He didn't begrudge the tobacco, he resented the interruption in his chain of thought. He smoked to stimulate his mind and to set his ideas flowing. But the moment he lighted a cigarette he read in several pairs of eyes an unspoken plea for the fag-end.

Tsezar turned to Shukhov and said:

'Take it, Ivan Denisovich.'

And with his thumb he pushed the smouldering fag-end out of the short amber holder.

Shukhov started (though it was exactly what he had expected of Tsezar) and gratefully hurried to take the fag-end with one hand, while slipping the other hand under it to prevent it from dropping. He didn't resent the fact that Tsezar felt squeamish about letting him finish the cigarette in the holder (some had clean mouths, some had foul) and he didn't burn his hardened fingers as they touched the glowing end. The main thing was, he had cut out that jackal Fetiukov, and now could go on drawing in smoke until his lips were scorched. Mmm. The smoke crept and flowed through his whole hungry body, making his head and feet respond to it.

Aleksandr Solzhenitsyn, *One Day in the Life of Ivan Denisovich*, 1962 (trans. Ralph Parker, 1962)

CHAPTER THIRTEEN

Soldiers and Smoking

At last he heard from along the road at the foot of the hill the clatter of a horse's galloping hoofs. It must be the coming of orders. He bent forward, scarce breathing. The exciting clickety-click, as it grew louder and louder, seemed to be beating upon his soul. Presently a horseman with jangling equipment drew rein before the colonel of the regiment. The two held a short, sharp-worded conversation. The men in the foremost ranks craned their necks. As the horseman wheeled his animal and galloped away he turned to shout over his shoulder, 'Don't forget that box of cigars!' The colonel mumbled in reply. The youth wondered what a box of cigars had to do with war.

Stephen Crane, *The Red Badge of Courage*, 1895

> Pack up your troubles in your old kit bag
> And smile, smile, smile.
> While you've a lucifer to light your fag,
> Smile boys, that's the style.
> What's the use of worrying,
> It never was worthwhile. So:
> Pack up your troubles in your old kit bag
> And smile, smile, smile.
>
> George Henry Powell, 1912

Wellington restricts smoking in the army, 1845

The Commander-in-Chief has been informed that the practice of smoking, by the use of pipes, cigars, or cheroots, has become prevalent among the officers of the Army, which is not only in itself a species of intoxication occasioned by the fumes of tobacco, but, undoubtedly, occasions drinking and tippling by those who acquire the habit; and he intreats the Officers commanding Regiments to prevent smoking in the Mess Rooms of their several Regiments, and in the adjoining apartments, and to discourage the practice among the Officers of Junior Rank in their Regiments.

G. L. Apperson *The Social History of Smoking*, 1914

Satirical pipe-head of Wellington made as a result.

The Crimea, less than 10 years later

But clear as it is that tobacco smoked to excess is injurious to health, cannot it be shown that there are circumstances and conditions of life in which the practice is not only harmless, but even salutary? Ask those heroic men who have returned from the ice-bound regions, too probably the grave of Franklin and his messmates – ask the late denizens of the Crimean trenches, and will they not all avow that one great solace and preservative under their incredible hardships was their pipe of tobacco?

Letter from W. H. Ranking to *The Lancet*, 28 February 1857

[Tuesday, 10 March 1874]

I found John Gough returned from the Bath United Hospital last Saturday, nothing better but rather worse. He seemed in much pain whenever he drew a deep breath and the children were noisy and worried him. He was twenty-one years in the army, and fought at Alma and Inkerman where he was wounded. 'No one but themselves who went through it,' he said, 'will ever know what our soldiers endured in the winter of 1854–1855. No firewood but what they cut down or the roots they grubbed up under the fire of the enemy's guns.

[205]

The coffee served out green to be roasted as the men could over their miserable fires in fragments of shell, and then when burnt or blackened a little pounded with two stones in a piece of canvas or coarse cloth, just something to flavour the water. A little grog and plenty of salt meat, but often no biscuit, and they were afraid to eat much of the salt meat for fear of scurvy. When they came in from the trenches or night fatigue duty, no fire, no straw to lie down on, only a blanket and greatcoat and the mud ankle-deep. On Christmas Day a little piece of butter and two ounces of 'figgy pudding' were served to each man out of casks. Tobacco was more precious than gold. 'If a man was lucky enough to have a pipe he doted on it as if it were Almighty God coming down upon him. Tobacco was so scarce that he hardly dared to put it into the pipe, only a very little bit, and then just two or three draws at a time. Then he stopped the pipe with a bit of rag and put it into his pocket. He could not afford himself more than that at once. If I had had tobacco I could have done with one meal a day. The French soldiers were in plenty while we were starving. The French managed everything well. In our lines there was nothing but shameful mismanagement. As many men died of neglect, mismanagement, cold, starvation and needless disease as died in battle. The French were four miles nearer to Balaclava and the provision stores, then they had hardy mules, while the English horses dropped under their loads and died by the roadside.'

Rev. Francis Kilvert, *Kilvert's Diary*, 1939

A lady told me a story of a man, M – , in her division, which shows how much some of them will venture for a smoke. He had just had one of his toes taken off, under the influence of chloroform. It bled profusely; and the surgeon, after binding it up, went away, giving her strict injunctions not to allow him to move, and ordered him some medicine, which he would send presently. She was called away to another patient for a few minutes, and went, leaving M – with strict orders not to put his foot down. On her return to his bedside, to her astonishment he was gone; and after some searching she discovered him, by the traces of blood on the stairs and corridor, sitting down in the yard, smoking his pipe with the greatest *sang froid*. She spoke to him seriously about disobeying orders and doing himself an injury; but he was perfectly callous on the subject of his toe. She succeeded, however, in working on his feelings at having disfigured the corridor with blood, and he came back, saying, 'Indeed, ma'am, I could not help going to have a pipe, for that was the nastiest stuff I ever got drunk on in my life' – alluding to the taste of the chloroform.

Ismeer, or Smyrna, and the British Hospital in 1855, by A Lady

First World War

We may surely brush aside much prejudice against the use of tobacco when we consider what a source of comfort it is to the sailor and soldier engaged in a nerve-racking campaign ... tobacco must be a real solace and joy when he can find time for this well-earned indulgence.

The Lancet, 3 October 1914

[France, 1916]

He found a tree that had not been damaged by shellfire and sat down beneath it, lighting a cigarette and sucking in the smoke. Before the war he had never touched tobacco; now it was his greatest comfort.

Sebastian Faulks, *Birdsong*, 1993

[Wilfred Owen]

Monday, [12] February 1917 [Advanced Horse Transport Depot]
My own dear Mother,
   ... Your 3 parcels came within 2 days of each other, 2 actually together. It is so unlucky that they did not reach me up the line, where everything has a tenfold value. Still nothing can take from the preciousness of the presents you send me.
   The Cigarettes are the most essential of all ...
   W. E. O. x x x

Sunday, 15 September 1918   *With the 2nd Batt., The Manchester Regt.*

My dear dear Mother,
   ... All thanks for the parcels – in anxious anticipation!
   Cigarettes are scarcer and scarcer. <u>Verb. Sap.</u> The poor boys were smoking grass in envelopes in the line last week ...
   W. E. O. x x x

Harold Owen and John Bell, editors, *Wilfred Owen: Collected Letters*, 1967

The excitement was finished, and O'Brien was somewhere down in the craters. The bombing and rifle fire had slackened when I started out to look for him. I went mechanically, as though I were drowning myself in the darkness. This is no fun at all, was my only thought as I groped my way down the soft clogging side of the left-hand crater; no fun at all, for they were still chucking an occasional bomb and firing circumspectly. I could hear the reloading click of rifle bolts on the lip of the crater above me as I crawled along with mud clogged fingers, or crouched and held my breath painfully. Bullets hit the water and little showers of earth pattered down from the banks. I knew that nothing in my previous experience of patrolling had ever been so grim as this, and I lay quite still for a bit, miserably wondering whether my number was up; then I remembered that I was wearing my pre-war raincoat; I could feel the pipe and tobacco-pouch in my pocket and somehow this made me less forlorn.

Siegfried Sassoon, *The Memoirs of an Infantry Officer*, 1930

[Geoffrey Studdert Kennedy, a.k.a. Woodbine Willie]

Towards the middle of the bitter winter of 1915–16 a very new chaplain arrived in France. Soon afterwards he was to be met, at most hours of the day and night, in a large and noisy shed on the *Rive Gauche* railway siding in the town of Rouen. The shed was a canteen, in which drafts for the front, having come up from Le Havre, could pause awhile before moving on a further stage towards what, in that old war, was likely to be fairly rapid extinction for the majority.

The new chaplain ... was thirty-two. He had bat-wing ears; his mouth gave the impression of being over large for its surroundings, and the man himself appeared astonished at the fact of his being rigged out in the officer's uniform of the day; Captain's pips at cuff and shoulder, the Maltese cross of a padre in cap and lapels. He wore it untidily. There were occasions later when the untidiness merged into disarray, as when he was discovered wearing immense spurs, one of them upside down.

The new chaplain's name was Geoffrey Anketell Studdert Kennedy, a man destined within a year or so to become known as Woodbine Willie, legendary padre of the first world war ... It was his custom to go down the train distributing cigarettes out of one haversack and

New Testaments out of the other. To the end he was still giving away Woodbines.

*Studdert Kennedy gives advice to a new army chaplain**
'I remember the conversation very well,' Geoffrey wrote. 'He asked me to tell him the best way of working. I said: "Live with the men; go everywhere they go. Make up your mind you will share all their risks, and more if you can do any good. The line is the key to the whole business. Work in the very front, and they will listen to you; but if you stay behind, you're wasting your time. Men will forgive you anything but lack of courage and devotion."'

'I remember walking up and down saying this very fiercely, because I was full of it. He took it so humbly and eagerly that I was ashamed of myself, and loved him. I said the more padres died in the battle doing Christian deeds the better; most of us would be more useful dead than alive. He asked me about purely spiritual work. I said: "There is very little; it is all muddled and mixed. Take a box of fags in your haversack and a great deal of love in your heart, and go up to them: laugh with them, joke with them. You can pray with them sometimes; but pray for them always."'

Studdert Kennedy's funeral, 1929
One thing became immediately apparent. Geoffrey had been a national figure to a degree which would probably have astonished him more than anyone else. The fact was soon made plain – touchingly, surprisingly so. A decent regret usually attends the passing of the captains and the kings of this world. The right, the expected things are said, the dignities of a formal mourning are observed from afar by the passing crowds. Only occasionally does a death seem to draw from those crowds themselves some special reaction, expressed in simple emotional acts.

The obsequies of Geoffrey, which were elaborate and prolonged, gave rise to many instances of such.

They began in Liverpool itself, when his body was taken from the vicarage to St Catherine's church to lie before the altar. Throughout that Friday some two thousand people of all sorts and conditions, including a coloured man wearing his war-medals, passed through

---

* The recipient of the advice was Theodore Bayley, who later became the oldest man to receive the Victoria Cross.

the church. The following morning two hundred were at the early celebration. Afterwards, at the removal of the coffin for its journey to Worcester, some man unknown stepped forward to lay a packet of Woodbines on it.

William Purcell, *An Anglican Incident: Being Some Account of the Life and Times of Geoffrey Anketell Studdert Kennedy, Poet, Prophet, Seeker after Truth, 1883–1929,* 1962

An explanation of the origin of the superstition which considers the lighting of three cigarettes with one match to be dangerous has at last been made.

'You see it was this way,' says James Valentine, Jr., the official explainer in Jersey State, U.S.A. 'The superstition originated with the British army in the Boer War. The sniping ability of the Boer sharpshooters was of a high order, most of them having been born and brought up in the wilds where all sorts of shooting was second nature to them.

The British Army soon learned that when lighting a smoke at night if the match was held long enough for three men to light from it, it was also just long enough to enable an alert sniper to draw a bead on the match flame, with the result that the last man was frequently killed. And so in this way arose the belief that it was "unhealthy" to light three cigarettes on a match. This belief grew into a superstition which was handed down through the British Army, and they brought it with them into the last war.'

B.A.T. (British-American Tobacco) *Bulletin*, November 1921

'Don't Forget the Cigarettes for Tommy.'

Song title, 1916*

Second World War

The troops I tramped Gibraltar to regale with the British Way and Purpose were not desperate, but they were certainly fed up, fucked up, and far from home. They astutely recognised that the war was no longer a concern of the British. It had been handed over to the Ameri-

---

* During the First World War, the public subscribed enough money to provide British soldiers with 232,599,191 cigarettes.

cans and the Russians, and the defence of the Rock belonged to an outworn strategy. A thing still rankled among the longer-settled orange-suckers, as members of the garrison were called by the visiting Royal Navy. A garrison notice had stated that much American money was, as it were, symbolically invested in Gibraltar. A great American insurance company used the Rock as an emblem of impregnability, and if the Rock fell to the enemy the company would be ruined. So it was the duty of the Gibraltar garrison to defend that segment of American finance. The cynicism of the troops was profound. The chief symbols of their alienation were the men who were leading them to victory – Field-Marshal Montgomery and Prime Minister Churchill.

Montgomery was primarily hated as a puritan who made his men run ten miles before breakfast and denounced smoking and drinking. There were too many unit commanders who transmitted this doctrine of austerity, in accents not too remote from Montgomery's own, to men who did not have ten miles to run, except into Spain, and who were stationed in a smoker's paradise. In Gibraltar it was sinful not to smoke. Cigarettes were duty-free, plentiful, and of a variety forgotten in wartime Britain. I became an eighty-a-day man. Drink was a different matter. Beer came from Britain in barrels, some of them filched by the Docks Operating Group, and it alternated between Tetley's, a very acceptable brew, and Simmonds's, which was an emetic with a court-martial in every cask. Large drunkenness was intermittent, depending on the arrival of the ships. But, to men deprived of women, smoking and drinking were the sole comforts, and that bastard Montgomery would, given a chance, take those comforts away.

Anthony Burgess, *Little Wilson and Big God*, 1987

Guerrilla warfare

A customary and extremely important comfort in the life of the guerrilla fighter is a smoke . . . a smoke in moments of rest is a great friend to the solitary soldier. Pipes are useful, because they permit using to the extreme all tobacco that remains in the butts of cigars and cigarettes at times of scarcity.

Che Guevara, *Guerilla Warfare*, 1961

We have heard how from the Thirty Years War onward soldiers have turned more and more gratefully to tobacco for consolation in time of war. This fact alone should be enough to close the lips and restrain the pens of those who denounce tobacco as the enemy of mankind. I shall not be extravagant when I claim that neither of the last two world wars would have been endurable for the vast majority of combatants and non-combatants alike without the help of tobacco.

Compton Mackenzie, *Sublime Tobacco*, 1957

Of course, I have to pay for drinks, and we all lift a few. I am melancholy: I'll be gone for six weeks; naturally I have to be thankful, but how will it be when I return? Will they still all be here? Haje and Kemmerich have already gone.

Whose turn is next?

We drink and I look them in the face, one after the other. Albert sits next to me and smokes, and slowly we all gather together . . . Over our heads a cloud of smoke spreads out. What would a soldier be without tobacco?

Erich Remarque, *All Quiet on the Western Front*, 1929

When a convoy got through, the whole city knew. The lorries brought vital supplies – flour. We really needed matches. And cigarettes! Cigarettes! Can you imagine soldiers without cigarettes? We were kept alive by the convoys from Tel Aviv.

Yitzhak Navon, Israeli Intelligence Officer, remembers defending the road to Jerusalem – in the BBC series *The 50 Years War: Israel and the Arabs*, 1998

Veteran groups were furious last week when Congress voted to finance the pending highway bill by denying billions of dollars to veterans suffering from tobacco-related illnesses. This week, the groups were stunned to discover that the lawmakers actually went further than that and declared any veteran who smoked on active duty could be considered to have engaged in 'wilful misconduct'.

The Washington Post, 30 May 1998

CHAPTER FOURTEEN

Smoking, Sex and Seduction

The habit of obtaining sexual satisfaction is less tyrannical than the tobacco habit, but it gains on one.
Colette, *The Pure and the Impure*, 1941

She introduced me to the Olympians of smoke. She taught me its mythology through black and white cinema, showed me its gods and rituals and villains. I marvelled at Greta Garbo and Sam Spade and the way the smoke of cigarettes made sophisticate the silver of the silver screen.

She took me to see the Gitanes series of pre-war film-noirs at the Arts Cinema, where a sign in the toilet said No Smoking Rauchen Verboten Ne Pas Fumer Non Fumare while the screen filled with unrepentant images of the twentieth century's most proficient smokers. Their lives and our lives were enhanced by tobacco, confirming beyond doubt that in times of stress like love and European war the only fully human action was always a smoke. Smoking was as decent a response to hysteria as it was to boredom. It was as reassuring in victory as it was in defeat. And most comforting of all, it was absolutely one hundred per cent safe. I saw nobody die of lung cancer, not on screen. Nobody even coughed or had a sore throat, except perhaps Marlene Dietrich.

Lucy told me that all this could be mine. That smoking and not smoking was the difference between entry and no entry into a cinematic world where post-coital cigarettes were shared in king-size beds in all the premier hotels of the world. By people like us. She held out cigarettes to me like an apple. It was love and desire. It was knowledge and everything.
Richard Beard, *X20*, 1996

Incidentally, I've noticed that girls that are very difficult to get into bed usually don't smoke. Women who are healthily promiscuous, not to the extent of being whores or something, nearly always are smokers. It's odd that. I suppose it's something to do with temperament. Non-smokers tend to be more judgemental.

Jeffrey Bernard, 'Last Word' in James Leavey, editor, *The Forest Guide to Smoking in London*, 1996

When I was young . . . whenever I went to a brothel with my friends I always picked the ugliest girl and insisted on making love to her in front of them without taking my cigar out of my mouth. It wasn't any fun for me: I just did it for the gallery.

Gustave Flaubert, in *The Goncourt Journal*, 1865 (trans. Robert Baldick, 1962)

IKE: *(Puffing on his cigarette, still looking at* TRACY*)* Mm. Oh, man, that is so great!
YALE: *(To* EMILY, *overlapping)* Mm.
TRACY: *(To* IKE, *chuckling)* You don't smoke.
IKE: I know I don't smoke. I don't inhale because it gives you cancer. But *(Exhaling)* I look so incredibly handsome with a cigarette –
TRACY: *(Interrupting)* Oh.
IKE: – that I can't *not* hold one. I know this. *(Still smoking the cigarette)* You like the way I look?
TRACY: Mm-hm.
She nods her head yes while YALE *chuckles with* EMILY *in the background.*
IKE: *(Looking at* TRACY*)* I know.
YALE: *(To* EMILY*)* Provocative.
IKE: *(To* TRACY*)* I'm getting through to you, right?
TRACY: *(Overlapping)* Yup. You'll have to excuse me.
She gets up from the table.
YALE: *(Looking at* TRACY *as she walks away)* Jesus, she's gorgeous.
IKE: *(Drinking his glass of wine and nodding his head)* Mm, but she's seventeen. *(Smacking his lips together)* I'm forty-two and she's seventeen. *(Coughing)* I-I'm dating a girl wherein I can beat up her father. It's the first time that phenomenon ever occurred in my life.

'Manhattan' (1979) in *Four Films of Woody Allen*, 1983 (Allen played Ike)

[A Seventeenth-Century Maiden Writes . . .]

In truth, maids, what thoughts possesseth ye,
Just such-like thoughts sometimes possesseth me,
Mine sometimes wanton are: maids, you all know
That we that maidens are, our thoughts are so.
To see a gallant gape (maids, your mouths wipe)
To entertain a fair tobacco-pipe.
Believe me maids, my maiden thoughts it moves
To think of what doth pass 'tween two that loves.
It, at a word, (Oh that I might come at her)
Does make my maiden-mouth o'erflow with water.

William Goddard (fl. 1599–1615), *Satire 14*

I swooned the first time I saw Charlo. I actually did. I didn't faint or
fall on the floor but my legs went rubbery on me and I giggled. I
suddenly knew that I had lungs because they were empty and col-
lapsing.
Charlo Spencer.
There he was, over there, leaning against the wall.
Fiona nudged me.
– There he is.
I saw him and I knew who she meant. It couldn't have been anyone
else, after all I'd heard about him, after all I'd expected. He was with
a gang but all by himself. His hands in his pockets with the thumbs
hooked over the denim and a fag hanging from his mouth. It got me
then and it gets me now: cigarettes are sexy – they're worth the
stench and the cancer. Black bomber jacket, parallels, loafers – he was
wearing what everyone wore back then but the uniform was made
specially for him. The other boys looked thick and deformed beside
him. Tallish, tough looking and smooth. In a world of his own but he
knew we were watching him.
We'd been dancing together in a circle, our jackets and jumpers and
bags on the floor in front of us, and I was sweating a bit. And I felt
the sweat when I saw Charlo. This wasn't a crush – this wasn't David
Cassidy or David Essex over there – it was sex. I wanted to go over
there and bite him.
He took the fag from his mouth – I could feel the lip coming part

of the way before letting go – and blew a gorgeous jet of smoke up into the light. It pushed the old smoke out of its way and charged into the ceiling. Then he fitted the fag back onto his lip and the hand went back to his pocket. He was elegant; the word doesn't seem to fit there but that was what he was.

Roddy Doyle, *The Woman Who Walked Into Doors*, 1996

[Mr Phillips and his son, Martin]

At the peacock enclosure a small crowd has gathered to watch the birds. One of the males is displaying, his tail fanned out in too many varieties of blue to name. To Mr Phillips, the intricate pattern of colours would be purely beautiful if it weren't for the eye motif imprinted on the tail. The hen peacock is sort-of-not-looking but hasn't wandered away, and the other peacocks and peahens are minding their own business. There is something ridiculous about the male's display, the lengths to which the bird is having to go to attract attention – but then there always is about males trying to seize the notice of females, whether it's to do with banging your head against another stag after a 40 mph run-up or simply wearing black clothes and trying to look fascinatingly uninterested in an irresistibly interesting way. Part of Martin's success with girls must be to do with his mastery of this proactive, highly visible and sexually signalling form of looking bored. And then, he is tremendously good at smoking.

John Lanchester, *Mr Phillips*, 2000

Sweet-brier and southernwood, jasmine, pink, and rose have long been yielding their evening sacrifice of incense: this new scent is neither of shrub nor flower; it is – I know it well – it is Mr Rochester's cigar. I look round and listen. I see trees laden with ripening fruit. I hear a nightingale warbling in a wood half a mile off: no moving form is visible, no coming step audible; but that perfume increases: I must flee. I make for the wicket leading to the shrubbery, and I see Mr Rochester entering. I step aside into the ivy recess; he will not stay long: he will soon return whence he came, and if I sit still he will never see me.

But no – eventide is as pleasant to him as to me, and this antique garden as attractive; and he strolls on, now lifting the gooseberry-tree branches to look at the fruit, large as plums, with which they are laden; now taking a ripe cherry from the wall; now stooping towards a knot of flowers, either to inhale their fragrance or to admire the dew-beads on their petals. A great moth goes humming by me; it alights on a plant at Mr Rochester's foot: he sees it, and bends to examine it.

Charlotte Bronte, *Jane Eyre*, 1847

The Scent of a Good Cigar

WHAT is it comes through the deepening dusk, –
Something sweeter than jasmine scent,
Sweeter than rose and violet blent,
More potent in power than orange or musk?
The scent of a good cigar.

I am all alone in my quiet room,
And the windows are open wide and free
To let in the south wind's kiss for me,
While I rock in the softly gathering gloom,
And that subtle fragrance steals.

Just as a loving, tender hand
Will sometimes steal in yours,
It softly comes through the open doors,
And memory wakes at its command, –
The scent of that good cigar.

And what does it say? Ah! that's for me
And my heart alone to know;
But that heart thrills with a sudden glow,
Tears fill my eyes till I cannot see, –
From the scent of that good cigar.

Kate A. Carrington, in William G. Hutchinson, editor, *Lyra Nicotiana: Poems and Verses Concerning Tobacco*, 1898

Carmen and the women of the Seville tobacco factory*

Voyez-les! Regards impudents,
Mines coquettes!
Fumant toutes, du bout des dents,
La cigarette!

Look at them! Their insolent stares,
Their flirtatious looks!
All smoking, at the end of their teeth
A cigarette!

The soldiers sing of the cigarette workers in Georges Bizet's
Carmen, 1873–4

... they were talking, singing, and disputing, in the same breath ...
Most of them were young, and several very pretty. The extreme carelessness of their dress allowed us to contemplate their charms at our
ease. Some of them had got the end of a cigar boldly stuck in the
corner of their mouth, with all the coolness of an officer of hussars ...

Théophile Gautier, *Wanderings in Spain*, 1853

The Tobacco Factory, where the unfortunate hero of Merimée's story
first sets eyes on Carmen, was an essential component of Romantic
Andalucía, and as obligatory to any visit to Seville as the cathedral.
Travellers' fanciful conceptions of the place, when compared with the
reality of the life which was led there, are an interesting reflection on
the Romantic distortion of Andalucía. Early visitors to the factory
had merely expressed wonder at the monumental dimensions of the
building, at the efficiency with which it was run, and at the great
number of people and mules employed there. By Merimée's day the
interest of foreigners was concentrated on four connected rooms at
the very centre of the immense complex, for here were gathered a
reputed three thousand female cigar makers, chattering away, their
colourful street clothes hanging around the walls. One of Andalucía's
great attractions was its beautiful women, and these four rooms,
with their steamy, hot-house atmosphere, seemed to offer travellers
unlimited possibilities for studying these women in a suitably sensual

* For Merimée's *Carmen* (1845), see the beginning of Chapter Five.

environment. Richard Ford greatly enhanced these women's reputation for animosity and provocative behaviour when he wrote that they were known to be 'more impertinent than chaste', and would sometimes smuggle out 'the weed in a manner her most Catholic majesty never dreamt of'; when A. C. Andros visited the place in 1860 he turned away on the grounds that 'owing to the intense heat, the *eight thousand* females employed in making cigars are working in all but *puris naturalibus*.' The strong-minded, cheeky, beautiful and overwhelmingly sensual Carmen represented all that Romantic travellers had come to expect of the women of the Tobacco Factory. Naturally, the hopes being so greatly raised, numerous travellers came away bitterly disappointed, and went afterwards to opposite extremes to describe the women. 'I have never beheld such an assemblage of uglinesses,' wrote George Dennis.

Michael Jacobs, *Andalucía*, 1998

Victorian flirting

[Becky Sharp and Rawdon Crawley before their engagement . . .]

. . . the walk over the Rectory fields, and in at the little park wicket, and through the dark plantation, and up the checkered avenue to Queen's Crawley, was charming in the moonlight to two such lovers of the picturesque as the Captain and Miss Rebecca.

'O those stars, those stars!' Miss Rebecca would say, turning her twinkling green eyes up towards them. 'I feel myself almost a spirit when I gaze upon them.'

'Oh – ah – Gad – yes, so do I exactly, Miss Sharp,' the other enthusiast replied. 'You don't mind my cigar, do you, Miss Sharp?' Miss Sharp loved the smell of a cigar out of doors beyond everything in the world – and she just tasted one too, in the prettiest way possible, gave a little puff, and a little scream, and a little giggle, and restored the delicacy to the Captain, who twirled his moustache, and straightaway puffed it into a blaze that glowed quite red in the dark plantation, and swore – 'Jove – aw – Gad – aw – it's the finest segaw I ever smoked in the world – aw,' for his intellect and conversation were alike brilliant and becoming to a heavy young dragoon.

[. . . and after their marriage]

A day or two before Christmas, Becky, her husband, and her son, made ready and went to pass the holidays at the seat of their ancestors at Queen's Crawley. Becky would have liked to leave the little brat behind, and would have done so but for Lady Jane's urgent invitations to the youngster; and the symptoms of revolt and discontent which Rawdon manifested at her neglect of her son. 'He's the finest boy in England,' the father said in a tone of reproach to her, 'and you don't seem to care for him, Becky, as much as you do for your spaniel. He shan't bother you much: at home he will be away from you in the nursery, and he shall go outside on the coach with me.'

'Where you go yourself because you want to smoke those filthy cigars,' replied Mrs Rawdon.

'I remember when you liked 'em though,' answered the husband.

Becky laughed: she was almost always good-humoured. 'That was when I was on my promotion, Goosey,' she said. 'Take Rawdon outside with you, and give him a cigar too if you like.'

William Makepeace Thackeray, *Vanity Fair*, 1848

Felix entered the room with a cigar in his mouth and threw himself upon the sofa.

'My dear boy,' she said, 'pray leave your tobacco below when you come in here.'

'What affectation it is, mother,' he said, throwing, however, the half-smoked cigar into the fire-place. 'Some women swear they like smoke, others say they hate it like the devil. It depends altogether on whether they wish to flatter or snub a fellow.'

Anthony Trollope, *The Way We Live Now*, 1875

————————

January 7. Sexual encounter.
Afterward, she and the President moved to the Oval Office and talked. According to Ms Lewinsky: '[H]e was chewing on a cigar. And then he had the cigar in his hand and he was looking at the cigar in . . . sort of a naughty way. And so . . . I looked at the cigar and I looked at him and I said, we can do that, too, some time.'

[220]

March 31. Sexual encounter.
In the hallway by the study, the President and Ms Lewinsky kissed. On this occasion, according to Ms Lewinsky, 'he focused on me pretty exclusively,' kissing her bare breasts and fondling her genitals. At one point, the President inserted a cigar into Ms Lewinsky's vagina, then put the cigar in his mouth and said: 'It tastes good.' After they were finished, Ms Lewinsky left the Oval Office and walked through the Rose Garden.

The Starr Report, 1998

CHAPTER FIFTEEN
Giving, Receiving, Bonding

Whatever Aristotle and all the philosophers may say, there is nothing equal to tobacco. All good fellows like it, and he who lives without tobacco does not deserve to live. It not only exhilarates and clears a man's brains but also teaches virtue, and one learns to become a good fellow through its means. Do you not plainly see that, as soon as we take it, we put on an agreeable manner towards everybody and are delighted to offer it right and left wherever we are? We do not even wait until it is asked of us ... so true is it that tobacco inspires all who take it with sentiments of ... generosity.

> Molière, *Dom Juan*, 1665 (being French, Molière was talking about snuff.)

[Carlyle on his father]

He was no niggard, but truly a wisely generous Economist. He paid his men *handsomely* and with overplus. He had known Poverty in the shape of actual want (in boyhood), and never had one penny which he knew not well how he had come by ('picked,' as he said, 'out of the hard stone'): yet he ever parted with money as a man that knew when he was getting money's worth; that could *give* also, and with a frank liberality, when the fit occasion called. I remember, with the peculiar kind of tenderness that attaches to many similar things in his life, one or I rather think two times, when he sent me to buy a quarter of a pound of Tobacco to give to some old women whom he had had gathering Potatoes for him: he nipt off for each a handsome leash [hank], and handed it her by way of over-and-above. This was a common principle with him. I must have been twelve or thirteen when I fetched this Tobacco. I love to think of it. 'The little that a just man hath.' The old women are now perhaps all dead; he too is dead: but the gift still lives.

> Thomas Carlyle, *Reminiscences*, 1881

In the morning, after breakfast and the doctor's inspection, the Tramp Major herded us all into the dining-room and locked the door upon us. It was a limewashed, stone-floored room, unutterably dreary, with its furniture of deal boards and benches, and its prison smell. The barred windows were too high to look out of, and there were no ornaments save a clock and a copy of the workhouse rules. Packed elbow to elbow on the benches, we were bored already, though it was barely eight in the morning. There was nothing to do, nothing to talk about, not even room to move. The sole consolation was that one could smoke, for smoking was connived at so long as one was not caught in the act. Scotty, a little hairy tramp with a bastard accent sired by Cockney out of Glasgow, was tobaccoless, his tin of cigarette ends having fallen out of his boot during the search and been impounded. I stood him the makings of a cigarette. We smoked furtively, thrusting our cigarettes into our pockets, like schoolboys, when we heard the Tramp Major coming.

Most of the tramps spent ten continuous hours in this comfortless, soulless room. Heaven knows how they put up with it. I was luckier than the others, for at ten o'clock the Tramp Major told off a few men for odd jobs, and he picked me out to help in the workhouse kitchen, the most coveted job of all. This, like the clean towel, was a charm worked by the word 'gentleman' ...

At three I went back to the spike. The tramps had been sitting there since eight, with hardly room to move an elbow, and they were now half mad with boredom. Even smoking was at an end, for a tramp's tobacco is picked-up cigarette ends, and he starves if he is more than a few hours away from the pavement. Most of the men were too bored even to talk; they just sat packed on the benches, staring at nothing, their scrubby faces split in two by enormous yawns. The room stank of *ennui* ...

Three hours dragged by. At six supper arrived, and turned out to be quite uneatable; the bread, tough enough in the morning (it had been cut into slices on Saturday night), was now as hard as ship's biscuit. Luckily it was spread with dripping, and we scraped the dripping off and ate that alone, which was better than nothing. At a quarter past six we were sent to bed. New tramps were arriving, and in order not to mix the tramps of different days (for fear of infectious diseases) the new men were put in the cells and we in dormitories. Our dormitory was a barn-like room with thirty beds close together, and a tub to serve as a common chamber-pot. It stank abominably, and the older men coughed and got up all night. But being so many together kept the room warm, and we had some sleep.

We dispersed at ten in the morning, after a fresh medical inspection, with a hunk of bread and cheese for our midday dinner. William and Fred, strong in the possession of a shilling, impaled their bread on the spike railings – as a protest, they said. This was the second spike in Kent that they had made too hot to hold them, and they thought it a great joke. They were cheerful souls, for tramps. The imbecile (there is an imbecile in every collection of tramps) said that he was too tired to walk and clung to the railings, until the Tramp Major had to dislodge him and start him with a kick. Paddy and I turned north, for London. Most of the others were going on to Ide Hill, said to be about the worst spike in England.

Once again it was jolly autumn weather, and the road was quiet, with few cars passing. The air was like sweet-briar after the spike's mingled stenches of sweat, soap, and drains. We two seemed the only tramps on the road. Then I heard a hurried step behind us, and someone calling. It was little Scotty, the Glasgow tramp, who had run after us panting. He produced a rusty tin from his pocket. He wore a friendly smile, like someone repaying an obligation.

'Here y'are, mate,' he said cordially. 'I owe you some fag ends. You stood me a smoke yesterday. The Tramp Major give me back my box of fag ends when we come out this morning. One good turn deserves another – here y'are.'

And he put four sodden, debauched, loathly cigarette ends into my hand.

George Orwell, *Down and Out in Paris and London*, 1933

Velisarios passed him, and the two men looked at one another with something like recognition. However thin and bedraggled he had become since he had gone to the front, Velisarios was still the biggest man that anyone had ever seen, and Carlo, despite his equivalent experiences on the other side of the line, was also the biggest man that anyone had ever seen. Both of these Titans had become accustomed to the saddening suspicion within themselves that they were freaks; to be superhuman was a burden that had seemed impossible to share and impossible to explain to ordinary people, who would have been incredulous.

They were both astonished, and for a moment forgot that they were enemies. 'Hey,' exclaimed Velisarios, raising his hands in a gesture of pleasure. Carlo, stumped for an exclamation that would make sense to a Greek, aimed inaccurately for a failed compromise that sounded very like 'Ung'. Carlo offered one of his atrocious cigarettes, Velisarios took one, and they gesticulated and made sour faces to each other as they drew on the smoke that was sharp as needles. 'Fuck the war,' said Carlo, by way of farewell, and the two went on their opposite ways, Carlo beginning to feel very content.

[And later . . .]

Velisarios buried Carlo Guercio's remains that night in the yard of the doctor's house. Struggling across the walls and fields, accompanied by that sticky smell of death, his hands slimy and slipping, he had felt like Atlas burdened by the world. It had not taken him long to discover that his load was too heavy to carry in his arms as he had carried the captain, and finally he staggered along with that great weight across his shoulders, as though it were a mighty sack of wheat.

In the darkness he bound up Carlo's shattered jaw with a strip of sheet, and then he hacked downwards, chopping through the olive's roots, unearthing ancient layers of stones and fires, tossing out shards of pottery and the ancient shoulder-blades of sheep. He did not know it, but he buried Carlo in the soil of Odysseus' time, as though he had belonged there from the first.

Just before dawn, when the surgery on the captain was complete at last, and father and daughter were both unutterably exhausted, they came out to say farewell to that heroic flesh.

Pelagia combed the hair and kissed the forehead, and the doctor, naturally a pagan and always moved by ancient ways, placed a silver coin over each eye and a flask of wine in the grave. Velisarios stood below and brought the body down. He straightened up, and a thought occurred to him. From his pocket he took a crushed pack of cigarettes, removed one, straightened it out, and placed it in the dead man's lips. 'I owed him one,' he said, and clambered out.

Louis de Bernières, *Captain Corelli's Mandolin*, 1994

My own college was short on lords. It was rich, or so it was said, but no richness ever seemed to percolate as far down as us. On a second glance I found I did know, or had met, one of its undergraduates, a certain Norman Iles. We had shared digs at Cambridge the previous year in vain pursuit of the same scholarship. He at once introduced me to the man with whom (under the doubling-up system wartime had brought) he shared a tutor, one Philip Larkin, whose first action was to offer me a cigarette, the equivalent in those days of a glass of rare malt whisky.

Kingsley Amis, *Memoirs*, 1991

———

On the Mountains of the Prairie,
On the great Red Pipe-stone Quarry,
Gitche Manito, the mighty,
He the Master of Life, descending,
On the red crags of the quarry
Stood erect, and called the nations,
Called the tribes of men together.
　From his footprints flowed a river,
Leaped into the light of morning,
O'er the precipice plunging downward
Gleamed like Ishkoodah, the comet.
And the Spirit, stooping earthward,
With his finger on the meadow
Traced a winding pathway for it,
Saying to it, 'Run in this way!'
　From the red stone of the quarry
With his hand he broke a fragment,
Moulded it into a pipe-head,
Shaped and fashioned it with figures;
From the margin of the river
Took a long reed for a pipe-stem,
With its dark green leaves upon it;
Filled the pipe with bark of willow,
With the bark of the red willow;
Breathed upon the neighboring forest,
Made its great boughs chafe together,
Till in flame they burst and kindled;
And erect upon the mountains,
Gitche Manito, the mighty,

Smoked the calumet, the Peace-Pipe,
As a signal to the nations.

Henry Wadsworth Longfellow, *The Song of Hiawatha*, 1855

[Smoking is] the sole habit that makes brothers of earth's people; for tobacco, in the three hundred years between its glorious discovery and our enlightened age has won more proselites [sic] than Christianity in two thousand, and without spilling a drop of blood.

D. F. Sarmiento, *Viajes por Europa, Africa i América 1845–1847*, 1849

The first time that Dr Creighton asked me to come down to Peterborough, in 1894, before he became Bishop of London, I was a little doubtful whether to go or not. As usual, I consulted my good clerk, Alfred, who said:

'Let me have a look at his letter, Sir.'

I gave him the letter, and he said:

'I see, Sir, there is a crumb of tobacco in it; I think you may go.'

I went and enjoyed myself very much. I should like to add that there are very few men who have ever impressed me so profoundly and so favourably as Dr Creighton. I have often seen him since, both at Peterborough and at Fulham, and like and admire him most cordially.

Samuel Butler, *The Notebooks of Samuel Butler*, 1912

CHAPTER SIXTEEN

All in the Mind: Smoking and Thinking

'You are quite a philosopher, Sam,' said Mr Pickwick. 'It runs in the family, I b'lieve, sir,' replied Mr Weller. 'My father's wery much in that line, now. If my mother-in-law blows him up, he whistles. She flies in a passion, and breaks his pipe; he steps out and gets another. Then she screams wery loud, and falls into 'sterics; and he smokes wery comfortably till she comes to agin. That's philosophy, sir, an't it?'

Charles Dickens, *The Pickwick Papers*, 1837

Carl Zuckmayer has described how he and Brecht came as somewhat erratic 'Dramaturgen' to Reinhardt's complex of Berlin theatres in 1924. Friedrich Holländer, who had engaged them, resigned from the direction of Reinhardt's affairs (and notably of the Deutsches Theater) before the beginning of the 1924–5 season, and neither of them took the administrative side of the job very seriously.

'Brecht seldom turned up there; with his flapping leather jacket he looked like a cross between a lorry driver and a Jesuit seminarist. Roughly speaking, what he wanted was to take over complete control: the season's programme must be regulated entirely according to his theories, and the stage be rechristened 'epic smoke-theatre', it being his view that people might actually be disposed to think if they were allowed to smoke at the same time. As this was refused him he confined himself to coming and drawing his pay.'

John Willett, *The Theatre of Bertolt Brecht: A Study from Eight Aspects*, 1959

The pipe-smoking philosopher

Forsaken of all comforts but these two,
My faggot and my pipe, I sit to muse
On all my crosses, and almost excuse
The Heavens for dealing with me as they do.
When Hope steps in, and with a smiling brow,
Such cheerful expectations doth infuse
As makes me think ere long I cannot choose
But be some grandee, whatsoe'er I'm now.
But having spent my pipe, I then perceive
That hopes and dreams are cousins – both deceive.
Then mark I this conclusion in my mind,
It's all one thing – both tend into one scope –
To live upon Tobacco and on Hope,
The one's but smoke, the other is but wind.

Sir Robert Aytoun (1570–1638)

Tobacco

The Indian weed witheréd quite,
Green at noon, cut down at night;
Shows thy decay, all flesh is hay,
Thus think, then drink Tobacco.

The Pipe that is so lily white
Shows thee to be a mortal wight,
And even such, gone with a touch,
Thus think, then drink Tobacco.

And when the smoke ascends on high,
Think, thou behold'st the vanity
Of wordly stuff gone with a puff:
Thus think, then drink Tobacco.

And when thy Pipe grows foul within,
Think on thy soul defil'd with sin,
And then the fire it doth require,
Thus think, then drink Tobacco.

The ashes that are left behind,
May serve to put thee still in mind,
That unto dust, return thou must,
Thus think, then drink Tobacco.

Anon.*, seventeenth century

The fact is, squire, the moment a man takes to a pipe he becomes a philosopher. It's the poor man's friend; it calms the mind, soothes the temper, and makes a man patient under difficulties. It has made more good men, good husbands, kind masters, indulgent fathers, than any other blessed thing on this universal earth.

Thomas Haliburton, *The Clockmaker: Or the Sayings and Doings of Sam Slick, of Slickville*, 1836

'Well, Watson,' said Holmes, when our visitor had left us, 'what do you make of it all?'

'I make nothing of it,' I answered, frankly. 'It is a most mysterious business.'

'As a rule,' said Holmes, 'the more bizarre a thing is the less mysterious it proves to be. It is your commonplace, featureless crimes which are really puzzling, just as a commonplace face is the most difficult to identify. But I must be prompt over this matter.'

'What are you going to do then?' I asked.

'To smoke,' he answered. 'It is quite a three-pipe problem, and I beg that you won't speak to me for fifty minutes.'

Arthur Conan Doyle, 'The Red-Headed League' in *The Adventures of Sherlock Holmes*, 1892

Dream and memory

Pictures in Smoke

IN a rapt, dreamy quietude I sit
Leisurely puffing clouds from my cigar,

* The poem, one of the most famous of all smoking lyrics, has been much argued over through the centuries – and attributed at various times to a repentant George Wither (see Chapter Two), Thomas Jenner and Robert Wisdome. It also exists in several other versions. 'Drinking' tobacco was the usual way of referring to smoking in the early seventeenth century.

And down the sunbeams, with a noiseless tread,
  A throng of elves come tripping from afar.
Half consciously the fairies I invoke
To paint me pictures in the tinted smoke.

Old scenes of boyhood's careless fun and sport;
  Faces of schoolmates, fresh and young and fair;
Grim pedagogues with frowning front and brow;
  Long shining curls and braids of silken hair;
White hands, red smarting 'neath the ferrule's stroke
Or clasped in browner ones – pictured in smoke.

Familiar fireside scenes; the light of home;
  The good-night kiss and trudging off to bed;
The petty quarrels and the making up;
  The mother's soft hand resting on the head;
The shadowy moonlight on a hillside oak;
Quaint boyhood fancies – radiant in the smoke.

The first coquetting with the first boy love;
  The awkward gallantry of unripe years;
The simple gifts; the long walks after school;
  The slights that brought a rush of angry tears;
The feuds and duels that such slights provoke –
How vividly they're painted in the smoke!

The first time leaving home; the last good-bye;
  The bitter pang of loneliness and pain;
New cares and trials, real life begun;
  The first sore yearning to be young again,
When worn and weary 'neath toil's cumbrous yoke –
How true to life these pictures are in smoke!

I pray you, my good fairies, leave me now;
  You've brought the past to me with memories glad;
The pictures vanish, but the trace is left –
  The boy was happy but the man is sad.
No longer young and fond: Time's ravens croak,
And youth has vanished with the fragrant smoke.

How life is like this vapour! Calm-eyed Hope
  In fairy guise paints it with pictures rare,

And while we gaze and stretch out eager hands,
  Behold the phantoms vanish in the air!
Urged by a fate no pleading can revoke,
We grow old watching pictures in the smoke.

T. H. Elliott in William G. Hutchinson, editor, *Lyra Nicotiana:
Poems and Verses Concerning Tobacco*, 1898

My Cigarette

My cigarette! The amulet
  That charms afar unrest and sorrow,
The magic wand that, far beyond
  To-day, can conjure up to-morrow.
Like love's desire, thy crown of fire
  So softly with the twilight blending;
And ah, meseems a poet's dreams
  Are in thy wreaths of smoke ascending.

My cigarette! Can I forget
  How Kate and I, in sunny weather,
Sat in the shade the elm-tree made
  And rolled the fragrant weed together?
I at her side, beatified
  To hold and guide her fingers willing;
She rolling slow the paper's snow,
  Putting my heart in with the filling.

My cigarette! I see her yet,
  The white smoke from her red lips curling,
Her dreaming eyes, her soft replies,
  Her gentle sighs, her laughter purling!
Ah, dainty roll, whose parting soul
  Ebbs out in many a snowy billow,
I too would burn, if I could earn
  Upon her lips so soft a pillow.

Ah, cigarette! The gay coquette
  Has long forgot the flame she lighted;
And you and I unthinking by
  Alike are thrown, alike are slighted.

[232]

The darkness gathers fast without,
    A raindrop on my window plashes;
My cigarette and heart are out,
    And naught is left me but the ashes.

Charles F. Lummis in William G. Hutchinson, editor,
*Lyra Nicotiana: Poems and Verses Concerning
Tobacco*, 1898

Pictures in the Smoke

Oh, gallant was the first love, and glittering and fine;
    The second love was water, in a white clear cup;
The third love was his, and the fourth was mine;
    And after that, I always get them all mixed up.

Dorothy Parker, 1926

The Duet

I was smoking a cigarette;
    Maud, my wife, and the tenor, McKey,
Were singing together a blithe duet,
And days it were better I should forget
    Came suddenly back to me, –
Days when life seemed a gay masque ball,
And to love and be loved was the sum of it all.

As they sang together, the whole scene fled,
    The room's rich hangings, the sweet home air,
Stately Maud, with her proud blonde head,
And I seemed to see in her place instead
    A wealth of blue-black hair,
And a face, ah! your face – yours, Lisette;
A face it were wiser I should forget.

We were back – well, no matter when or where;
    But you remember, I know, Lisette.
I saw you, dainty and debonair,
With the very same look that you used to wear
    In the days I should forget.
And your lips, as red as the vintage we quaffed,
Were pearl-edged bumpers of wine when you laughed.

Two small slippers with big rosettes
  Peeped out under your kilt-skirt there,
While we sat smoking our cigarettes
(Oh, I shall be dust when my heart forgets!)
    And singing that self-same air;
And between the verses, for interlude,
I kissed your throat and your shoulders nude.

You were so full of a subtle fire,
  You were so warm and so sweet, Lisette;
You were everything men admire;
And there were no fetters to make us tire,
  For you were – a pretty grisette.
But you loved as only such natures can,
With a love that makes heaven or hell for a man.

They have ceased singing that old duet,
  Stately Maud and the tenor, McKey.
'You are burning your coat with your cigarette,
And *qu'avez vous*, dearest, your lids are wet,'
  Maud says, as she leans o'er me.
And I smile, and lie to her, husband-wise,
'Oh it is nothing but smoke in my eyes.'

Ella Wheeler Wilcox (1850–1919)

One Cigarette

No smoke without you, my fire.
After you left,
your cigarette glowed on in my ashtray
and sent up a long thread of such quiet grey
I smiled to wonder who would believe its signal
of so much love. One cigarette
in the non-smoker's tray.
As the last spire
trembles up, a sudden draught
blows it winding into my face.
Is it smell, is it taste?
You are here again, and I am drunk on your tobacco lips.
Out with the light.

Let the smoke lie back in the dark.
Till I hear the very ash
sigh down among the flowers of brass
I'll breathe, and long past midnight, your last kiss.

Edwin Morgan, *The Second Life*, 1968

Contentment / idleness

Smokers, male and female, inject and excuse idleness in their lives every time they light a cigarette.

Colette, *The Pure and the Impure*, 1941

What a glorious creature was he who first discovered the use of tobacco! – the industrious retires from business – the voluptuous from pleasure – the lover from a cruel mistress – the husband from a curs'd wife – and I from all the world to my pipe.

Sir Owen Apshinken in Henry Fielding's *The Grub Street Opera*, 1731

Little tube of mighty pow'r,
Charmer of an idle hour,
Object of my warm desire,
Lip of wax, and eye of fire:
And thy snowy taper waist,
With my finger gently brac'd;
And thy pretty swelling crest,
With my little stopper prest,
And the sweetest bliss of blisses,
Breathing from thy balmy kisses.
Happy thrice, and thrice agen,
Happiest he of happy men;
Who when agen the night returns,
When agen the taper burns;
When agen the cricket's gay,
(Little cricket, full of play)
Can afford his tube to feed
With the fragrant Indian weed:
Pleasure for a nose divine,

Incense of the god of wine.
Happy thrice, and thrice agen,
Happiest he of happy men.

Isaac Hawkins Browne (1705–60), *A Pipe of Tobacco: In*
Imitation of Six Several Authors, Imitation II (of John Philips)

'May be you knows Mass Pilbeam? No! doant ye? Well, he was a
very sing'lar marn was Mass Pilbeam, a very sing'lar marn! He says
to he's mistus one day, he says, 'tis a long time, says he, sence I've
took a holiday – so cardenly, nex marnin' he laid abed till purty nigh
seven o'clock, and then he brackfustes, and then he goos down to the
shop and buys fower ounces of barca, and he sets hisself down on
the maxon [manure heap], and there he set, and there he smoked and
smoked and smoked all the whole day long, for, says he, 'tis a long
time sence I've had a holiday! Ah, he was a very sing'lar marn – a
very sing'lar marn indeed.'

Rev. W. D. Parish, *A Dictionary of the Sussex Dialect*, 1875

Some opponents (and all 'worshipful men,' who write M.D. after their
names, and are greatly in earnest) find every disease under the sun
originating in tobacco-smoke. Others (equally good men, who also
dignify their patronymics with a sprinkling of additional letters never
given at christenings) declare as loudly in its favour, and quote quite
as many instances of good resulting from the practice. Truth, as usual,
seems to lie between, undiscovered by the belligerents, but perfectly
well known to 'the honest smoker' (as old Izaak Walton would style
him) who wonders from amid his peaceful cloud what all the turmoil
means. Can the smoking of 'the pipe of peace'; the harmless sedative
of an amiable man, raise all this storm? Can his quiet and consoling
habit be the cause why so many 'decent men' should grow quarrelsome
and even vindictive about the matter?

F. W. Fairholt, *Tobacco: Its History and Associations*, 1859

Tobacco has been a blessing to us idlers. What the civil service clerks
before Sir Walter's time found to occupy their minds with, it is hard
to imagine. I attribute the quarrelsome nature of the Middle Ages
young men entirely to the want of the soothing weed. They had no
work to do, and could not smoke, and the consequence was they were
for ever fighting and rowing. If, by any extraordinary chance, there

was no war going, then they got up a deadly family feud with the next-door neighbour, and if, in spite of this, they still had a few spare moments on their hands, they occupied them with discussions as to whose sweetheart was the best looking, the arguments employed on both sides being battle-axes, clubs, &c. Questions of taste were soon decided in those days . . .

Now-a-days we light a pipe, and let the girls fight it out amongst themselves.

They do it very well. They are getting to do all our work. They are doctors, and barristers, and artists. They manage theatres, and promote swindles, and edit newspapers. I am looking forward to the time when we men shall have nothing to do but lie in bed till twelve, read two novels a day, have nice little five o'clock teas all to ourselves, and tax our brains with nothing more trying than discussions upon the latest patterns in trousers, and arguments as to what Mr Jones's coat was made of and whether it fitted him. It is a glorious prospect – for idle fellows.

Jerome K. Jerome, *The Idle Thoughts of an Idle Fellow*, 1886

Lying in a hot bath, smoking a pipe. And Elagabalus himself, after driving his white horses through the gold-dusted streets of Rome, never knew anything better; nor indeed anything as good, not having either pipe or tobacco. People still say to me 'The way you work!', and behind the modest smirk I laugh secretly, knowing myself to be one of the laziest and most self-indulgent men alive. Long after they have caught the 8.20, opened the morning mail, telephoned to the managing director of the Cement Company, dictated yet another appeal to the Board of Trade, I am lying in my hot bath, smoking a pipe. I am not even soaping and scrubbing, but simply lying there, like a pink porpoise, puffing away. In a neighbouring room, thrown on the floor, are the morning papers, loud with more urgent demands for increased production, clamouring for every man and woman to save the country. And there I am, lost in steam, the fumes of Latakia, and the vaguest dreams. Just beyond the bolted door, where the temperature drops to nearly freezing point, are delicate women, who have already been up for hours, toiling away. And do I care? Not a rap. Sometimes I pretend, just to test the credulity of the household, that I am planning my day's work; but I am doing nothing of the kind. Often I do not intend to do any work at all during the day; and even when I know I must do some, I could not possibly plan it, in or out of a bath. No, I am just lying there, a pampered slug, with my saurian little eyes half-closed, cancelling the Ice Ages, lolling again in the steamy hot morning of the world's time, wondering dimly what is happening to Sir Stafford Cripps. ' . . . One of the most energetic and prolific of our authors . . .' *Gertcha!*

    J. B. Priestley, *Delight*, 1949

Lastly (and this is, perhaps, the golden rule), no woman should marry a teetotaller, or a man who does not smoke. It is not for nothing that this 'ignoble tabagie,' as Michelet calls it, spreads over all the world. Michelet rails against it because it renders you happy apart from thought or work; to provident women this will seem no evil influence in married life. Whatever keeps a man in the front garden, whatever checks wandering fancy and all inordinate ambition, whatever makes for lounging and contentment, makes just so surely for domestic happiness.

    Robert Louis Stevenson, *Virginibis Puerisque*, 1881

She was about twenty-eight years old. She had a rather narrow forehead of more height than is considered elegant. Her nose was small and inquisitive, her upper lip a shade too long and her mouth more than a shade too wide. Her eyes were grey-blue with flecks of gold in them. She had a nice smile. She looked as if she had slept well. It was a nice face, a face you get to like. Pretty, but not so pretty that you would have to wear brass knuckles every time you took it out . . .

    I filled a pipe and reached for the packet of paper matches. I lit the pipe carefully. She watched that with approval. Pipe smokers were solid men. She was going to be disappointed in me.

    Raymond Chandler, *Farewell, My Lovely*, 1940

The Cigar

Some sigh for this and that;
My wishes don't go far;
The world may wag at will,
So I have my cigar.

Some fret themselves to death
With Whig and Tory jar;

I don't care which is in,
So I have my cigar . . .

Some want a German row,
Some wish a Russian war;
I care not – I'm at peace,
So I have my cigar.

I never see the Post,
I seldom read the Star;
The Globe I scarcely heed,
So I have my cigar.

They tell me that Bank Stock
Is sunk much under par;
It's all the same to me,
So I have my cigar.

Honours have come to men
My juniors at the Bar;
No matter – I can wait,
So I have my cigar.

Ambition frets me not;
A cab or glory's car
Are just the same to me,
So I have my cigar . . .

The ardent flame of love
My bosom cannot char,
I smoke, but do not burn,
So I have my cigar.

They tell me Nancy Low
Has married Mr R.;
The jilt! but I can live,
So I have my cigar.

Thomas Hood (1799–1845)

It is not that the Englishman can't feel – it is that he is afraid to feel.
He has been taught at his public school that feeling is bad form. He

must not express great joy or sorrow, or even open his mouth too
wide when he talks – his pipe might fall out if he did.

E. M. Forster, 'Notes on the English Character' (1920), in *Abinger Harvest*, 1936

Silent companionship

The pipe with solemn interposing puff
Makes half a sentence at a time enough;
The dozing sages drop the drowsy strain,
Then pause, and puff, – and speak, and pause again.

William Cowper, *Conversation*, 1782

Honest men, with pipes and cigars in their mouths, have great physical
advantages in conversation. You may stop talking if you like – but the
breaks of silence never seem disagreeable, being filled up by the puffing
of the smoke . . . the cigar harmonises the society, and soothes at once
the speaker and the subject whereon he converses. I have no doubt
that it is from the habit of smoking that . . . American Indians are
such monstrous well-bred men. The pipe draws wisdom from the lips
of the philosopher, and shuts up the mouth of the foolish: it generates
a style of conversation, contemplative, thoughtful, benevolent, and
unaffected: in fact . . . I must come out with it – I am an old smoker.
At home I have done it up the chimney rather than not do it (the
which I own is a crime).

I vow and believe that the cigar has been one of the greatest creature
comforters of my life – a kind companion, a gentle stimulant, an
amiable anodyne, a cementer of friendship. May I die if I abuse that
kindly weed which has given me so much pleasure.

William Makepeace Thackeray, *Sketches and Travels in London*, 1853

Tobacco-smoke is the one element in which, by our European manners,
men can sit silent together without embarrassment, and where no man
is bound to speak one word more than he has actually and veritably
got to say. Nay, rather every man is admonished and enjoined by the
laws of honour, and even of personal ease, to stop short of that point;
at all events, to hold his peace and take to his pipe again the instant
he *has* spoken his meaning, if he chance to have any. The results of

which salutary practice, if introduced into Constitutional Parliaments, might evidently be incalculable.

Thomas Carlyle, *Frederick the Great*, 1858–65

[Emerson and Carlyle]

The friendship formed by these two men at Craigenputtock lasted during their lives. There is an unpublished legend to the effect that on the one evening passed at Craigenputtock by Emerson, in 1833, Carlyle gave him a pipe, and, taking one himself, the two sat silent till midnight, and then parted, shaking hands, with congratulations on the profitable and pleasant evening they had enjoyed.

Tobacco Talk and Smokers' Gossip: An Amusing Miscellany of Fact and Anecdote, 1884

['That goodly tavern']

Mr Willet sat in what had been his accustomed place five years before, with his eyes on the eternal boiler; and had sat there since the clock struck eight, giving no other signs of life than breathing with a loud and constant snore (though he was wide awake), and from time to time putting his glass to his lips, or knocking the ashes out of his pipe, and filling it anew. It was now half-past ten. Mr. Cobb and long Phil Parkes were his companions, as of old, and for two mortal hours and a half, none of the company had pronounced one word.

Whether people, by dint of sitting together in the same place and the same relative positions, and doing exactly the same things for a great many years, acquire a sixth sense, or some unknown power of influencing each other which serves them in its stead, is a question for philosophy to settle. But certain it is that old John Willet, Mr. Parkes, and Mr. Cobb, were one and all firmly of opinion that they were very jolly companions – rather choice spirits than otherwise; that they looked at each other every now and then as if there were a perpetual interchange of ideas going on among them; that no man considered himself or his neighbour by any means silent; and that each of them nodded occasionally when he caught the eye of another, as if he would say 'You have expressed yourself extremely well, sir, in relation to that sentiment, and I quite agree with you.'

Charles Dickens, *Barnaby Rudge*, 1841

CHAPTER SEVENTEEN
Young Smokers

... But then to teen-age hunger many things are delicious. Cigarettes, for example, were delicious: the sleek cellophane-wrapped rectitude of the pack, the suave tapping out of a single 'weed,' the chalky rasping initial inhale, the little crumbs to be picked from the lower lip without breaking conversational stride, the airy pluming gesturingness of it all.

John Updike, *Self-Consciousness: Memoirs*, 1989

[Mackenzie at nine]

It was some time early in the New Year that my father discovered – I do not remember how – that my brother and myself were smoking the stubs of his cigars in a Petersen pipe.

'And so you boys enjoy smoking?' he enquired.

I assured him that we thought it was ripping, or perhaps 'spiffing' was the adjective chosen.

'Well, since you enjoy smoking so much I will give you two of my cigars to smoke.'

With this he went to the corner cupboard of Dutch marquetry in which he kept his cigars, and selected the two largest he had. They must have been two of those shilling ones; I imagine it cost him a pang to administer the lesson he believed he was about to administer.

'Light them properly,' he commanded.

He passed us a big Bryant and May's box of safety-matches, one of which would light a cigar properly whereas it takes three of the matches in the shrunken boxes of to-day to light a cigar as it should be lit before it is put between the lips. When he saw that we were puffing away, my father lit a cigar for himself from the same box. I wish I could remember what the brand was, but I know it took a full hour to smoke that cigar. Soon I noticed a questioning look in my father's eyes, and this in turn was gradually succeeded by a puzzled and finally by a baffled expression. At that date my father was just thirty-eight years old, and I was conscious of the emotion of triumphing over his venerability. I realized that he was searching our complexions for that greenish pallor which in the *Boys' Own Paper* always appeared on the cheeks of young readers who defied the threat of early blindness and stunted growth; this the editor continually insisted was the inevitable result of smoking in early youth. Alas for my poor father's self-abnegation in parting with two of his best and biggest cigars to give a lesson to his offspring, our cheeks remained rosy, our foreheads unclammy.

'Are you feeling all right?' he asked when the cigars had been smoked.

We beamed at him gratefully: filial good manners forebade us to crow over a parent whose morale was for the moment a wreck.

Compton Mackenzie, *Sublime Tobacco*, 1957

[Stephen Dedalus's father]

I'm talking to you as a friend, Stephen. I don't believe in playing the stern father. I don't believe a son should be afraid of his father. No, I treat you as your grandfather treated me when I was a young chap. We were more like brothers than father and son. I'll never forget the first day he caught me smoking. I was standing at the end of the South Terrace one day with some maneens like myself and sure we thought we were grand fellows because we had pipes stuck in the corners of our mouths. Suddenly the governor passed. He didn't say a word, or stop even. But the next day, Sunday, we were out for a walk together and when we were coming home he took out his cigar case and said: *By the bye, Simon, I didn't know you smoked:* or something like that. Of course I tried to carry it off as best I could. *If you want a good smoke*, he said, *try one of these cigars. An American captain made me a present of them last night in Queenstown.*

Stephen heard his father's voice break into a laugh which was almost a sob.

– He was the handsomest man in Cork at that time, by God he was! The women used to stand to look after him in the street.

James Joyce, *A Portrait of the Artist as a Young Man*, 1916

So I remember that never was there such a dame-school as ours: so firm and kind and smelling of galoshes, with the sweet and fumbled music of the piano-lessons drifting down from upstairs to the lonely schoolroom where only the sometimes tearful wicked sat over undone sums or to repent a little crime, the pulling of a girl's hair during geography, the sly shin-kick under the table during prayers. Behind the school was a narrow lane where the oldest and boldest threw pebbles at windows, scuffled and boasted, lied about their relations –

'My father's got a chauffeur.'

'What's he want a chauffeur for, he hasn't got a car.'

'My father's the richest man in Swansea.'

'My father's the richest man in Wales.'

'My father's the richest man in the world' –

and smoked the butt-ends of cigarettes, turned green, went home, and had little appetite for tea.

Dylan Thomas, 'Reminiscences of Childhood' in *Miscellany One: Poems, Stories, Broadcasts*, 1963

There was one young gentleman in an India-rubber cloak, who smoked cigars all day; and there was another young gentleman in a parody upon a great coat, who lighted a good many, and feeling obviously unsettled after the second whiff, threw them away when he thought nobody was looking at him.

Charles Dickens, *The Pickwick Papers*, 1837

[Jarvis Cocker interviews David Bowie about Smoking]

DB: When you're a kid it's really a kind of perverse need to try something that's risky, because it's frowned upon by older people. Also because you know it's inherently bad for you.

JC: I remember when I first started that I couldn't believe it made me go dizzy and really light-headed.

DB: Yeah – I never understood why you just grit your teeth and carry on smoking just so you can get it right because it makes you so sick and feel so awful. It has to be what it symbolises and what it gives you of that 'I'm old enough to have attitude'. With you it was different 'cos you were 21, but I was still very gawky and awkward and wanting to find my attitude. Cigarettes sort of supplied it quite easily.

The Big Issue, 8–14 December 1997 (edited by Damien Hirst)

[Eugene Gant, 13-year-old paperboy]

Assembled with three or four of the carriers in the lunch room, he learned to smoke: in the sweet blue air of Spring, as he sloped down to his route, he came to know the beauty of Lady Nicotine, the delectable wraith who coiled in his brain, left her poignant breath in his young nostrils, her sharp kiss upon his mouth.

Thomas Wolfe, *Look Homeward, Angel*, 1929

If the statistics are right . . . then Joe Besser is personally responsible for my cancer. The last I heard of Joe he was working in the jewellery business in Hatton Garden, but that was 25 years ago. When I knew Joe properly we were both 13-year-olds at the same Jewish youth club in Hackney.

It was Joe who as we were walking along Clarence Road in Hackney in 1965 said 'I've decided. I'm going to start smoking. It'll help me pull. Do it for a few years, pull women, give it up when I'm 18.' We bought a packet of ten Consulate ('Cool as a Mountain Stream') between us, and we smoked . . .

So: there's me and Joe Besser with our ten Consulate trying to pull. It worked for Joe, but then Joe didn't need the outside agency of cigarettes. I was different. The reason that 30 and some years later I can still remember so precisely the conversation we had that night in Clarence Road is because there is some unreconstructed part of me which still believes what Joe told me then. I don't think that in any literal way smoking helps me pull, but I still believe that I look cooler, more assured, more *me* with a cigarette in my hand – and never mind that I know they stink, I know they kill.

It took me a while to get up to nicotinic speed from the ten a week smoked behind the youth club, but by the time I was earning a living I was on a pack a day. By the time, in my mid-30s, that I took an hour to get my breath back after playing ten minutes of an office football match and decided to quit, I was on two packs a day.

Not that I ever did stop smoking properly. Instead I switched to Nicorette – the nicotine chewing gum. I became addicted to it instead and by the day of diagnosis had been chewing the gum for something over ten years.

I can't tell you that the smoking was definitely responsible for my cancer. I can tell you that 90 per cent of all such cancers occur in smokers. I've had dozens of letters from armchair libertarians telling me that I shouldn't blame the cigarettes because their old auntie died of cancer and she never smoked so much as a Christmas cheroot. Maybe, but they really shouldn't confuse their impotent libertarian argument with the epidemiological one. By all means campaign for some phantom 'right' to smoke, but don't believe that right derives from corrupting the statistics about what smoking does to you. Understand it for what it is: the right to play Russian roulette, as I did, with the immune system.

John Diamond, C: *Because cowards get cancer too*, 1998

CHAPTER EIGHTEEN

A Packet of Twenty

Poisoning cats

So to the 'Change and thence home to dinner, and so out to Gresham College, and saw a cat killed with the Duke of Florence's poyson, and saw it proved that the oyle of tobacco drawn by one of the Society do the same effect, and is judged to be the same thing with the poyson both in colour and smell and effect.

Diary of Samuel Pepys, 3 May 1665

But besides the two volatile substances which exist ready formed in the tobacco-leaf, another substance of an oily nature is produced when tobacco is distilled alone in a retort, or is burned, as we do it, in a tobacco-pipe. This oil resembles one which is obtained in a similar way from the leaf of the poisonous foxglove (Digitalis purpurea). It is acrid and disagreeable to the taste, narcotic and poisonous. One drop applied to the tongue of a cat brought on convulsions, and in two minutes occasioned death.

James F. W. Johnston, *The Chemistry of Common Life*, 1855

Ode to Tobacco

Thou who, when fears attack,
Bidst them avaunt, and Black
Care, at the horseman's back
Perching, unseatest;
Sweet, when the morn is gray;
Sweet, when they've cleared away
Lunch; and at close of day
Possibly sweetest;

I have a liking old
For thee, though manifold
Stories, I know, are told,

Not to thy credit;
How one (or two at most)
Drops make a cat a ghost –
Useless, except to roast –
Doctors have said it:

How they who use fusees
All grow by slow degrees
Brainless as chimpanzees,
Meagre as lizards:
Go mad, and beat their wives;
Plunge (after shocking lives)
Razors and carving knives
Into their gizzards.

Confound such knavish tricks!
Yet know I five or six
Smokers who freely mix
Still with their neighbours;
Jones – (who, I'm glad to say,
Asked leave of Mrs J.) –
Daily absorbs a clay
After his labours.

Cats may have had their goose
Cooked by tobacco-juice;
Still why deny its use
Thoughtfully taken?
We're not as tabbies are:
Smith, take a fresh cigar!
Jones, the tobacco-jar!
Here's to thee, Bacon!

C. S. Calverley (1831–84)

It can scarcely have escaped the notice of thinking men, I think, that the forces of darkness opposed to those of us who like a quiet smoke are gathering momentum daily and starting to throw their weight about more than somewhat. Each morning I read in the papers a long article by another of those doctors who are the spearhead of the movement. Tobacco, they say, hardens the arteries and lowers the temperature of the body extremities, and if you reply that you like your arteries hard and are all for having the temperature of your body extremities lowered, especially in the summer months, they bring up that cat again.

The cat to which I allude is not the cat Poona which I chase at night but the one that has two drops of nicotine placed on its tongue and instantly passes beyond the veil.

'Look,' they say. 'I place two drops of nicotine on the tongue of this cat. Now watch it wilt.'

I can't see the argument. Cats, as Charles Stuart Calverley once observed, may have had their goose cooked by tobacco juice, but, as he went on to point out, we're not as tabbies are. Must we deprive ourselves of all our modest pleasures just because indulgence in them would be harmful to some cat which is probably a perfect stranger?

Take a simple instance such as occurs every Saturday afternoon on the Rugby football field. A scrum is formed, the ball is heeled out, the scrum-half gathers it, and instantaneously two fourteen-stone forwards fling themselves on his person, grinding him into the mud. Are we to abolish Twickenham and Murrayfield because some sorry reasoner tells us that if the scrum-half had been a cat he would have been squashed flatter than a Dover sole? And no use trying to drive into these morons' heads that there is no recorded instance of a team lining up for the kick-off with a cat playing scrum-half. Really, one feels inclined at times to give it all up and not bother to argue.

To me, and to you, too, probably, Winkler, it is pitiful to think that that is how these men spend their lives, placing drops of nicotine on the tongues of cats day in, day out all the year round, except possibly on bank holidays. But if you tell them that, like that Phantom fellow, they have become slaves to a habit, and urge them to summon up their manhood and throw off the shackles, they just stare at you with fishy eyes and mumble that it can't be done. Of course it can be done. If they were to say to themselves, 'I will not start placing nicotine on cats' tongues till after lunch', they would have made a beginning. After that it would be simple to knock off during the afternoon, and by degrees they would find that they could abstain altogether. The first cat of the day is the hard one to give up. Conquer the impulse for the after-breakfast cat, and the battle is half won.

P. G. Wodehouse, 'Healthward Ho!' in *Over Seventy: An Autobiography with Digressions*, 1957

———

Self-rationing

Ding Dong! A quarter past three. Light up at half past. Four and
three-quarter hours till closing time. Five and a quarter hours till
supper. Twopence halfpenny in pocket. No tobacco tomorrow. Suddenly a ravishing, irresistible desire to smoke came over Gordon. He
had made up his mind not to smoke this afternoon. He had only four
cigarettes left. They must be saved for tonight, when he intended to
'write'; for he could no more 'write' without tobacco than without
air. Nevertheless, he had got to have a smoke. He took out his packet
of Player's Weights and extracted one of the dwarfish cigarettes. It
was sheer stupid indulgence; it meant half an hour off tonight's
'writing' time. But there was no resisting it. With a sort of shameful
joy he sucked the soothing smoke into his lungs.

    George Orwell, *Keep the Aspidistra Flying*, 1936

Dixon paused in the portico to light the cigarette which, according to
his schedule, he ought to be lighting after breakfast on the next day
but one.

    Kingsley Amis, *Lucky Jim*, 1954

The speed of modern life

Even though a travel humidor is designed for a multiday trip and
a case is not, your expectations for both products should be
similar. Again, remember the size and shape of your cigars, and
be certain that the box will accommodate them. Then inspect the
details. Look for features like solid rear hinges, preferably of the
'piano' variety, which stretch the length of the box. Also, be certain
that the humidification unit inside the box will stay put while
you sprint to catch a plane or toss your luggage into the back of a
taxicab.

    If all goes well, both you and your cigars will arrive in fine condition,
ready to smoke away the troubles of an all-too-fast modern age.

    Cigar Aficionado's Buying Guide, 3rd edition, 1997

Richard sat there, smoking. Nicotine is a relaxant. Cigarettes are for the unrelaxed.

We are the unrelaxed.

Martin Amis, *The Information*, 1995

It is not necessary to be a member of the Tobacco Trade to realise that the world-wide practice of smoking is rapidly becoming, except for a small minority, a lost art and a limited pleasure. Indeed, many smokers in the furious tempo of modern life have freely admitted that it is only an essential narcotic for frayed nerves. For them choice Havana cigars, hand-made cigarettes and lustrous meerschaum pipes, which graced the smoking-rooms of fifty years ago, must seem almost as remote as the elaborate smoking paraphernalia which brought such excitement to Elizabethan England. To-day the ubiquitous cigarette has robbed most of us of these former glories and gripped us by the throat. Smoking has become habit, and habit, proverbially, blunts the edge of pleasure.

Alfred H. Dunhill, *The Gentle Art of Smoking*, 1954

In these days of spasmodic speed, volcanic rush, and eternal hurry, when quiet has lost its meaning and speed, not perfection, is the universal aim, tobacco affords man a resting-place and shelter from storm and stress. Smoking leads to contemplation and meditation. There are people who cannot do nothing; inaction is impossible to them, and yet though eternally busy they do nothing. A smoking man may be slow to commence, but he accomplishes his task better than the fraternity of fuss.

W. A. Penn, *The Soverane Herbe: A History of Tobacco*, 1901

Sir,

You will perhaps allow me the privilege of further contending for the moderate use of tobacco. Believing as I firmly do that in the chain of creation no link is deficient in its allotted use, I would ask the question of the infidels in the tobacco-blessing, Why was the tobacco-plant created? – what is its use? Shall we, arrogating to ourselves a greater power of reason than the Author of creation, deny ourselves one of the greatest blessings, which, in the present age of over-excitement of the nervous system, is peculiarly indicated as a counter-acting sedative?

Letter from W. Sumpter Esq., *The Lancet*, 28 February 1857

What are the real evils and plagues of this age? What but its breathless fuss and brainless flutter, its bother and din and hurry-scurry, its glare and stare and pretension? Now, the pipe calms a man; it slackens his pulse, lulls his restlessness, lays unruly haste and anxiety to sleep, and makes a man willing to stay in the arm-chair and enjoy it as one of the pleasantest and most comfortable things in life, and let the world, if it will, go a-gadding. Your true smoker – he that keeps his pipe in, I mean; and that is the mark by which you may know the true from the sham smoker – your true smoker is a pattern man for consistency. He takes his time about things.

Adam Hornbrook, *The Family Feud*, 1855

The introduction of tobacco into Europe in the sixteenth century corresponded with the arrival of the Age of Anxiety, the beginning of modern consciousness ... The Age of Anxiety gave itself an incomparable and probably indispensable remedy in the form of tobacco; it was an antidote brought by Columbus from the New World against the anxiety that his discoveries occasioned in the Eurocentered consciousness of Western culture ... It is tempting to think that Aristotle could not have known tobacco even if he knew it. Tobacco, the avid enjoyment of which quickly spread to every corner of the Continent and promptly beyond to Asia, defines modernity ...

Richard Klein, *Cigarettes Are Sublime*, 1993

Smoking under siege

[The siege of Lucknow]

Reduced though they were to living on the kind of mash of which Rees complained, or, in outposts like Anderson's where there were no cooks, on biscuits and sardines, what most of the soldiers and volunteers missed far more than good food was decent tobacco. When tea and coffee ran out they managed to make 'a tolerably good substitute' for these by roasting grain. But they found no palatable alternative to tobacco. They tried to smoke green leaves and became ill in consequence. They filled their pipes with tea leaves and dried guavas. They picked up wet and crumpled stubs of cheroots as though they had come upon priceless treasure. They stole precious stocks from men for whom, when under attack, they were prepared to risk their lives. They sold valued possessions – Rees sold his gold watch and chain – so as to be able to bid for cigars that might be offered at the auctions regularly held of dead men's effects.

Christopher Hibbert, *The Great Mutiny, India 1857*, 1978

In the latter months of the siege of Ladysmith tobacco was sold for £6 per pound, and a threepenny packet of cigarettes for 7s. 6d. Tobacco was the starving garrison's first request when the long-looked-for relief came.

W. A. Penn, *The Soverane Herbe: A History of Tobacco*, 1901

In long-besieged Leningrad all military rations were dwindling in the later months of 1941. Besides food, soldiers and sailors were entitled to 10 grammes of tobacco or 20 of *makhorka* (the inferior local species) daily. It is remarkable that in a city on the edge of famine people had to be urged to give up their tobacco ration in exchange for chocolate or sugar, and that the attempt failed.

V. G. Kiernan, *Tobacco: A History*, 1991

INT: DAY. PAUL'S APARTMENT

Morning. PAUL *and* RASHID *sitting at the table, eating breakfast.* RASHID *is wearing a red T-shirt with the word 'FIRE' emblazoned on the back in white letters. We catch them in mid-conversation.*

PAUL: It's 1942, right? And he's caught in Leningrad during the siege. I'm talking about one of the worst moments in human history. Five hundred thousand people died in that one place, and there's Bakhtin, holed up in an apartment, expecting to be killed any day. He has plenty of tobacco, but no paper to roll it in. So he takes the pages of a manuscript he's been working on for ten years and tears them up to roll his cigarettes.

RASHID: *(Incredulous)* His only copy?

PAUL: His only copy. *(Pause)* I mean, if you think you're going to die,

what's more important, a good book or a good smoke? And so he
huffed and he puffed, and little by little he smoked his book.

RASHID: *(Thinks, then smiles)* Nice try. You had me going for a
second, but no . . . no writer would ever do a thing like that. *(Slight
pause. Looking at* PAUL*)* Would he?

PAUL: *(Amused)* You don't believe me, huh? *(Stands up from the table
and begins walking to the bookcase)* Look, I'll show you. It's all in
this book.

'Smoke' in *Smoke and Blue in the Face: Two Films by Paul Auster*, 1995

Smoking and diplomacy

The art of diplomacy is the judicious administration of tobacco.

Lord Clarendon, British Foreign Secretary in the 1850s and 1860s, in 'Alpha of the
Plough', *Leaves in the Wind*, 1920

[Disraeli at the Congress of Berlin]

Berlin, 23 June 1878

I wanted to keep you tolerably *au courant* of my life here, but I
have so much to do, so many persons to see, so many papers to
write, have to talk, scribble, and think so much, that it has been
impossible. I can't even recollect where it was we last stopped. I think
on my return to Potsdam last Monday. I hope I gave you some account
of my visit there.

On that Monday of my return there was Congress and a grand
banquet at Bismarck's; I sate on his right hand, and though he ate
and drank a great deal, he talked as much: most entertaining and
picturesque; a sweet and gentle voice striking from such an ogre-
looking body, and recklessly frank. Then there have been other ban-
quets: notably one at the Italian Ambassador's: but talking of dinners,
the most interesting by far was my dinner with Bismarck alone. Affairs
were rather critical here and I was engaged at a 'banquet' at the
English Embassy, when he called on me – though he never calls on
anyone – and after some time proposed that, if not engaged, I should
dine with him alone and talk over matters.

He was in the bosom of his family who are interesting and devoted to him: the Princess, a daughter, 2 sons, and a married niece, pretty. After dinner he and I retired and smoked. It is the last blow to my shattered constitution, but had I refrained from smoking I should have made no way. So we spent a couple of memorable hours.

Affairs are progressing here and well.

Yours ever,

B

Letter to Lady Bradford, in Marquis of Zetland, editor, *The Letters of Disraeli to Lady Bradford and Lady Chesterfield*, 1929

[Churchill and Stalin]

19 January 1944

Maynard told me one amusing story about Stalin & W. on the Moscow visit when things weren't going too well over the 2nd Front. Stalin said goodbye to him when he went back one night & added 'I have carried out an old rite of Russian hospitality & put a pretty girl in yr. bed.' – W. rather embarrassed replied 'I shld prefer a good cigar'. When he got back he found a little girl of 4 with a placard round her neck on which was written 'I shall be ready as soon as the 2nd front'.

Mark Pottle, editor, *Champion Redoubtable: The Diaries and Letters of Violet Bonham Carter 1914–1945*, 1988

Smoking and the Germans

It would be well if the German nation would use the fruits and plants derived from the Indians moderately, and would distinguish between use and abuse. But now things have come to such a pass (Lord have mercy on us!) that we poor people of the Old World get something from the New World which right soon packs us off into the next world. Especially is this true of the beloved herb tobacco, a noble plant, but sore misused among us.

Franciscus Philippus Florinus, *Œconomus prudens et legalis; oder, Allgemeiner kluger und rechtsverständiger Hausvatter*, 1750

[Samuel Taylor Coleridge writes . . .]

A man here seldom sees his wife till dinner – they take their coffee in separate rooms, & never eat at breakfast; only as soon as they are up, they take their coffee – & about 11 o clock eat a bit of bread & butter; & with the coffee, the men at least take a pipe. (Indee[d, a] pipe at Breakfast is a great addition to the comforts of Life: I shall [smoke] at no other time in England. *Here* I smoke four times a day – 1 at breakfast, 1 half an hour before dinner, 1 in the afternoon at Tea, and one just before bed time – but I shall give it all up, unless, as before observed, you should happen to like the smoke of a pipe at Breakfast.) Once when I first came here, I smoked a pipe immediately after dinner; the Pastor expressed his surprize: I expressed mine that he could smoke before breakfast – 'O – Herr Gott! (i.e. Lord God) quoth he – it is delightful – it invigorates the frame, & *it cleans out the moutt so!*' A common amusement at the German Universities is for a number of young men to smoke out a Candle – i.e. to fill a room with Tobacco-smoke till the Candle goes out. – Pipes are quite the rage – a pipe of a particular kind, that has been smoked for a year or so, will sell here for twenty Guineas – the same pipe, when new, costs about four or five. They are called Meerschaums.

Letter to Mrs S. T. Coleridge, 14 January 1799

SIR, – Having had much experience of the baneful effects of smoking in my own country, Germany, which may be considered the great tobacco furnace of the age, which is affected by her reeking atmosphere in many ways, I trust that my opinion may have some weight with your readers.

The tendency of Germans to disease of the lungs may be traced to their incredible passion for smoking; and *our* principal medical men and physiologists compute that, out of twenty deaths of men between eighteen and twenty-five, ten originate in the waste of the constitution by smoking. So frequently is vision impaired by the constant use of tobacco, that spectacles may be said to be as much a part and parcel of a German as a hat is of an Englishman.

J. G. Schneider, Letter to *The Lancet*, 31 January 1857

Professor Schlafhaube, of the University of Heidelberg. *A Portrait from the Life*

Lazily runs the tide of human life –
There is no effort in our German land –
Of what avail are ceaseless moil and strife?
Is there not time? Why move, if we can stand?
There is no object the wide world can show,
Worth English hurry, sweat, and sore distress;
Let the moons wane and wax, and come and go,
And let us Germans doze in happiness!

Why should we turn and spin in frantic haste
When we have seventy years to live and dream?
Through cloud and vapour speed is perilous waste, –
Anchor the ship, there's fog upon the stream!
And let us sit and smoke the live-long day,
With deep-drawn whiffs, and drink the fattening beer;
Gazing on earth, or on the wreathlets grey
That curl above the pipes we love so dear!

Pipes! blessed pipes! There were no good on earth
Without tobacco. Give us that, and peace,
A little sunshine, and the children's mirth;
We'll ask no more! And if our wealth increase
Like growing corn; – why let it! We are glad!
But trouble us, O men of other climes,
No more with whistling steam, and efforts mad,
That make us languish for the ancient times.

Perish the Sultan! What is he to us?
Let Russia flourish! Why should we complain?
Are *we* the avengers? Work thy pleasure, Russ!
And let us smoke and sleep – and smoke again!
Firm as a rock let Germany endure;
Not like a rocket, blazing from the west;
Japan in Europe – slow, but very sure; –
Oh, give us pipes and peace, and let us rest!

Dresden, April 1855

Charles Mackay (1814–89)

[On a German tour]

... The German nation is still young, and its maturity is of importance to the world. They are a good people, a lovable people, who should help to make the world better. The worst that can be said against them is that they have their failings. They themselves do not know this; they consider themselves perfect, which is foolish of them. They even go so far as to think themselves superior to the Anglo-Saxon: this is incomprehensible. One feels they must be pretending. 'They have their points,' said George; 'but their tobacco is a national sin. I'm going to bed.'

Jerome K. Jerome, *Three Men on the Bummel*, 1900

Smoking and the Burmese

I have left to the last that country which is the spiritual home of all good smokers. In the course of this history I may be able to learn who brought tobacco to Burma and salute his memory with a pious epitaph, but known or unknown I give thanks to his spirit for the pleasure that smoking in Burma gave me . . .

A scene to warm the heart of a devoted smoker is of a Burmese family watching a play that goes on all night, and to observe how first father and then mother hands his or her cheroot round to the family of children who are enjoying the play with them . . .

That tobacco has played a vital part in preserving Burmese freedom I am convinced, but I begin to trespass on the fanciful aspect of smoking . . .

Machine-made cigarettes are much enjoyed, but at present they are too expensive except for the well-to-do Burmans; no doubt they will conquer Burma as they have conquered every other country. That will be a pity, because nowhere except in Cuba and a little bit of Louisiana can the devotee of tobacco in its noble strength feel himself in such accord with his fellow-smokers, and it can safely be claimed that the peculiar charm of the Burman owes much to his being an inveterate smoker from early childhood to old age.

Compton Mackenzie, *Sublime Tobacco*, 1957

By the old Moulmein Pagoda, lookin' lazy at the sea,
There's a Burma girl a-settin', and I know she thinks o' me;
For the wind is in the palm-trees, and the temple-bells they say:
'Come you back, you British soldier; come you back to Mandalay!'
  Come you back to Mandalay,
  Where the old Flotilla lay:
  Can't you 'ear their paddles chunkin' from Rangoon to
                Mandalay?

  On the road to Mandalay,
  Where the flyin'-fishes play,
  An' the dawn comes up like thunder outer China 'crost the
                  Bay!

'Er petticoat was yaller an' 'er little cap was green,
An' 'er name was Supi-yaw-lat – jes' the same as Theebaw's Queen,
An' I seed her first a-smokin' of a whackin' white cheroot,
An' a-wastin' Christian kisses on an 'eathen idol's foot:
  Bloomin' idol made o' mud –
  Wot they called the Great Gawd Budd –
  Plucky lot she cared for idols when I kissed 'er where she
                 stud!

  On the road to Mandalay . . .
  Rudyard Kipling, 'Mandalay', 1890

The Burmese are taught to smoke as to eat. A Burmese mother takes the cheroot from her mouth and puts it to the lips of her nursing babe; the child purses its tiny lips and puffs away with every indication of pleasure.
  W. A. Penn, *The Soverane Herbe: A History of Tobacco*, 1901

Postscript

A little before curfew on my last night in Albania, I was sitting in a café with the wire-service reporter and a couple other fellow stateside hacks. 'Albanians are just like anybody else,' I was saying.

 'They're crazy,' said the wire-service reporter.

 'No, they're not,' I said. 'They just have a different history, different traditions, a different set of political and economic circumstances. They're acting exactly the way we would if we . . .'

There was an Albanian family at the next table: handsome young husband, pretty wife, baby in a stroller, cute four-year-old girl bouncing on her dad's knee. The girl grabbed the cigarette from between her father's lips and tried a puff. Mom and Dad laughed. Dad took the cigarette back. Then he pulled a pack of Marlboros from his shirt pocket, offered a fresh cigarette to the little girl, and gave her a light.

P. J. O'Rourke, *Eat the Rich*, 1998

The pipe as companion

TO

THE VERY DEAR AND WELL-BELOVED

𝕱𝖗𝖎𝖊𝖓𝖉

OF MY PROSPEROUS AND EVIL DAYS –

TO THE FRIEND

WHO, THOUGH, IN THE EARLY STAGES OF OUR

ACQUAINTANCESHIP,

DID OFTTIMES DISAGREE WITH ME, HAS SINCE BECOME

TO BE MY VERY WARMEST COMRADE –

TO THE FRIEND

WHO, HOWEVER OFTEN I MAY PUT HIM OUT, NEVER (NOW)

UPSETS ME IN REVENGE –

TO THE FRIEND

WHO, TREATED WITH MARKED COLDNESS BY ALL THE FEMALE

MEMBERS OF MY HOUSEHOLD, AND REGARDED WITH SUSPICION

BY MY VERY DOG, NEVERTHELESS, SEEMS DAY BY DAY

TO BE MORE DRAWN BY ME, AND, IN RETURN, TO

MORE AND MORE IMPREGNATE ME WITH THE

ODOUR OF HIS FRIENDSHIP –

TO THE FRIEND

WHO NEVER TELLS ME OF MY FAULTS, NEVER WANTS TO

BORROW MONEY, AND NEVER TALKS ABOUT HIMSELF –

TO THE COMPANION OF MY IDLE HOURS,

THE SOOTHER OF MY SORROWS,

[260]

THE CONFIDANT OF MY JOYS AND HOPES –
MY OLDEST AND STRONGEST
𝔓𝔦𝔭𝔢,
THIS LITTLE VOLUME
IS
GRATEFULLY AND AFFECTIONATELY
DEDICATED.

Jerome. K. Jerome, Dedication to *The Idle Thoughts of an Idle Fellow*, 1886

'Halloa! that's not your pipe on the table! He must have left his behind him. A nice old briar, with a good long stem of what the tobacconists call amber. I wonder how many real amber mouthpieces there are in London. Some people think a fly in it is a sign. Why, it is quite a branch of trade, the putting of sham flies into the sham amber. Well, he must have been disturbed in his mind to leave a pipe behind him which he evidently values highly.'

'How do you know that he values it highly?' I asked.

'Well, I should put the original cost of the pipe at seven-and-six-pence. Now it has, you see, been twice mended: once in the wooden stem and once in the amber. Each of these mends, done, as you observe, with silver bands, must have cost more than the pipe did originally. The man must value the pipe highly when he prefers to patch it up rather than buy a new one with the same money.'

'Anything else?' I asked, for Holmes was turning the pipe about in his hand and staring at it in his peculiar pensive way.

He held it up and tapped on it with his long, thin forefinger as a professor might who was lecturing on a bone.

'Pipes are occasionally of extraordinary interest,' said he. 'Nothing has more individuality save, perhaps, watches and bootlaces. The indications here, however, are neither very marked nor very important. The owner is obviously a muscular man, left-handed, with an excellent set of teeth, careless in his habits, and with no need to practise economy.'

Arthur Conan Doyle, 'The Adventure of the Yellow Face' in *The Memoirs of Sherlock Holmes*, 1893

To my Pipe

To you, my Pipe, the latest verse,
To you, for better or for worse,
My best, most constant, closest friend,
I give requital at the end
Of this small volume all compact
Of fancy, folly, sober fact,
Wherein a-many bards combine
Hosannas to the Herb divine,
Sounding with no uncertain phrase
The diapason of its praise.
Small cause for wonderment indeed
That poets thus should sing the weed;
A weed! There never was a flow'r
Of greater worth in Eden bow'r,
For quite unparadised were we
Lacking its genial amity.

Dear Cloud-compeller, many a fill
Shall be your easy burden still, –
With you between his lips alight
A disillusioned anchorite
Might cast away his cankered scorn
And know that night's the womb of morn:
For you have power to cheer and bless
The man of deepest dolefulness,
I come to you for peace, and lo
A tranquil quietude I know –
Foreboded sorrow grows remote,
Out of your glowing embers float
My cares with wings of smoke unfurl'd
And go to seek another world.

Undying as the fire divine
That burned in Vesta's votive shrine,
You and the like of you shall be
Dowered with immortality.

Epilogue in William G. Hutchinson, editor, *Lyra Nicotiana:
Poems and Verses Concerning Tobacco*, 1898

'My lord, like one's cranium, it will endure till broken. I have smoked this one of mine more than half a century.'

'But unlike our craniums, stocked full of concretions, our pipe-bowls never need cleaning out,' observed another counsellor.

'True,' said Mohi, 'they absorb the oil of the smoke to incrust . . . like a good wife a pipe is a friend and companion for life . . . After many vexations, he may go home to that faithful counsellor, and find it full of kind consolations and suggestions. But not thus with cigars or cigarrets; the acquaintances of a moment, . . . their existence so fugitive, uncertain, unsatisfactory . . .'

Herman Melville, *Mardi and a Voyage Thither*, 1849

Choosing a Wife by a Pipe of Tobacco

Tube, I love thee as my life;
By thee I mean to chuse a wife.
Tube, thy *colour* let me find,
In her *skin*, and in her *mind*.
Let her have a *shape* as fine;
Let her breath be sweet as thine:
Let her, when her lips I kiss,
Burn like thee, to give me bliss:
Let her in some *smoke* or other
All my failings kindly smother.
Often when my thoughts are *low*,
Send them where they *ought to go*.
When to study I incline,
Let her aid be such as thine:
Such as thine her charming pow'r
In the vacant social hour.
Let her live to give delight,
Ever *warm* and ever *bright*:
Let her deeds, when'er she dies,
Mount as incense to the skies.

Anon., in *The Gentleman's Magazine*, February 1857

Then Jean was given final instructions on using the cap. When to put it in; how long afterwards to take it out; how to wash it, dry it, powder it, and put it away in its tin until next time. This reminded her of Father and his pipe: he always seemed to spend much longer filling and cleaning and poking it than he ever did smoking it. But perhaps all pleasures were like that.

Julian Barnes, *Staring at the Sun*, 1986.

The pleasures of a pipe. The tapping, the poking, the twisting, the cleaning, the stuffing, the lighting: those first cheek-hollowing puffs, and the dramatic way the match flame is sucked deep into the tobacco, leaps high in release, and is sucked deep again. And then the mouth-filling perfume, the commanding clouds of smoke. Oddly, I find the facial expressions and mannerisms of other men who smoke pipes stagy, prissy, preening, and offensive. But ever since I, as an unheeded admonition to Esther some years ago, gave up cigarettes, the pipe has been my comfort, my steeplejack's grab, my handhold on the precipitous cliff of life.

John Updike, *Roger's Version*, 1986

Favourite brands

[Thomas Carlyle to Jean Carlyle Aitken]

Friday Morning [30 January 1835]

Dear Jean,

... I am going into the City (that is the old part of London five miles East from this) to, among other things, order tobacco. Mundell's man holds out there, and furnishes me with an excellent unadulterated article, which he keeps in a separate Barrel and never shows to the Cockneys ...

Charles Richard Sanders *et al.*, editors, *The Collected Letters of Thomas and Jane Welsh Carlyle*, 1981

Pettigrew will be welcomed if he comes, but he is a married man, and we seldom see him nowadays. Others will be regarded as intruders. If they are smoking common tobaccos, they must either be allowed to try ours or requested to withdraw. One need only put his head in at my door to realize that tobaccos are of two kinds, the Arcadia and others. No one who smokes the Arcadia would ever attempt to describe its delights, for his pipe would be certain to go out. When he was at school, Jimmy Moggridge smoked a cane-chair, and he has since said that from cane to ordinary mixtures was not so noticeable as the change from ordinary mixtures to the Arcadia. I ask no one to believe this, for the confirmed smoker in Arcadia detests arguing with anybody about anything. Were I anxious to prove Jimmy's statement, I would merely give you the only address at which the Arcadia is to be had. But that I will not do. It would be as rash as proposing a man with whom I am unacquainted for my club. You may not be worthy to smoke the Arcadia Mixture.

J. M. Barrie, *My Lady Nicotine*, 1890*

Smoking etiquette

If you are so unfortunate as to have contracted the low habit of smoking, be careful to practise it under certain restrictions; at least, so long as you are desirous of being considered fit for civilised society.

The first mark of a gentleman is a sensitive regard for the feelings of others; therefore, smoke where it is least likely to prove personally offensive by making your clothes smell; then wash your mouth, and brush your teeth. What man of delicacy could presume to address a lady with his breath smelling of onions? Yet tobacco is equally odious. The tobacco smoker, in *public*, is the most selfish animal imaginable; he perseveres in contaminating the pure and fragrant air, careless whom he annoys, and is but the fitting inmate of a tavern.

Smoking in the streets, or in a theatre, is only practised by shop-boys, pseudo-fashionables – and the 'SWELL MOB'.

All songs that you may see written in praise of smoking in magazines or newspapers, or hear sung upon the stage, are *puffs*, paid for by the proprietors of cigar divans and tobacco shops, to make their trade popular – therefore, never believe nor be deluded by them.

---

* The original for Barrie's Arcadia Mixture was the Craven Mixture, available only from one tobacconist's in Wardour Street. After Barrie admitted as much, *My Lady Nicotine* was used to advertise the brand – with the result that the tobacconist, who had bought the shop for £3,000 just before the book's publication, sold it three years later for £100,000.

Never be seen in cigar divans or billiard rooms; they are frequented, at best, by an equivocal set. *No good* can be gained there – and a man loses his respectability by being seen entering or coming out of such places.

Aγωγòς, *Hints on Etiquette and the Usages of Society with a Glance at Bad Habits*, 3rd edition, 1836

Smoking

THE etiquette in this, as in many other matters, has quite altered during the last few years. At one time it was considered a sign of infamously bad taste to smoke in the presence of women in any circumstances. But it is now no longer so. So many women smoke themselves, that in some houses even the drawing-room is thrown open to Princess Nicotine. The example of the Prince of Wales has been largely instrumental in sweeping away the old restrictions. He smokes almost incessantly. On one occasion, at the Ranelagh Club, I noticed that he consumed four cigars in rapid succession, almost without five minutes' interval between them . . .

It is now no uncommon thing to see a man in evening dress smoking in a brougham with a lady on their way to opera, theatre, or dinner engagement. This is going rather far, for a woman's evening dress implies shut windows, except in the height of summer, and her garments become as much impregnated with the odour of tobacco as if she had herself been smoking . . .

There are also men round whom cling the odours of stale tobacco with a very disagreeable constancy. Why it should be so I cannot pretend to say. It must be due to carelessness of some kind, and carelessness in such matters amounts to bad manners. Even to men who smoke – and much more to those who do not – the smell of stale tobacco is revolting. Fancy, then, how it must offend the olfactory nerves of women. Such men suggest the stableyard while they are yet several feet away!

Mrs C. E. Humphrey, *Manners for Men*, 1898

It should be unnecessary to say that no guest may smoke at meals in anyone's house; the hotel and restaurant habit has made some young people terribly lax on this point, so that it is well to mention that such a thing is not to be tolerated for a moment. This matter of smoking is one of those in which fashion has had its say. More recently, cocktails enter into the question, and are generally offered as a prelude to dinner, or lunch either, for that matter. Shades of our grandmothers! How horrified they would be!

Mrs U. Massey Lyon, *Etiquette: A Guide to Public and Social Life*, 1927

Nowadays a woman smokes at any time or in any place. There are a few men left who wax sentimental when a girl says she doesn't smoke, but even they automatically go on offering her cigarettes. It's just smug to say: 'No, I don't smoke,' when confronted with a cigarette-case. 'No, thank you,' is quite sufficient. But it's still not the thing for a woman to smoke on the street, except that, although for a long time no real lady puffed on a cigarette in a car or a taxi, she now does it with the nonchalance she would display in her own drawing-room. The dance floor is the one place where it is unforgivable for either a woman or a man to carry a lighted cigarette. This last, however, has nothing to do with etiquette – it's merely a measure of safety, for it is too simple to ignite your partner (don't misunderstand) or set a diaphanous dress ablaze.

Alice-Leone Moats, *No Nice Girl Swears*, 1933*

Cigarettes should be to hand in every reception room whether you smoke yourself or not. It is unnecessary and even tiresome to supply only cigarettes of expensive quality; the cheaper Virginian brands are much more popular in all classes. A wisely-filled box will contain two kinds or more sorted into different compartments.

June Langley and Doris Moore, *The Pleasure of Your Company: A Text-book of Hospitality*, 1933

It had taken him an hour or more to get himself ready. Social life is so complicated when your income is two quid a week. He had had a painful shave in cold water immediately after dinner. He had put on his best suit – three years old but just passable when he remembered to press the trousers under his mattress. He had turned his collar inside out and tied his tie so that the torn place didn't show. With the point of a match he had scraped enough blacking from the tin to polish his shoes. He had even borrowed a needle from Lorenheim and

---

* Definitely a racier book than Mrs Massey Lyon's. The sentence before this passage, for example, reads: 'By all means, sit in any position you like, so long as you have pretty legs.'

darned his socks – a tedious job, but better than inking the places where your ankle shows through. Also he had procured an empty Gold Flake packet and put into it a single cigarette extracted from the penny-in-the-slot-machine. That was just for the look of the thing. You can't, of course, go to other people's houses with *no* cigarettes. But if you have even one it's all right, because when people see one cigarette in a packet they assume that the packet has been full. It is fairly easy to pass the thing off as an accident.

'Have a cigarette?' you say casually to someone.

'Oh – thanks.'

You push the packet open and then register surprise. 'Hell! I'm down to my last. And I could have sworn I had a full packet.'

'Oh, I won't take your last. Have one of *mine*,' says the other.

'Oh – thanks.'

And after that, of course, your host and hostess press cigarettes upon you. But you must have *one* cigarette, just for honour's sake.

George Orwell, *Keep the Aspidistra Flying*, 1936

There are those who will not permit any smoking in their home. It is their prerogative but of course their smoking guests may consider this anti-social. It is very unkind to confront a heavy smoker in your home with the fact that he or she will have to suffer a smoke-free evening. Better to warn your guests when you invite them, so they can decide whether or not to turn down your invitation.

There are some hosts who don't like smoking but permit their guests to do so. Hosts are no longer obliged to provide cigarettes for guests (although we would argue that thoughtful people who can afford to do so will always keep spare tobacco for their friends and acquaintances) but should have a sufficient number of ashtrays, preferably too many rather than too few. All ashtrays should be emptied regularly, rather than left to overflow. And always ensure your stub is out, not still burning away.

Some hosts may even politely ask smoking guests to wait until after dinner, where they can go to a separate room or be ushered out of doors (in the nicest possible way, and only in good weather) for a communal smoke. The polite guest will accept this suggestion, gracefully.

If this is your first visit and you've had no warning, look for the ashtrays, as this will give you some indication of whether you can light up, or not. Even if there are none it may be all right to light up but first you must ask permission. It's also polite to carry a little tin or, in smart company, a portable ashtray, in case the response to your request is: 'Oh, yes, of course, but I don't know if we've got an ashtray.' You can then reply: 'I've got one of my own!'

There's nothing to stop you carrying a small canister of air freshener (Neutradol is particularly effective, doesn't smell like a tart's boudoir and one squirt obliterates most known smells). This is also useful if the place you're visiting reeks of other things, which is all too often in these days of central heating, double-glazing and odd diets.

A non-smoker who allows you to light up in their home is doing you the biggest favour – they've got to live with the fumes long after you've gone. So be polite and don't take advantage of other people's generosity.

Most caring smokers go out into the garden or just outside the front door, or smoke next to an open window exhaling through it, out of courtesy. However, if your host is downright unpleasant and tells you not to smoke anywhere near the house, never mind inside it, the best response is to say nothing at all. Whether you return for a second visit, or not, is entirely up to you.

James Leavey, editor, *The FOREST Guide to Smoking in London*, 1996

[Can a host ban Smoking? Two 'society experts' give their advice.]

MARY KILLEN: Most people are actually pleased to smoke less than they would if they had a free rein. It is bossy to tell people they cannot, but, at Nigel Nicolson's house, Sissinghurst, if anyone tries to have a fag in secret, the smoke alarms go off and the fire brigade arrives. It would be quite a good idea to have extra-sensitive smoke alarms, though not linked to the police station.

CELESTRIA NOEL: You can ban smoking but, if you do, you may have to put up with the two-party syndrome – all the most amusing people standing outside in the garden.

Harpers & Queen, May 1999

Smoking snobbery

The luxuries of the cigar-smoker, in the way of ornamental receptacles for cigars, need not here be descanted on. Some, in their elaboration and costliness, belong to the wealthy, and are merely to be considered as the vanities of selfish pride. When men enshrine cigars in pearl cases, elaborated with metal work, that make them seem only fitted for the scent-cases of a lady's boudoir, they may be looked upon with due contempt, not only by ladies, but by those of their own sex who adhere to the honest useful case of plain Russia leather.

F. W. Fairholt, *Tobacco: Its History and Associations*, 1859

People who claim to know say I smoke the worst cigars in the world . . .

Now then observe what superstition, assisted by a man's reputation, can do. I was to have twelve personal friends to supper one night. One of them was as notorious for costly and elegant cigars as I was for cheap and devilish ones. I called at his house and when no one was looking borrowed a double handful of his very choicest . . . I removed the labels and put the cigars into a box with my favorite brand on it – a brand which those people all knew, and which cowed them as men are cowed by an epidemic.

They took these cigars when offered at the end of the supper, and lit them and sternly struggled with them – in dreary silence for hilarity died when the fell brand came into view and started around – but their fortitude held for a short time only; then they made excuses and filed out, treading on one another's heels with indecent eagerness; and in the morning when I went out to observe results the cigars all lay between the front door and the gate.

All except one – that one lay in the plate of the man from whom I had cabbaged the lot. One or two whiffs was all he could stand. He told me afterward that some day I would get shot for giving people that kind of cigar to smoke.

Mark Twain, *Concerning Tobacco*, 1890

And, as you sample different cigars, perhaps lighting (so to speak) on one that is particularly to your taste, you may want to keep a smoking journal . . . If you're not interested in creating cigar-band designs, you can paste the bands in your smoking journal as a memento.

John-Manuel Andriote, Andrew E. Falk and B. Henry Pérez, *The Art of Fine Cigars*, 1996

The components of a good humidor can be judged easily. Starting from the inside of the box, look for details like perfectly squared and fitted seams. You shouldn't see any glue, and a gap in a joint spells trouble because it provides an exit for moisture, eventually resulting in warping. Cedar is the best wood for the inside of a humidor because of its ability to enhance the aging process. It allows the various tobaccos in a cigar the chance to 'marry' so that the cigar is not composed of separate tobacco flavors, but of subtle nuances of taste.

The rim of the box should be constructed uniformly, with tight tolerances, so that the lid closes with the solid feel of a Mercedes Benz car door.

Cigar Aficionado's Buying Guide, 3rd Edition, 1997

May 1996
Dana Gould, a stand-up comedian, takes the stage at a West Hollywood nightclub, eyes a crowd of young hipsters puffing away and offers a succinct analysis: 'Ah, cigars . . . the ponytail of the 90's.'

Tom McNichol, 'Cigar Asphyxionado . . . the short history of a stinky fad' in *The New York Times Magazine*, 29 June 1997

The poor man's friend

[The trade union leader]

He smirked in acknowledgement of their uncouth greetings, and sat down; then glancing round, he inquired whether it would not be agreeable to the gentlemen present to have pipes and liquor handed round; adding, that he would stand treat.

As the man who has had his taste educated to love reading, falls devouringly upon books after a long abstinence, so these poor fellows, whose tastes had been left to educate themselves into a liking for tobacco, beer, and similar gratifications, gleamed up at the proposal of the London delegate. Tobacco and drink deaden the pangs of hunger, and make one forget the miserable home, the desolate future.

Elizabeth Gaskell, *Mary Barton: A Tale of Manchester Life*, 1848

[In a London pub]

... the deep perpetual groan of London misery seemed to swell and swell and form the whole undertone of life. The filthy air came into the place in the damp coats of silent men, and hung there till it was brewed to a nauseous warmth ... strong-smelling pipes contributed their element in a fierce, dogged manner which appeared to say that it now had to stand for everything – for bread and meat and beer, for shoes and blankets and the poor things at the pawnbroker's and the smokeless chimney at home.

Henry James, *The Princess Casamassima*, 1886

A door that locked, a fire in winter, a pipe of tobacco – these were things essential; and granted these, I have been often richly content in the squalidest garret.

George Gissing, *The Private Papers of Henry Ryecroft*, 1903

Smoking myths

Many years ago a Bushongo returned from a long journey and after surprising his companions by smoking persuaded them to try it with these words:

'When you have a quarrel with your brother, in your fury you may wish to slay him: sit down and smoke a pipe. When the pipe is finished you will think that perhaps death is too great a punishment for your brother's offences, and you will decide to let him off with a thrashing. Relight your pipe and smoke on. As the smoke curls upwards you will come to the conclusion that a few hard words might take the place of blows. Light up your pipe once more, and when it is smoked through you will go to your brother and ask him to forget the past.'

M. W. Hilton-Simpson, *Land and Peoples of the Masai*, 1911

Now to descend from the substance and the smoak to the ashes, 'tis well known that the medicinall virtues thereof are very many, but they are so common that I will spare the inserting of them heer: But if one would try a pretty conclusion how much smoak ther is in a pound of Tobacco, the ashes will tell him, for let a pound be exactly weighed, and the ashes kept charily and weigh'd afterwards, what wants of a pound weight in the ashes cannot be denied to have bin smoak, which evaporated into air: I have bin told that Sir *Walter Rawleigh* won a wager of Queen *Elizabeth* upon this nicity.*

James Howell, *Epistolæ Ho-Elianæ*, 1650

*This reference to the wager between Elizabeth and Raleigh in Howell's *Letters* appears to be the only authority for the full story by a later writer which is often quoted in books about tobacco. The story runs that the Queen having wagered twenty angels that Raleigh could not solve her doubt as to his vaunted ability to weigh smoke, he accepted the challenge. After smoking a pipe, weighing the ashes, and arriving at the weight which had been smoked away –

' "Your Majesty cannot deny that the difference hath been evaporated in smoke."

"Truly I cannot," answered the Queen.

Ordering the wager to be paid, she turned to the courtiers around her, and said: "Many alchemists have I heard of who turned gold into smoke, but Raleigh is the first who has turned smoke into gold." '

The authorship of this excellent story has, so far as I can trace, never been attributed, but there is no doubt that it was based on the letter quoted here. Howell was private secretary to the Earl of Leicester; then Clerk of Council; and after languishing for eight years in the Fleet Prison became the first Historiographer Royal.

W. Partington, editor, *Smoke Rings and Roundelays: Blendings from Prose and Verse since Raleigh's Time*, 1924

When the connoisseur is sauntering at his ease, inhaling with delight one of those cigars, *de la Reina*, relishing with the *gusto* of a true amateur its delicious flavour, and admiring its aptitude to catch and retain fire, let him know, then, that cigar, so fiery and yet so mild, has been – well, this cigar has been, like most others he has ever smoked, rolled – yes, rolled, upon the *bare thigh* of one of the country girls, called a *guajira* in Cuba.

The Countess Merlin, 'The Introduction of Tobacco into Europe' in *Bentley's Miscellany*, April 1844

A sudden outburst is heard from the area near the counter.

YOUNG MAN: *(Aghast)* Ninety-two dollars?

The focus of the scene shifts to AUGGIE *and the* YOUNG MAN.

AUGGIE: They don't come cheap, son. These little honeys are works of art. Rolled by hand in a tropical climate, most likely by an eighteen-year-old girl in a thin cotton dress with no underwear on. Little beads of sweat forming in her naked cleavage. The smooth, delicate fingers nimbly turning out one masterpiece after another . . .

YOUNG MAN: *(Pointing)* And how much are these?

AUGGIE: Seventy-eight dollars. The girl who rolled these was probably wearing panties.

'Smoke' in *Smoke and Blue in the Face: Two Films by Paul Auster*, 1995

Some distinctive smokers (in Raymond Chandler)

I looked at Spangler. He was leaning forward so far he was almost out of his chair. He looked as if he was going to jump. I couldn't think of any reason why he should jump, so I thought he must be excited. I looked back at Breeze. He was about as excited as a hole in the wall. He had one of his cellophane-wrapped cigars between his thick fingers and he was slitting the cellophane with a penknife. I watched him get the wrapping off and trim the cigar end with the blade and put the knife away, first wiping the blade carefully on his trousers. I watched him strike a wooden match and light the cigar carefully, turning it around in the flame, then hold the match away from the cigar, still burning, and draw on the cigar till he decided it was properly lighted. Then he shook the match out and laid it down beside the crumpled cellophane on the glass top of the cocktail table. Then he leaned back and pulled up one leg of his trousers and smoked peacefully. Every motion had been exactly as it had been when he lit a cigar in Hench's apartment, and exactly as it always would be whenever he lit a cigar. He was that kind of man, and that made him dangerous.

Raymond Chandler, *The High Window*, 1943

Sexy was very faint praise for her. The jodphurs, like her hair, were coal black. She wore a white silk shirt with a scarlet scarf loose around her throat. It was not as vivid as her mouth. She held a long brown cigarette in a pair of tiny golden tweezers. The fingers holding it were more than adequately jewelled. Her black hair was parted in the middle and a line of scalp as white as snow went over the top of her head and dropped out of sight behind. Two thick braids of her shining black hair lay one on each side of her slim brown neck. Each was tied with a small scarlet bow. But it was a long time since she was a little girl.

Raymond Chandler, *The Little Sister*, 1949

She picked a cigarette out of a box, tossed it in the air, caught it between her lips effortlessly and lit it with a match that came from nowhere.

Raymond Chandler, *The Little Sister*, 1949

After a moment the man on the couch slowly raised the arm with the cigarette at the end of it. He got the cigarette wearily into his mouth and drew on it with the infinite languor of a decadent aristocrat mouldering in a ruined château.

Raymond Chandler, *The Little Sister*, 1949

Smoking and sport

The sporting community's concerns about loss of sponsorship revenue from tobacco companies are misplaced. Successful participation in sport and tobacco advertising, and by implication consumption, are mutually exclusive.

Letter in *The Sunday Times*, 25 May 1997

What was good enough for Johan Cruyff and Bobby Charlton is good enough for Paul Gascoigne, was the message from Glenn Hoddle yesterday.

Gascoigne picked up a smoking habit while he was playing for Lazio and he has returned to cigarettes in recent weeks as he helped his new club Middlesbrough return to the Premiership.

The England coach, though, has continued his softly-softly approach in his dealings with the wayward midfielder who is battling to be fit for the World Cup.

Guardian, 13 May 1998

All-time smoking soccer eleven

Before going let's return to the issue of footballers smoking. On paper, at least, we've gathered together some footballing legends. So here's the *Free Choice* smoker first team: Dino Zoff (Italy); Socrates (Brazil); Gerson (Brazil); Jack Charlton (England); Frank Leboeuf (France); Jimmy Greaves (England); David Ginola (France); Osvaldo Ardiles (Argentina); Malcolm Macdonald (England); Bobby Charlton (England); Robert Prosinecki (Croatia). Sub: Gazza (England). Coach: Cesar Luis Menotti (Argentina).

Free Choice (FOREST magazine) July/August 1998

Tobacco, taxes and smuggling

Sugar, rum and tobacco, are commodities which are no where necessaries of life, which are become objects of almost universal consumption, and which are therefore extremely proper subjects of taxation.

Adam Smith, *An Inquiry into the Nature and Causes of the Wealth of Nations*, 1776

How far do such tenacious Sots exceed,
The Ratio of those Brutes which cannot think?
Who sacrifice their Lives to such a Weed?
Whose only Virtues are to Smoak and Stink.

Wine is a Cordial that revives the Soul,
Yet that's destructive, drank to an Extream,
But damn'd Tobacco makes the Fancy dull,
And surely was, long since, the Devil's Dream.

What wondrous Vertues must be first ascrib'd,
To make the pois'nous fi'ry Leaf go down,
Or Man its stinking Fumes had ne'er imbib'd,
But the curs'd Plant had rotted still unknown.

Well might the Royal *Scot* so much exclaim,
Against an Herb, that did such Mischief breed,
Which in his happy Days had scarce a Name,
Besides that odious Term of *Indian* Weed.

Nor would the nauseous Product e'er have grown,
Within these Realms, so popular a Vice,
Had it not brought large Incomes to the Crown,
And been a grand Promoter of Excise.

> Edward Ward (1667–1731), *How Far Do Such Tenacious Sots Exceed*

[Thomas Carlyle in 1860]

Apparently it was this summer that one of the most welcome callers from America, Milburn the blind preacher, came many times to 'tea at six o'clock.' By-and-by he dictated to a faithful scribe what he remembered. 'Never,' said he, 'had I any idea of what eloquent talk meant until I listened to Carlyle.'

'At their first interview,' as soon as tea was done, Carlyle said: –

'I hope, sir, that, unlike many of your countrymen, you sometimes indulge in the solace of a pipe?'

Milburn declared he did and Carlyle led him into the garden, where there were seats under an awning, a table with a canister of tobacco and new clay pipes. As they lit up he said: –

'People in moderate circumstances in this country can not afford to offer their friends a good cigar, and I suppose only what you would consider very middling tobacco. The Government finds it needful to have such a revenue that it must needs lay a tax of some hundreds per cent upon the poor man's pipe, while the rich man's glass of wine pays scarcely one-tenth of this impost. But I learn that there is as much tobacco smuggled into England as pays the duty. Thus, as you see, it is as it ever will be when the laws are unjust and onerous; for the smuggler is the Lord Almighty of the Chancellor of the Exchequer, saying to him, "Thus far shalt thou go, and no farther, and here shall thy proud waves be stayed."'

> David Alec Wilson, *Carlyle to Threescore-and-Ten*, 1929

If you wake at midnight, and hear a horse's feet,
Don't go drawing back the blind, or looking in the street,
Them that asks no questions isn't told a lie.
Watch the wall, my darling, while the Gentlemen go by!
 Five and twenty ponies
 Trotting through the dark –
 Brandy for the Parson,
 'Baccy for the Clerk;
 Laces for a lady, letters for a spy,
And watch the wall, my darling, while the Gentlemen go by!

  Rudyard Kipling, *A Smuggler's Song*, 1906

Tobacco as currency

[South Africa, 10 April 1652]

Skipper Davit Conick together with two assistants and two soldiers
with fowling-pieces and muskets, having gone on a fishing-expedition
to the Salt River, encountered nine Saldania [aborigines] who adopted
such an amicable and pleasant attitude that it was almost a wonder:
they took the skipper round the neck as if with great joy and made
signs that if we had copper and tobacco they would bring us enough
cattle.

[. . . and 6 December, 1652]

If we had no tobacco there would hardly be any trade, as a whole
cow would often be withheld for a finger's length of tobacco or a
pipe. We should therefore be provided with 1,000 lbs. annually, which
should moreover be of good quality, for if there is the least rot in the
tobacco, they can taste it immediately and will not look at it, calling
it stinking tobacco.

  Diary of Jan van Riebeeck, quoted in Compton Mackenzie, *Sublime Tobacco*, 1957

In the rude ages of society, cattle are said to have been the common
instrument of commerce; and, though they must have been a most
inconvenient one, yet in old times we find things were frequently
valued according to the number of cattle which had been given in

exchange for them. The armour of Diomede, says Homer, cost only nine oxen; but that of Glaucus cost an hundred oxen. Salt is said to be the common instrument of commerce and exchanges in Abyssinia; a species of shells in some parts of the coast of India; dried cod at Newfoundland; tobacco in Virginia; sugar in some of our West India colonies; hides or dressed leather in some other countries; and there is at this day a village in Scotland where it is not uncommon, I am told, for a workman to carry nails instead of money to the baker's shop or the ale-house.

Adam Smith, *An Inquiry into the Nature and Causes of the Wealth of Nations*, 1776

[Letter from Virginia]

To Mr John Norton
Mercht. in London
By Capt. Lilly

4th Jany. 1767

Sir,

By Capt. Lilly have sent you 4 hds. Tobo and shall be oblig'd to you, to send me the following articles on it viz: 3 Tooth brushes, a green silk Tippet, 1 pr. womens pattins, 1 pr. clogs, 1 fashionable muft with a hair tippet to it, a red Silk Bonnet and Cloke for a child three years old, three mourning rings according to the inclosed directions, a Silver lac'd hatt for a Boy four years old. These things shall be glad to have by the first ship in York or Rappak.

I am, Sir,
Your humble sert.
Augustine Smith.

P.S. 2 fans at 2s. 6d. each for a Child 5 years old.

Frances Norton Mason, editor, *John Norton & Sons, Merchants of London and Virginia. Being the Papers from their Counting House for the Years 1750 to 1795*, 1937

In Virginia tobacco had become king . . .

Ministers and the military were to be paid in the best Virginia leaf. The clergy, quite naturally, thought they could best serve God in those parishes where tobacco of superior quality was grown. The fact that in these places more marriages and more funeral services were to be performed was said to be quite irrelevant. (Only a historian of tobacco could be expected to comment on this circumstantial evidence.) Superb sermons were often thundered from pulpits on the importance of raising good tobacco and the moral necessity of curing it properly. A law of 1624 required that 'no man dispose of his tobacco before the minister be satisfied.' This occasioned the comment by a later observer:

> We perceive in this law that the custom of passing tobacco current in payments had so far obtained ground, that the parson made no scruple of receiving this luxurious article for preaching, or the clerk for bawling out amen!

Frequent disputes arose between ministers and their parishioners over the amounts of fees or salaries and the quality of receipts. Shrewd evaluation of a crop became a routine of ministerial activity. At a later period, when tobacco was scarce, the Assembly ordered that the clergy be paid in cash. This indecent proposal, clearly inspired by Satan, was indignantly rejected by the ministers as a body.

Jerome E. Brooks, *The Mighty Leaf: Tobacco through the Centuries*, 1953

West Beirut can also be toured on foot. You'll find the city is full of surprises – a sacking of the Saudi embassy because of long lines for visas to Mecca, for instance, or shelling of the lower town by an unidentified gunboat or car bombs several times a day. Renaults are the favoured vehicles. Avoid double-parked Le Cars. Do not, however, expect the population to be moping around glassy eyed. There's lots of jewellery and make-up and the silliest Italian designer jeans on earth. The streets are jammed. Everyone's very busy, though not exactly working. They're rushing from one place to another in order to sit around drinking hundreds of tiny cups of Turkish coffee and chat at the top of their lungs. The entire economy is fuelled, as far as I could see, by everyone selling cartons of smuggled Marlboros to each other.

P. J. O'Rourke, 'A Ramble through Lebanon' (1984) in *Holidays in Hell*, 1988

The first smokers

The Iroquois believed that tobacco was given to them as the means of communicating with the spiritual world. By burning tobacco they could send up their petitions with its ascending incense, to the Great Spirit, and render their acknowledgements acceptably for his blessings. Without this instrumentality, the ear of Ha-wen-ne-yu could not be gained. In like manner they returned their thanks at each recurring festival to the Invisible Aids, for their friendly offices, and protecting care.

J. W. Springer, 'An Ethnohistoric Study of the Smoking Complex in Eastern North America' in *Ethnohistory* 28, 1981

[A Winnebago myth]

Earthmaker created the spirits who live above the earth, those who live on the earth, those who live under the earth, and those who live in the water; all these he created and placed in charge of some powers . . . In this fashion he created them and only afterwards did he create us. For that reason we were not put in control of any of these blessings. However, Earthmaker did create a weed and put it in our charge, and he told us that none of the spirits he had created would have the power to take this away from us without giving us something in exchange. Thus said Earthmaker. Even he, Earthmaker, would not have the power of taking this from us without giving up something in return. He told us if we offered him a pipeful of tobacco, if this we poured out for him, he would grant us whatever we asked of him. Now all the spirits come to long for this tobacco as intensely as they longed for anything in creation, and for that reason, if at any time we make our cry to the spirits with tobacco, they will take pity on us and bestow on us the blessings of which Earthmaker placed them in charge. Indeed so it shall be, for thus Earthmaker created it.

Elisabeth Tooker, editor, *Native North American Spirituality of the Eastern Woodlands*, 1979

It is remarkable how often versions of the Winnebago origin myth crop up throughout the New World. In the mythology of the Pilaga Indians of the Gran Chaco, in Paraguay, for example, tobacco first appeared out of the ashes of a cannibal-woman killed by the culture hero.

The Fox Indians, on the western side of Lake Michigan, inherited tobacco from the Great Manitou . . . As the Manitous were addicted to the plant, and as they could not grow it themselves, they entered into a contract of mutual benefit with humans, tobacco in return for care and protection... Among the Chippewa of Lake Superior, tobacco was held in a similar supernatural esteem... The Yecuana of Venezuela believe that women were created from clay over which tobacco smoke was blown; among the Yaqui, on the other hand, tobacco came into existence through the metamorphosis of a woman.

Jordan Goodman, *Tobacco in History: The Cultures of Dependence*, 1993

Sometimes the Indians grow tired of a war which they have carried on against some neighbouring nation for many years without much success, and in this case they seek for mediators to begin a negotiation. These being obtained, the treaty is thus conducted.

A number of their own chiefs, joined by those who have accepted the friendly office, set out together for the country of their enemies. Such as are chosen for this purpose are chiefs of the most extensive abilities and of the greatest integrity. They bear before them the Pipe of Peace, which I need not inform my readers is of the same nature as a Flag of Truce among the Europeans, and is treated with the greatest respect and veneration, even by the most barbarous nations. I never heard of an instance wherein the bearers of this sacred badge of friendship were ever treated disrespectfully, or its rights violated. The Indians believe that the Great Spirit never suffers an infraction of this kind to go unpunished.

The Pipe of Peace, which is termed by the French the Calumet, for what reason I could never learn, is about four feet long. The bowl of it is made of red marble, and the stem of it of a light wood, curiously painted with hieroglyphicks in various colours and adorned with the feathers of the most beautiful birds. It is not in my power to convey an idea of the various tints and pleasing ornaments of this much esteemed Indian implement.

Every nation has a different method of decorating these pipes, and they can tell at first sight to what band it belongs. It is used as an introduction to all treaties, and great ceremony attends the use of it on these occasions.

The assistant or aid-du-camp of the great warrior, when the chiefs are assembled and seated, fills it with tobacco mixed with herbs, taking care at the same time that no part of it touches the ground. When it is filled, he takes a coal that is thoroughly kindled from a fire which is generally kept burning in the midst of the assembly, and places it on the tobacco.

As soon as it is sufficiently lighted, he throws off the coal. He then turns the stem of it towards the heavens, after this towards the earth and, now holding it horizontally, moves himself round till he has completed a circle. By the first action he is supposed to present it to the Great Spirit, whose aid is thereby supplicated; by the second, to avert any malicious interposition of the evil spirits; and by the third to gain the protection of the spirits inhabiting the air, the earth, and the waters. Having thus secured the favour of those invisible agents, in whose power they suppose it is either to forward or obstruct the issue of their present deliberations, he presents it to the hereditary chief who, having taken two or three whiffs, blows the smoke from his mouth first towards heaven, and then around him upon the ground.

It is afterwards put in the same manner into the mouths of the ambassadors or strangers who observe the same ceremony; then to the chiefs of the warriors and to all the other chiefs in turn according to their gradation. During this time the person who executes this honourable office holds the pipe slightly in his hand, as if he feared to press the sacred instrument; nor does any one presume to touch it but with his lips.

Norman Gelb, editor, *Jonathan Carver's Travels through America 1766–1768: An Eighteenth-Century Explorer's Account of Uncharted America*, 1993

The last smoke

[The death of Sir Walter Raleigh]

He tooke a pipe of tobacco a little before he went to the scaffolde, which some female persons were scandalised at; but I think 'twas well and properly donne to settle his spirits.

John Aubrey, *Lives*, 1693

> A Fleming late that killed one with a knife,
> Carried by cart to end his wretched life,
> Toward Tyburn riding did tobacco take,
> (To purge his head against his heels did shake).
> But I durst lay ten pounds to twenty shilling,
> To take his purge no wise-man will be willing:
> Though Englishman are apt for imitation,

Yet masters, let the Dutchman keep his fashion:
For howsoe'er it with his liking stood,
The smoking did his choking little good.

Samuel Rowlands (1570?–1630?), Tobacco Carted to Tyburn

A poor Roman Catholic priest, named Kemble, was hanged in 1679, in his eightieth year, he having been implicated in the plot of Titus Oates. He marched to his fate, amidst a crowd of weeping friends, with the tranquillity of a primitive martyr, and smoking a pipe of tobacco. In memory of this, the people of Herefordshire to this day call the last pipe they take at a sitting a Kemble pipe.

Tobacco Talk and Smokers' Gossip: an Amusing Miscellany of Fact and Anecdote, 1884

Smoking in bed. Sharing a cigarette. Watching David Bowie in *Merry Christmas, Mr. Lawrence*. This is heaven: the convergence of bed, you, smoking, and David Bowie. Bowie, a prisoner of war, is in his cell awaiting execution. The guards come to fetch him, but he makes them wait while he prepares for the end. He picks up his hat, holding it upside down in the palm of his hand like a bowl, and turns to the wall. Peering into the wall as though into a mirror, he rubs his chin, dips an imaginary shaving brush into the bowl, picks up an imaginary razor, and begins to shave. Slowly, ritualistically, he mimes the act of shaving and then of drinking a cup of tea, and then he reaches out and takes an imaginary cigarette between his fingers. My hand reaches out for the pack and starts shaking a cigarette loose, but your fingers close around my wrist, and you whisper, 'Wait.'

He inhales deeply, luxuriously, you can feel the nicotine spreading through his being. And then he exhales, running his tongue over his lips, tasting, catching a stray strand of tobacco. He savors that cigarette. When it is almost finished he throws it to the ground – cut to a high-angle medium shot of his boot stepping on the imaginary stub. Then he moves off, out of frame.

Lesley Stern, The Smoking Book, 1999

DYING FOR A CIGGIE – death-row inmate Larry White was refused his last request – a cigarette – because the jail in Huntsville, Texas, is non-smoking.

News of the World, 17 May 1998

The future

It may well seem ... that there will shortly be no more cigarette smokers left at all, anywhere. What was once the unique prerogative of the most refined and futile dandies, having become the luxury of billions of people, may abruptly vanish. Will anything have been lost? On the day when some triumphant antitabagist crushes under his heel the last cigarette manufactured on the face of the earth, will the world have any reason to grieve, perhaps to mourn the loss of a cultural institution, a social instrument of beauty, a wand of dreams?

Richard Klein, *Cigarettes are Sublime*, 1993

I turned about. She was in a saffron-yellow dress of an ancient cut. This was a thousandfold more wicked than if she had had absolutely nothing on. Two sharp points, glowing roseately through the thin tissue: two embers smouldering among ashes. Two tenderly rounded knees –

She was seated in a rather squat armchair; on a small square table before her stood a flagon of some poisonously green stuff and two diminutive stemmed glasses. In the corner of her mouth was the slenderest of paper tubes, sending up the smoke of that combustible substance the ancients used (I have now forgotten what they called it) ... She poured some of the liquid in the flagon into one of the tiny glasses, sipped some off.

'An exquisite liqueur. Care for some?'

It was only then that I grasped what the green stuff was: alcohol. I saw in a flash of lightning the things that had taken place yesterday: the stony hand of The Benefactor; the unbearably bright blade of the electric ray; but above all, up there on the Cube – that fellow with his head thrown back, his spread-eagled body. I shuddered.

'Listen,' I said, 'you surely must know that The One State is merciless to all who poison themselves with nicotine and, especially, with alcohol – '

Yevgeny Zamyatin, *We*, 1920 (trans. Bernard Guilbert Guerney)

CHAPTER NINETEEN

Giving Up

I have known Spaniards in Española who had become accustomed to taking [tobacco] and who, after I had reprimanded them, saying that it was a vice, answered that they were unable to stop taking it . . .

> Bishop, Bartholomé de Las Casas, *History of the Indies, c.* 1535

Any habit carries with it the endlessly repeated belief that one has sufficient self-control to stop, abruptly, at any moment: believing one can stop is the preeminent condition of continuing.

> Richard Klein, *Cigarettes Are Sublime*, 1993

Prepare carefully

He stopped smoking at least once a month. He went through with it like the solid citizen he was: admitted the evils of tobacco, courageously made resolves, laid out plans to check the vice, tapered off his allowance of cigars, and expounded the pleasures of virtuousness to every one he met. He did everything, in fact, except stop smoking.

> Sinclair Lewis, *Babbitt*, 1922

Name a day, and stick to it

February 11, 1896: While waiting, I will tell you that after so many, many promises, I have now, at this moment, smoked my last cigarette.

Later that afternoon: 7 minutes before 4 afternoon, still smoking, still and always for the last time.

February 13, 1896: Last night I promised Livia not to smoke any more.

Later that afternoon: Thanks to this outburst, with your permission, I smoked for the last time, and let's not speak about it any more.

February 19, 1896: The cigarette that I am in the process of smoking is the last cigarette!

Italo Svevo's journal in *Ecrits Intimes, Essais and Lettres* (trans. Mario Fusco, 1973)

I was about twenty. For several weeks I suffered from a violent sore throat accompanied by fever. The doctor ordered me to stay in bed and to give up smoking entirely. I remember being struck by that word *entirely* which the fever made more vivid. I saw a great void, and no means of resisting the fearful oppression which emptiness always produces.

When the doctor had left, my father, who was smoking a cigar, stayed on a little while to keep me company (my mother had already been dead some years). As he was going away he passed his hand gently over my feverish brow and said:

'No more smoking, mind!'

I was in a state of fearful agitation. I thought: 'As it's so bad for me I won't smoke any more, but I must first have just one last smoke.' I lit a cigarette and at once all my excitement died down, though the fever seemed to get worse, and with every puff at the cigarette my tonsils burned as if a firebrand had touched them. I smoked my cigarette solemnly to the end as if I were fulfilling a vow. And though it caused me agony I smoked many more during that illness. My father would come and go, always with a cigar in his mouth, and say from time to time:

'Bravo! A few days more of no smoking and you will be cured!'

It only needed that phrase to make me long for him to get out of the room instantly so that I might begin smoking again at once. I would pretend to be asleep in order to get rid of him quicker.

This illness was the direct cause of my second trouble: the trouble I took trying to rid myself of the first. My days became filled with cigarettes and resolutions to give up smoking, and, to make a clean sweep of it, that is more or less what they are still. The dance of the last cigarette which began when I was twenty has not reached its last figure yet. My resolutions are less drastic and, as I grow older, I become more indulgent to my weaknesses. When one is old one can afford to smile at life and all it contains. I may as well say that for some time past I have been smoking a great many cigarettes and have given up calling them the last.

I find the following entry on the front page of a dictionary, beautifully written and adorned with a good many flourishes:

2 February, 1886. To-day I finish my law studies and take up chemistry. Last cigarette!!

That was a very important last cigarette . . .

While I sit here analysing myself a sudden doubt assails me: did I really love cigarettes so much because I was able to throw all the responsibility for my own incompetence on them? Who knows whether, if I had given up smoking, I should really have become the strong perfect man I imagined? Perhaps it was this very doubt which bound me to my vice, because life is so much pleasanter if one is able to believe in one's own latent greatness. I only put this forward as a possible explanation of my youthful weakness, but without any very great conviction.

Now that I am old and no one expects anything of me, I continue to pass from cigarette to resolution and back again. What is the point of such resolutions to-day? Perhaps I am like that aged dyspeptic in Goldoni, who wanted to die healthy after having been ill all his life!

Once when I was a student I changed my lodgings, and had to have the walls of my room repapered at my own expense, because I had covered them with dates. Probably I left that room just because it had become the tomb of my good resolutions, and I felt it impossible to form any fresh ones there.

I am sure a cigarette has a more poignant flavour when it is the last. The others have their own special taste too, peculiar to them, but it is less poignant. The last has an aroma all its own, bestowed by a sense of victory over oneself and the sure hope of health and strength in the immediate future. The others are important too, as an assertion of one's own freedom, and when one lights them one still has a vision of that future of health and beauty, though it has moved a little farther off.

The dates on my walls displayed every variety of colour and I had painted some of them in oils. The latest resolution, renewed in the most ingenuous good faith, found appropriate expression in the violence of its colours which aimed at making those of the preceding one pale before it. I had a partiality for certain dates because their figures went well together. I remember one of last century which seemed as if it must be the final monument to my vice: 'Ninth day of the ninth month, in the year 1899.' Surely a most significant date! The new century furnished me with other dates equally harmonious, though in a different way. 'First day of the first month in the year 1901.' Even to-day I feel that if only that date could repeat itself I should be able to begin a new life.

But there is no lack of dates in the calendar, and with a little imagination each of them might be adapted to a good resolution. I remember the following, for instance, because it seemed to me to contain an undeniable categorical imperative: 'Third day of the sixth month, in the year 1912, at 24 o'clock.' It sounds as if each number doubled the one before.

The year 1913 gave me a moment's pause. The thirteenth month, which ought to have matched the year, was missing. But of course such exact mathematical correspondence is hardly necessary to set off a last cigarette. Some dates which I have put down in books or on the backs of favourite pictures arrest one's attention by their very inconsequence. For example, the third day of the second month of the year 1905 at six o'clock! It has its own rhythm, if you come to think of it, for each figure in turn contradicts the one that went before. Many events too, in fact all from the death of Pius IX to the birth of my son, I thought deserved to be celebrated by the customary iron resolution. All my family marvel at my memory for anniversaries, grave or gay, and they attribute it to my nice sympathetic nature!

In order to make it seem a little less foolish I tried to give a philosophic content to the malady of 'the last cigarette.' You strike a noble attitude, and say: 'Never again!' But what becomes of the attitude if you keep your word? You can only preserve it if you keep on renewing your resolution. And then Time, for me, is not that unimaginable thing which never stops. For me, but only for me, it comes again.

Italo Svevo, *Confessions of Zeno*, 1923 (trans. Beryl de Zoete, 1948)

Saturday 12 August

9st 3 (still in very good cause), alcohol units 3 (v.g.), cigarettes 32 (v.v. bad, particularly since first day of giving up), calories 1800 (g.), Instants 4 (fair), no. of serious current affairs articles read 1.5, 1471 calls 22 (OK), minutes spent having cross imaginary conversations with Daniel 120 (v.g.), minutes spent imagining Daniel begging me to come back 90 (excellent).

Right. Determined to be v. positive about everything. Am going to change life: become well informed re: current affairs, stop smoking entirely and form functional relationship with adult man.

8.30 a.m. Still have not had fag. Vg.

8.35 a.m. No fags all day. Excellent.

8.40 a.m. Wonder if anything nice has come in post?

8.45 a.m. Ugh. Hateful document from Social Security Agency asking for £1452. What? How can this be? Have not got £1452. Oh God, need fag to calm nerves. Mustn't. Mustn't.

8.47 a.m. Just had fag. But no-smoking day does not start officially till have got dressed. Suddenly start thinking of former boyfriend Peter with whom had functional relationship for seven years until finished with him for heartfelt, agonizing reasons can no longer remember. Every so often – usually when he has no one to go on holiday with – he tries to get back together and says he wants us to get married. Before know where am, am carried away with idea of Peter being answer. Why be unhappy and lonely when Peter wants to be with me? Quickly find telephone, ring Peter and leave message on his answerphone – merely asking him to give me call rather than whole plan of spending rest of life together, etc.

1.15 p.m. Peter has not rung back. Am repulsive to all men now, even Peter.

4.45 p.m. No-smoking policy in tatters. Peter finally rang. 'Hi, Bee.' (We always used to call each other Bee and Waspy.) 'I was going to ring you anyway. I've got some good news. I'm getting married.'

Ugh. V. bad feeling in pancreas area. Exes should never, never go out with or marry other people but should remain celibate to the end of their days in order to provide you with a mental fallback position.

'Bee?' said Waspy. 'Bzzzzzzz?'

'Sorry,' I said, slumping dizzily against the wall. 'Just, um, saw a car accident out of the window.'

I was evidently superfluous to the conversation, however, as Waspy gushed on about the cost of marquees for about twenty minutes, then said, 'Have to go. We're cooking Delia Smith venison sausages with juniper berries tonight and watching TV.'

Ugh. Have just smoked entire packet of Silk Cut as act of self-annihilating existential despair. Hope they both become obese and have to be lifted out of the window by crane.

Helen Fielding, *Bridget Jones's Diary*, 1996

ARSENAL V LIVERPOOL
25.10.89

I remember the game for conventional reasons, for substitute Smith's late winner and thus a handy Cup win over the old enemy. But most of all I remember it as the only time in the 1980s and, hitherto, the 1990s, that I had no nicotine in my bloodstream for the entire ninety minutes. I have gone through games without smoking in that time: during the first half of the 83/84 season I was on nicotine chewing gum, but never managed to kick that, and in the end went back to the cigarettes. But in October '89, after a visit to Allen Carr the anti-smoking guru, I went cold turkey for ten days, and this game came right in the middle of that unhappy period.

I want to stop smoking and, like many people who wish to do the same, I firmly believe that abstinence is just around the corner. I won't buy a carton of duty-frees, or a lighter, or even a household-sized box of matches because, given the imminence of my cessation, it would be a waste of money. What stops me from doing so now, today, this minute, are the things that have always stopped me: a difficult period of work up ahead, requiring the kind of concentration that only a Silk Cut can facilitate; the fear of the overwhelming domestic tension that would doubtless accompany screaming desperation; and, inevitably and pathetically, the Arsenal.

They do give me some leeway. There's the first half of the season, before the FA Cup begins, and before the Championship has warmed up. And there are times like now, when with my team out of everything by the end of January I am looking at almost five months of dull but tension-free afternoons. (But I've got this book to write, and deadlines, and . . .) And yet some seasons – the 88/89 Championship year, for example, or the chase for the Double in 90/91 where every game between January and May was crucial – I cannot contemplate what it would be like to sit there without a smoke. Two down against Tottenham in a Cup semi-final at Wembley with eleven minutes gone and no fag? Inconceivable.

Nick Hornby, *Fever Pitch*, 1992

The easy method

The Easy Method is basically this: initially to forget the reasons we'd like to stop, to face the cigarette problem and to ask ourselves the following questions:

1 What is it doing for me?
2 Do I actually enjoy it?
3 Do I really need to go through life paying through the nose just to stick these things in my mouth and suffocate myself?

The beautiful truth is that it does absolutely nothing for you at all. Let me make it quite clear. I do not mean that the disadvantages of being a smoker outweigh the advantages; all smokers know that all their lives. I mean there are not *any* advantages from smoking. The only advantage it ever had was the social 'plus'; nowadays even smokers themselves regard it as an antisocial habit . . .

Imagine having a cold sore on your face. I've got this marvellous ointment. I say to you, 'Try this stuff.' You rub the ointment on, and the sore disappears immediately. A week later it reappears. You ask, 'Do you have any more of that ointment?' I say, 'Keep the tube. You might need it again.' You apply the ointment. Hey presto, the sore disappears again. Every time the sore returns, it gets larger and more painful and the interval gets shorter and shorter. Eventually the sore covers your whole face and is excruciatingly painful. It is now returning every half hour. You know that the ointment will remove it temporarily, but you are very worried. Will the sore eventually spread over your whole body? Will the interval disappear completely? You go to your doctor. He can't cure it. You try other things, but nothing helps except this marvellous ointment.

By now you are completely dependent on the ointment. You never go out without ensuring that you have a tube of the ointment with you. If you go abroad, you make sure that you take several tubes with you. Now, in addition to your worries about your health, I'm charging you £100 per tube. You have no choice but to pay.

You then read in the medical column of your newspaper that this isn't happening just to you; many other people have been suffering from the same problem. In fact, pharmacists have discovered that the ointment doesn't actually cure the sore. All that it does is to take the sore beneath the surface of the skin. It is the ointment that has caused the sore to grow. All you have to do to get rid of the sore is to stop using the ointment. The sore will eventually disappear in due course.

Would you continue to use the ointment?

Would it take willpower not to use the ointment? If you didn't believe the article, there might be a few days of apprehension, but once you realized that the sore was beginning to get better, the need or desire to use the ointment would go.

Would you be miserable? Of course you wouldn't. You had an awful problem, which you thought was insoluble. Now you've found the solution. Even if it took a year for that sore to disappear completely, each day, as it improved, you'd think, 'Isn't it marvellous? I'm not going to die.'

Allen Carr, *Easy Way to Stop Smoking*, 1985

The whole problem is a particularly difficult one because of the well-known *law of temporal succession*. This law, put quite briefly and baldly, states that if an act has two consequences, one rewarding and the other punishing, which would be strictly equal if simultaneous, then the influence of those consequences upon later performances of the act will vary depending upon the order in which they occur. If the punishing consequence comes first and the rewarding one later the difference between the inhibiting and the reinforcing effect will be in favour of the inhibition, but if the rewarding consequence comes first and the punishing one later the difference will be in favour of the reinforcement . . .

If we apply this law to the smoking of cigarettes we can see how very strongly it works against the giving up of smoking. The reward is immediate; the punishing consequences are not only very problematical but they are also in the far distance.

H. J. Eysenck, *Smoking, Health and Personality,* 1965

The philosophical approach

With *all* possession there is made the crystallizing synthesis which Stendhal has described for the one case of love. Each possessed object which raises itself on the foundation of the world, manifests the entire world, just as a beloved woman manifests the sky, the shore, the sea which surrounded her when she appeared. To appropriate this object is then to appropriate the world symbolically. Each one can recognize it by referring to his own experience: for myself, I shall cite a personal example, not to prove the point but to guide the reader in his inquiry.

Some years ago I brought myself to the decision not to smoke any more. The struggle was hard, and in truth, I did not care so much for the *taste* of the tobacco which I was going to lose, as for the *meaning* of the act of smoking. A complete crystallization had been formed. I used to smoke at the theater, in the morning while working, in the evening after dinner, and it seemed to me that in giving up smoking I was going to strip the theater of its interest, the evening meal of its savor, the morning work of its fresh animation. Whatever unexpected happening was going to meet my eye, it seemed to me that it was fundamentally impoverished from the moment that I could not welcome it while smoking. To-be-capable-of-being-met-by-me-smoking: such was the concrete quality which had been spread over everything. It seemed to me that I was going to snatch it away from everything and that in the midst of this universal impoverishment, life was scarcely worth the effort. But to smoke is an appropriative, destructive action. Tobacco is a symbol of 'appropriated' being, since it is destroyed in the rhythm of my breathing, in a mode of 'continuous destruction,' since it passes into me and its change in myself is manifested symbolically by the transformation of the consumed solid into smoke. The connection between the landscape seen while I was smoking and this little crematory sacrifice was such that as we have just seen, the tobacco symbolized the landscape. This means then that the act of destructively appropriating the tobacco was the symbolic equivalent of destructively appropriating the entire world. Across the tobacco which I was smoking was the world which was burning, which was going up in smoke, which was being reabsorbed into vapor so as to reenter into me. In order to maintain my decision not to smoke, I had to realize a sort of decrystallization; that is, without exactly accounting to myself for what I was doing, I reduced the tobacco to being nothing but itself – an herb which burns. I cut its symbolic ties with the world; I persuaded myself that I was not taking anything away from the play at the theater, from the landscape, from the book which I was reading, if I considered them without my pipe; that is, I rebuilt my possession of these objects in modes other than that sacrificial ceremony. As soon as I was persuaded of this, my regret was reduced to a very small matter; I deplored the thought of not perceiving the odor of the smoke, the warmth of the bowl between my fingers and so forth. But suddenly my regret was disarmed and quite bearable.

Jean-Paul Sartre, *Being and Nothingness: An Essay on Phenomenological Ontology*, 1943 (trans. Hazel E. Barnes, 1957)

[In 1977]

I went back to the hospital the next morning. Sartre had had dinner, had watched a little television, and had slept well. They were now carrying out a long X-ray examination – thorax, legs, hands, and so on. They brought him back to his bed and Dr Housset appeared. He spoke forcibly. Sartre could save his legs only by giving up tobacco. If he did not smoke anymore, his state could be much improved and he could be assured of a quiet old age and a normal death. Otherwise his toes would have to be cut off, then his feet, and then his legs. Sartre seemed impressed. Liliane and I took him home without too much difficulty. As for tobacco, he said he wanted to think it over. He saw Melina and Arlette and then the next day Pierre and Michèle. When I arrived late in the afternoon he was walking a little better. But the day after that, in the evening, he told me that his leg hurt every night for about an hour . . .

We spent the evening reading and talking. He had made up his mind to stop smoking the next day, Monday. I said, 'Doesn't it make you sad to think you're smoking your last cigarette?' 'No. To tell you the truth I find them rather disgusting now.' No doubt he associated them with the idea of being cut to pieces little by little. The next day he handed me his cigarettes and lighters to give to Sylvie. And that evening he told me that he was in an astonishingly good mood *because* he had stopped smoking. It was a final renunciation and he never seemed to find it burdensome. He was not affected even when his friends smoked in front of him – indeed, he even encouraged them to do so.

Simone de Beauvoir, *Adieux: A Farewell to Sartre*, 1981 (trans. Patrick O'Brian, 1984)

At the beginning of February 1980 a check-up at the Broussais hospital confirmed [Sartre's] condition was unchanged. He was still enjoying life and still finding it easy to make friends with young girls who were glad to spend time with him. Freedom now meant freedom to forget the restrictions imposed by his deteriorating body. In the same way that he had fought fatigue by swallowing corydrane, he fought back against the doctors' regime and the surveillance of the loyal de Beauvoir. Michelle had been wrong to think he wanted to die but right about his antipathy to discipline. The caring de Beauvoir seemed like a reactionary enemy who could be outwitted by subversive friends willing to smuggle in cigarettes, whisky, vodka, which he hid behind books.

Ronald Hayman, *Writing Against: A Biography of Sartre*, 1986

Don't backslide

Then Pete and his sisters sang Mexican songs, in gay heartbroken tones. And I was asked to read poetry out of a drugstore anthology – which I did – the tequila beginning to take effect – with reckless freedom of expression. The mother and father listened to Browning's 'Youth and Art' with the greatest pleasure, not understanding a single word. It seemed perfectly natural that I should be drinking, and smoking one cigarette after another. (It is an extraordinary psychological fact, which I've tested several times, that an ex-smoker can smoke when drunk without reviving the nicotine addiction.)

Christopher Isherwood, Entry for 22 September 1943 in Katherine Bucknell, editor, *Diaries Volume One 1939–1960*, 1996

Ernest felt now that the turning point of his life had come. He would give up all for Christ – even his tobacco . . .

In one matter only, did he openly backslide. He had, as I said above, locked up his pipes and tobacco, so that he might not be tempted to use them. All day long on the day after Mr Hawke's sermon he let them lie in his portmanteau bravely; but this was not very difficult, as he had for some time given up smoking till after hall. After hall this day he did not smoke till chapel time, and then went to chapel in self-defence. When he returned he determined to look at the matter from a common sense point of view. On this he saw that, provided tobacco did not injure his health – and he really could not see that it did – it stood much on the same footing as tea or coffee.

Tobacco had nowhere been forbidden in the Bible, but then it had not yet been discovered, and had probably only escaped proscription for this reason. We can conceive of St Paul or even our Lord Himself as drinking a cup of tea, but we cannot imagine either of them as smoking a cigarette or a churchwarden. Ernest could not deny this, and admitted that Paul would almost certainly have condemned tobacco in good round terms if he had known of its existence. Was it not then taking rather a mean advantage of the Apostle to stand on his not having actually forbidden it? On the other hand, it was possible that God knew Paul would have forbidden smoking, and had purposely arranged the discovery of tobacco for a period at which Paul should be no longer living. This might seem rather hard on Paul, considering all he had done for Christianity, but it would be made up to him in other ways.

These reflections satisfied Ernest that on the whole he had better smoke, so he sneaked to his portmanteau and brought out his pipes and tobacco again. There should be moderation he felt in all things, even in virtue; so for that night he smoked immoderately.

Samuel Butler, *The Way of All Flesh*, 1903

Again days of trial arrived. The Count seemed possessed by a fever of renunciation. Now had come the turn of tobacco. Oh, unfortunate man! How hard it was to part from tobacco, and from the cigarettes he used to smoke so awkwardly yet with such enjoyment! 'Smoking is harmful,' announced the Count, one morning, 'it is a luxury! Instead of tobacco, barley might be grown to feed the famished.' And his horn cigar-holder was set aside on the shelf, where it lay beside the works of Rousseau, Stendhal, Bernardin de Saint-Pierre, & c.

The Count gained a new, extremely difficult victory over himself. He suffered unendurable torment, positively not knowing what to do with himself. He would pick up a cigarette-end here and there like a schoolboy, to have but a single whiff, or dilating his nostrils he would eagerly inhale the smoke when others smoked in his presence. And after a while, despite his convictions, he again yielded to his inclination, for smoking really soothed his nerves and those who supposed the Count to be an ascetic in the full sense of the word are much mistaken. He has had, and still has, times when he is capable of any amount of self-denial, but with his physique and his senses the Count can never be a Saint.

The Tolstoys' governess, Anna Seuron, quoted in Aylmer Maude, *The Life of Tolstoy: Later Years*, 1910

In Hannibal, when I was about fifteen, I was for a short time a Cadet of Temperance, an organization which probably covered the whole United States during as much as a year – possibly even longer. It consisted in a pledge to refrain, during membership, from the use of tobacco; I mean it consisted partly in that pledge and partly in a red merino sash, but the red merino sash was the main part. The boys joined in order to be privileged to wear it – the pledge part of the matter was of no consequence. It was so small in importance that, contrasted with the sash, it was, in effect, non-existent. The organization was weak and impermanent because there were not enough holidays to support it. We could turn out and march and show the red sashes on May Day with the Sunday schools, and on the Fourth of July with the Sunday schools, the independent fire company, and the militia company. But you can't keep a juvenile moral institution alive on two displays of its sash per year. As a private, I could not have held out beyond one procession, but I was Illustrious Grand Worthy Secretary and Royal Inside Sentinel, and had the privilege of inventing the passwords and of wearing a rosette on my sash. Under these conditions, I was enabled to remain steadfast until I had gathered the glory of two displays – May Day and the Fourth of July. Then I resigned straightway, and straightway left the lodge.

I had not smoked for three full months, and no words can adequately describe the smoke appetite that was consuming me. I had been a smoker from my ninth year – a private one during the first two years, but a public one after that – that is to say, after my father's death. I was smoking, and utterly happy, before I was thirty steps from the lodge door. I do not now know what the brand of the cigar was. It was probably not choice, or the previous smoker would not have thrown it away so soon. But I realized that it was the best cigar that was ever made. The previous smoker would have thought the same if he had been without a smoke for three months. I smoked that stub without shame. I could not do it now without shame, because now I am more refined than I was then. But I would smoke it, just the same. I know myself, and I know the human race, well enough to know that.

Mark Twain, *Autobiography*, 1906

Success

It seems marvellous to me that once I smoked. Old photographs in which I am holding a cigarette have in my eyes the black-and-white glamour of stills from Hollywood films noirs. I smoked a great deal, in fact, beginning at the age of fifteen (or could it have been fourteen?) when, as part of my campaign to become more 'popular,' I bought a pack in Reading, at the railroad station on Seventh Street, and lit my first cigarette as I walked along past the little banistered porches, beneath the buttonwood trees. At the initial puff, the sidewalk lifted as if to strike my forehead, but I fought the dizziness and persevered. The beckoning world of magazines (loaded with cigarette ads) demanded this, not to mention the world of girls. With some determined tutorial work in Stephens' Luncheonette, I learned how to inhale, to double-inhale, to French-inhale, and (just barely) to blow smoke rings. At Harvard, I was up to three packs a day, and my fingertips turned orange. In Oxford, the little stiff cardboard packages of five or ten Churchman's were a novelty, as was, at the back of the slideout part of the package, the lined blank space entitled 'Notes' – conjuring up an empire full of Englishmen coolly taking notes, amid grapeshot and cavalry hoofbeats, on their cigarette boxes. In New York, getting worried, I began to experiment with holders, including that awkwardly long type which employs as a filter an entire other cigarette, replaced when it darkens through and through and drips with tar juice. By the time of the move to Ipswich, my self-glamorization in other respects had proceeded far enough that I almost felt able to do without cigarettes as a prop. Now I have long since, in deference to my emphysema, given up smoking, even the smoking of little cigars that, after I broke the cigarette habit, used to get me through the stress of composition. Also, I have given up salt and coffee in deference to high blood pressure and alcohol in deference to methotrexate. The big-bellied Lutheran God within me looks on scoffingly. '*Hunde, wollt ihr ewig leben?*' Frederick the Great thundered at his battle-shy soldiers – 'Dogs, would you live forever?'

John Updike, *Self-Consciousness: Memoirs*, 1989

Giving Up Smoking

There's not a Shakespeare sonnet
Or a Beethoven quartet
That's easier to like than you
Or harder to forget.

You think that sounds extravagant?
I haven't finished yet –
I like you more than I would like
To have a cigarette.

Wendy Cope, *Making Cocoa for Kingsley Amis*, 1986

Failure

A Farewell to Tobacco*

May the Babylonish curse
Straight confound my stammering verse,
If I can a passage see
In this word-perplexity,

* Lamb sent the poem to William and Dorothy Wordsworth on 28 September 1805 – and in the accompanying letter, wrote: 'I wish you may think this a handsome farewell to my "Friendly Traitress." Tobacco has been my evening comfort and my morning curse for these five years; and you know how difficult it is from refraining to pick one's lips even, when it has become a habit.'

Or a fit expression find,
Or a language to my mind,
(Still the phrase is wide or scant)
To take leave of thee, *great plant*!
Or in any terms relate
Half my love, or half my hate:
For I hate, yet love, thee so,
That, whichever thing I shew,
The plain truth will seem to be
A constrain'd hyperbole,
And the passion to proceed
More from a mistress than a weed . . .

Brother of Bacchus, later born,
The old world was sure forlorn,
Wanting thee, that aidest more
The god's victories than before
All his panthers, and the brawls
Of his piping Bacchanals.
These, as stale, we disallow,
Or judge of *thee* meant; only thou
His true Indian conquest art;
And, for ivy round his dart,
The reformed god now weaves
A finer thyrsus of thy leaves.

Scent to match thy rich perfume
Chemic art did ne'er presume
Through her quaint alembic strain,
None so sov'reign to the brain.
Nature, that did in thee excel,
Fram'd again no second smell.
Roses, violets, but toys
For the smaller sort of boys,
Or for greener damsels meant;
Thou art the only manly scent.

Stinking'st of the stinking kind,
Filth of the mouth and fog of the mind,
Africa, that brags her foyson,

Breeds no such prodigious poison,
Henbane, nightshade, both together,
Hemlock, aconite –

Nay, rather,
Plant divine, of rarest virtue;
Blisters on the tongue would hurt you.
'Twas but in a sort I blam'd thee;
None e'er prosper'd who defam'd thee;
Irony all, and feign'd abuse,
Such as perplext lovers use,
At a need, when, in despair
To paint forth their fairest fair,
Or in part but to express
That exceeding comeliness
Which their fancies doth so strike,
They borrow language of dislike;
And, instead of Dearest Miss,
Jewel, Honey, Sweetheart, Bliss,
And those forms of old admiring,
Call her Cockatrice and Siren,
Basilisk, and all that's evil,
Witch, Hyena, Mermaid, Devil,
Ethiop, Wench, and Blackamoor,
Monkey, Ape, and twenty more;
Friendly Trait'ress, loving Foe, –
Not that she is truly so,
But no other way they know
A contentment to express,
Borders so upon excess,
That they do not rightly wot
Whether it be pain or not.

Or, as men, constrain'd to part
With what's nearest to their heart,
While their sorrow's at the height,
Lose discrimination quite,
And their hasty wrath let fall,
To appease their frantic gall,
On the darling thing whatever,

Whence they feel it death to sever,
Though it be, as they, perforce,
Guiltless of the sad divorce.

For I must (nor let it grieve thee,
Friendliest of plants, that I must) leave thee.
For thy sake, *tobacco*, I
Would do any thing but die,
And but seek to extend my days
Long enough to sing thy praise.
But, as she, who once hath been
A king's consort, is a queen
Ever after, nor will bate
Any tittle of her state,
Though a widow, or divorced,
So I, from thy converse forced,
The old name and style retain,
A right Katherine of Spain;
And a seat, too, 'mongst the joys
Of the blest Tobacco Boys;
Where, though I, by sour physician,
Am debarr'd the full fruition
Of thy favours, I may catch
Some collateral sweets, and snatch
Sidelong odours, that give life
Like glances from a neighbour's wife;
And still live in the by-places
And the suburbs of thy graces;
And in thy borders take delight,
An unconquer'd Canaanite.

Charles Lamb, 1805

... I am going to leave off smoke. In the meantime I am so smoky
with last night's ten pipes that I must leave off ...

Charles Lamb, Letter to William Hazlitt, 19 February 1806

This very night I am going to *leave off tobacco*! Surely there must
be some other world in which this unconquerable purpose shall be
realised.

Charles Lamb, Letter to Thomas Manning, 26 December 1815

I design to give up smoking; but have not fixed upon the equivalent vice. I must have *quid pro quo* . . .

Charles Lamb, Letter to Thomas Hood, postmarked 10 August 1824

[Lost in the wilderness]

We huddled together on our knees in the deep snow, and the horses put their noses together and bowed their patient heads over us; and while the feathery flakes eddied down and turned us into a group of white statuary, we proceeded with the momentous experiment. We broke twigs from a sage-bush and piled them on a little cleared place in the shelter of our bodies. In the course of ten or fifteen minutes all was ready, and then, while conversation ceased and our pulses beat low with anxious suspense, Ollendorff applied his revolver, pulled the trigger, and blew the pile clear out of the country! It was the flattest failure that ever was.

This was distressing, but it paled before a greater horror – the horses were gone! . . .

Nobody said a word for several minutes. It was a solemn sort of silence; even the wind put on a stealthy, sinister quiet, and made no more noise than the falling flakes of snow. Finally a sad-voiced conversation began, and it was soon apparent that in each of our hearts lay the conviction that this was our last night with the living . . .

Poor Ollendorff broke down, and the tears came. He was not alone, for I was crying too, and so was Mr Ballou. Ollendorff got his voice again, and forgave me for things I had done and said. Then he got out his bottle of whisky and said that whether he lived or died he would never touch another drop. He said he had given up all hope of life, and although ill prepared, was ready to submit humbly to his fate; that he wished he could be spared a little longer, not for any selfish reason, but to make a thorough reform in his character, and by devoting himself to helping the poor, nursing the sick, and pleading with the people to guard themselves against the evils of intemperance, make his life a beneficent example to the young, and lay it down at last with the precious reflection that it had not been lived in vain. He ended by saying that his reform should begin at this moment, even here in the presence of death, since no longer time was to be vouchsafed wherein to prosecute it to men's help and benefit – and with that he threw away the bottle of whisky.

Mr Ballou made remarks of similar purport, and began the reform he could not live to continue, by throwing away the ancient pack of cards that had solaced our captivity during the flood and made it bearable. He said he never gambled, but still was satisfied that the meddling with cards in any way was immoral and injurious, and no man could be wholly pure and blemishless without eschewing them. 'And therefore,' continued he, 'in doing this act I already feel more in sympathy with that spiritual saturnalia necessary to entire and obsolete reform.' These rolling syllables touched him as no intelligible eloquence could have done, and the old man sobbed with a mournfulness not unmingled with satisfaction.

My own remarks were of the same tenour as those of my comrades, and I know that the feelings that prompted them were heartfelt and sincere. We were all sincere, and all deeply moved and earnest, for we were in the presence of death and without hope. I threw away my pipe, and in doing it felt that at last I was free of a hated vice, and one that had ridden me like a tyrant all my days. While I yet talked, the thought of the good I might have done in the world and the still greater good I might *now* do, with these new incentives and higher and better aims to guide me if I could only be spared a few years longer, overcame me, and the tears came again. We put our arms about each other's necks and awaited the warning drowsiness that precedes death by freezing.

It came stealing over us presently, and then we bade each other a last farewell. A delicious dreaminess wrought its web about my yielding senses, while the snow-flakes wove a winding-sheet about my conquered body. Oblivion came. The battle of life was done . . .

I do not know how long I was in a state of forgetfulness, but it seemed an age. A vague consciousness grew upon me by degrees, and then came a gathering anguish of pain in my limbs and through all my body. I shuddered. The thought flitted through my brain, 'this is death – this is the hereafter.'

Then came a white upheaval at my side, and a voice said, with bitterness,

'Will some gentleman be so good as to kick me behind?'

It was Ballou – at least, it was a towzled snow image in a sitting posture, with Ballou's voice.

I rose up, and there in the grey dawn, not fifteen steps from us, were the frame buildings of a stage station, and under a shed stood our still saddled and bridled horses! . . .

I have scarcely exaggerated a detail of this curious and absurd adventure. It occurred almost exactly as I have stated it. We actually went into camp in a snowdrift in a desert, at midnight in a storm, forlorn and hopeless, within fifteen steps of a comfortable inn.

For two hours we sat apart in the station and ruminated in disgust. The mystery was gone now, and it was plain enough why the horses had deserted us. Without a doubt they were under that shed a quarter of a minute after they had left us, and they must have overheard and enjoyed all our confessions and lamentations.

After breakfast we felt better, and the zest of life soon came back. The world looked bright again, and existence was as dear to us as ever. Presently an uneasiness came over me – grew upon me – assailed me without ceasing. Alas, my regeneration was not complete – I wanted to smoke! I resisted with all my strength, but the flesh was weak. I wandered away alone and wrestled with myself an hour. I recalled my promises of reform and preached to myself persuasively, upbraidingly, exhaustively. But it was all vain: I shortly found myself sneaking among the snowdrifts hunting for my pipe. I discovered it after a considerable search, and crept away to hide myself and enjoy it. I remained behind the barn a good while, asking myself how I would feel if my braver, stronger, truer comrades should catch me in my degradation. At last I lit the pipe, and no human being can feel meaner and baser than I did then. I was ashamed of being in my own pitiful company. Still dreading discovery, I felt that perhaps the further side of the barn would be somewhat safer, and so I turned the corner. As I turned the one corner, smoking, Ollendorff turned the other with his bottle to his lips, and between us sat unconscious Ballou deep in a game of 'solitaire' with the old greasy cards!

Absurdity could go no further. We shook hands and agreed to say no more about 'reform' and 'examples to the rising generation.'

Mark Twain, *Roughing It*, 1872

[Kenneth Williams's attempts to stop smoking]

16 March 1962 With Henri Davies to Hammersmith where we got Herbal Cigarettes. I will go on to these for a bit, but I will never go back to tobacco. This I do know. I'm finished with Nicotine.

15 January 1964 This morning I suddenly took stock of myself. From here on, I thought, start making some sort of gesture to God. Like in Lent. Give up things. Things you really like. Start with fags, then drink. On every page hereafter, I will record this progress. I had to rush off to Berman's for the fitting at 3 o'c. for *Carry On Spying*. Came out of that at 4 o'c. and walked thro' to Regent St to get the 59 bus home but a revolting pouff sat next to me so I got off at Portman Sq. and walked home.

19 January 1964 My 5th day of no smoking. In future I shall write this as NS. After having a bath today, I looked in the mirror & thought 'How lovely I am ... how very lovely ...'

30 January 1964 I had 4. So bang goes my word about not smoking. I have to accept this weakness I suppose: and ask the forgiveness for being such an abject creature.

8 April 1971 I had smoked 3 cigarettes today by 2 o'c. and then I decided to kick it. Did not smoke for the rest of the day. By the end of the evening my breathing was better. I will give up drink as well for certainly I've never really enjoyed it.

19 April 1971 Pinewood – everyone expressing their derision at my smoking again! Gerald said the next one is *Carry On Matron* – it seems the hospital jokes are unending. Felt quite buoyant on the set today. I notice that whenever I'm volatile etc., Sid James gets really irritated!! He doesn't like it when he's alongside someone who is getting the attention in an amusing way: as an entertainer himself he's talentless & resents it in others – but as a man he is kind and generous, albeit a philistine.

17 June 1981 The plane arrived at Sydney about 6 o'c. in the morning and I got a taxi to the Town House Hotel. I got postcards to send to the chums. Had the fags! So my resolution to give up smoking has gone bust! The surprise has been the weather! Sunny and bright ... not unlike April or May in England.

25 March 1988 Up at 7 o'c. after lousy night. Went for papers. After I'd had coffee I realised I can't have anything to eat or drink till tomorrow! What a life! Now I have to drear about starving till I go to the Cromwell Hospital for these tests. Got cab at 1.20. Arrived on time. Waited in bedroom in the surgical gown for Sonic Scan scheduled for 2.30. Eventually I was done at 3.50!! 'So sorry, we thought you were coming as an out-patient & didn't know you were *in* the hospital.' One forgets the world is full of idiots. Murray-Lyon did the gastroscopy & said there was a huge ulcer in the same place. Then I was wheeled back to the room. I asked him 'Is there anything which exacerbates this condition' and he said 'Smoking' adding that there was *proof* that ulcers were the result of smoking. Had a meal at about 8 o'c. and everything tasted marvellous. Twinge of regret when it came to the coffee and one realised . . . no fags . . . shame. The habit of a lifetime taken away from one.

The Kenneth Williams Diaries, ed. Russell Davies, 1993

Some disadvantages of giving up

I own many books full of my annotations, proving that once I read them, though I have no memory of it. In writing a sentence some twenty lines above, I had to get up and go ask my wife what the five senses were; I could think of only four. 'Smell,' she said, when I had named my four. She was in the bathtub, up to her neck in bubbles, and though the bathroom smelled nicely of vitamin-enhanced soap I was not sorry I had suppressed 'smell,' since of the five senses it delivers most unpleasantness to us, and least well illustrated the point I was trying to make. When I stopped smoking, a whole unwelcome new world of odors came upon me, of dead rats in the wall and what people had eaten for lunch hours before. When I get out of bed in the morning, my own smell surprises me: stale flesh, warmed over. My body's ugly obstinacy in keeping on living strikes me as admirable, like an ungenial but impressive moral position; it makes me, still half-asleep, stop and think.

John Updike, *Self-Consciousness: Memoirs*, 1989

[A doctor writes . . .]

Since returning to Toronto I had acquired another and in some respects more intimate friend than Brocky. He was Hugh McWearie, the editor of the religious stuff in the *Colonial Advocate*. I met him because a colleague asked me to take a look at him and give an opinion about his wheezes, which were troublesome. Of course he smoked too much and his foul old pipes made him wheeze. But was I to launch an evangelical campaign upon him, to make him ashamed of his habit, and thereby to provide him with somewhat better health but a vastly deprived life? This was the sort of problem that was now uppermost in my thoughts about my profession. Was I an apostle of health, and if so what was health? If it was bodily well-being, that was a reasonable if not a simple answer. But if it included mental well-being, or spiritual well-being, the whole thing became greatly complicated. There are people who must have their poisons, or they are not themselves. So it was with Hugh, with his whisky and his disgusting pipes.

As he was a man of broad intelligence, I explained the problem to him. I told him that if he gave up tobacco, he might expect to live longer, but would he live better? I also told him that if he did not give up tobacco he might live a long life anyhow. Lots of puffers do. I had no plan of salvation to offer him. In the end he decided on his own regime; he stopped smoking from morning till night, and confined himself to eight large pipes a day. He bought two new pipes and threw away his stinkers. He stopped getting through most of a bottle of whisky every day, and cut out entirely his habit of having a hearty snort in bed before rising. But I forbade nothing . . .

I say (and of late years I am astonished that the World Health Organization agrees with me) that health is when nothing hurts very much; but the popular idea is of health as a norm to which we must all seek to conform. Not to be healthy, not to be in 'top form' is one of the few sins that modern society is willing to recognize and condemn. But are there not as many healths as there are bodies? If whatever we are demands certain physical frailties, why struggle to get rid of them? And what have the exemplars of health, our cherished and greatly rewarded athletes, ever done for mankind? They are entertainers, of a lesser sort. If McWearie's contribution to the public good, and his own deepest satisfaction, demands booze and stink, why try to turn him into a discontented ghost of himself, and kill him with what is popularly supposed to be kindness.

Robertson Davies, *The Cunning Man*, 1994

I do not want a cigarette.

To say this is terrifying. It's tantamount to saying: 'I do not want.'

To not-want: this is to be dead, or if not dead, then boring. Dead boring.

Yet sometimes I want, passionately, to not-want. Too much wanting kills. At times like this I want to forget.

I want a smoke.

Lesley Stern, *The Smoking Book*, 1999

It is the premise of this book that cigarettes, though harmful to health, are a great and beautiful civilizing tool and one of America's proudest contributions to the world. Seen in this light, the act of giving up cigarettes should perhaps be approached not only as an affirmation of life but, because life is not merely existing, as an occasion for mourning. Stopping smoking, one must lament the loss to one's life of something – or someone! – immensely, intensely beautiful, must grieve for the passing of a star.

Richard Klein, *Cigarettes Are Sublime*, 1993

CHAPTER XXXIII:
WHEN MY WIFE IS ASLEEP AND ALL THE HOUSE IS STILL

Perhaps the heading of this chapter will deceive some readers into thinking that I smoke nowadays in camera. It is, I know, a common jest among smokers that such a promise as mine is seldom kept . . . But never shall it be said of me with truth that I have broken my word. I smoke no more, and, indeed, though the scenes of my bachelorhood frequently rise before me in dreams . . . I am glad, when I wake up, that they are only dreams. Those selfish days are done, and I see that though they were happy days, the happiness was a mistake. As for the struggle that is supposed to take place between a man and tobacco after he sees smoking in its true colours, I never experienced it . . .

But when my wife is asleep and all the house is still, I listen to the man through the wall. At such times I have my briar in my mouth, but there is no harm in that, for it is empty. I did not like to give away my briar, knowing no one who understood it, and I always carry it about with me now to remind me of my dark past. When the man through the wall lights up I put my cold pipe in my mouth and we have a quiet hour together.

I have never to my knowledge seen the man through the wall, for his door is round the corner, and, besides, I have no interest in him until half-past eleven p.m. We begin then. I know him chiefly by his pipes, and them I know by his taps on the wall as he knocks the ashes out of them . . .

. . . Though I am compelled to say that I do not consider his character very lovable he has his good points, and I like his attachment to his briar. He scrapes it, on the whole, a little roughly, but that is because he is so anxious to light up again, and I discovered long ago that he has signed an agreement with his wife to go to bed at half-past twelve . . . Therefore when his last tap says good-night to me I take my cold briar out of my mouth, tap it on the mantelpiece, smile sadly, and so to bed.

J. M. Barrie, *My Lady Nicotine*, 1890

Sir, – Dr Johnston has given one account of the effects of giving up smoking. Let me, from a much shorter experience of abstinence, give another.

For thirty years I smoked heavily. The threat of lung carcinoma affected me not at all; I would willingly risk that possibility to continue to have the pleasure and comfort of smoking. But about six weeks ago I decided, for financial reasons, to stop smoking.

Instead of a 'sustained uplift of spirits and of general interest' I have been morose, irritable, and unable to concentrate. Time hangs heavily on my hands, I have lost interest in my work and my hobbies, and I have nothing to look forward to. I have acquired an enormous appetite which is impossible to satisfy, and a great increase in flatulence and flatus. I have become lazy and depressed, and only my sexual potency, of which I had no complaints, remains unaffected.

Until I read your contributor's article I was well content not to touch my many comforting pipes. Since reading it my resolve has weakened, and I can see no reasonable future without tobacco.

Temporary Non-smoker

Letter in *The Lancet*, 13 September 1952

It was supposed to change everything, like when you give up smoking and everyone has gone on about it for so long that you think When I Give Up Everything Will Be Different, and actually everything is the same, your job is still shit and you are still full of fear and worry and longing, you just . . . don't smoke. Or when you are sixteen and everyone has talked about fucking for so long, you think when you first actually fuck it will be like dying and rising again as A MAN.

That's what I felt like. I had done it, I had just kicked the door down and all I found inside was pictures of me BEFORE and AFTER, but they were the same.

James Hawes, *A White Merc with Fins*, 1996

The final farewell

My Last Cigar

'TWAS off the blue Canary isles,
　　A glorious summer day,
I sat upon the quarter-deck
　　And whiffed my cares away;
And as the volumed smoke arose
　　Like incense in the air,
I breath'd a sigh to think, in sooth,
　　It was my last cigar.

I leaned upon the quarter-rail
　　And looked down in the sea,
E'en there the purple wreath of smoke
　　Was curling gracefully.
Oh! what had I at such a time
　　To do with wasting care,
Alas! the trembling tear proclaimed
　　It was my last cigar.

I watched the ashes as it came
　　Fast drawing toward the end,
I watched it as a friend would watch
　　Beside a dying friend;
But still the flame crept slowly on,
　　It vanished into air,
I threw it from me, spare the tale,
　　It was my last cigar.

I've seen the land of all I love
　　Fade in the distant dim,
I've watched above the blighted heart

Where once proud hope hath been.
But I've never known a sorrow
That could with that compare,
When, off the blue Canaries,
I smoked my last cigar.

Joseph Warren Fabens, in William G.
Hutchinson, editor, *Lyra Nicotiana: Poems
and Verses Concerning Tobacco*, 1898

When Stubb had departed, Ahab stood for a while leaning over the bulwarks; and then, as had been usual with him of late, calling a sailor of the watch, he sent him below for his ivory stool, and also his pipe. Lighting the pipe at the binnacle lamp and planting the stool on the weather side of the deck, he sat and smoked.

In old Norse times, the thrones of the sea-loving Danish kings were fabricated, saith tradition, of the tusks of the narwhale. How could one look at Ahab then, seated on the tripod of bones, without bethinking him of the royalty symbolized? For a Khan of the plank, and a king of the sea, and a great lord of Leviathans was Ahab.

Some moments passed, during which the thick vapor came from his mouth in quick and constant puffs, which blew back again into his face. 'How now,' he soliloquized at last withdrawing the tube, 'this smoking no longer soothes. Oh my pipe! hard must it go with me if thy charm be gone! Here have I been unconsciously toiling, not pleasuring, – aye, and ignorantly smoking to windward all the while; to windward, and with such nervous whiffs, as if, like the dying whale, my final jets were the strongest and fullest of trouble. What business have I with this pipe? This thing that is meant for sereneness, to send up mild white vapors among mild white hairs, not among torn iron-grey locks like mine. I'll smoke no more – '

He tossed the still lighted pipe into the sea. The fire hissed in the waves; the same instant the ship shot by the bubble the sinking pipe made. With slouched hat, Ahab lurchingly paced the planks.

Herman Melville, *Moby-Dick, or The Whale*, 1851

INT: DAY. THE BROOKLYN CIGAR CO.

BOB, *a regular customer, has just come in and is standing at the counter with* AUGGIE. JIMMY *is working off to the side.*

AUGGIE: A pack of Luckies?

BOB: You know what? No. I'll tell you what . . . I've got one cigarette left . . . and I've decided, you know, I was going to come here, I'm going to quit. But I wanted to smoke this with you. So I thought, 'last cigarette,' smoke it with Auggie . . .

AUGGIE: You're kidding. I'm touched.

BOB: Hey Jimmy, will you take a picture of me and Auggie with my last cigarette? *(Hands* JIMMY *a camera)* You just push this. *(To* AUGGIE*)* This is it, man.

AUGGIE: All right, where do you want me to stand?

BOB: I don't know. You want to come over here?

AUGGIE: Bob, you know . . .

BOB: The last cigarette. With Auggie.

AUGGIE: I'm touched that you would want to smoke your last cigarette with me.

BOB: Hey, man, twelve years I've been coming in here . . . Luckies.

Dissolve. BOB *and* AUGGIE *pose for the camera.*

BOB: Wait, Jimmy. Your finger's in front there. All right. Thanks.

JIMMY *takes the photo.*

AUGGIE: You got it, Jimmy.

BOB *and* AUGGIE *sit down.*

BOB: So that's it. One more cigarette. *(Dissolve)* I remember my first cigarette, man. These friends of mine, they stole cigarettes from this store, Bueler's Pharmacy. I still remember. It's in like a suburb of Akron, Ohio, where I grew up. So we walked home along the railroad tracks . . . opened the pack . . . I still remember . . . it was like a pack of Newports. We smelled them first . . . you know that menthol . . . smelled like candy or something. Then we lit them up . . . we started inhaling . . . coughing. Couples of minutes later, we're sick, nauseous . . . dizzy. But we felt so cool. Like, real bad-ass ten-year-old kids . . . smoking. *(Dissolve)* But sex and cigarettes, you've got to admit . . . that's one thing I'm really going to miss . . .

AUGGIE: Sex?

BOB: Well . . .

AUGGIE: You're giving up sex also?

BOB: No.

AUGGIE: Because you can't smoke afterwards?

BOB: Maybe. You know, I've never had a girlfriend who didn't smoke. Maybe that means if I quit I'll never have sex again. *(Dissolve)* But

having a cigarette after sex . . . that's like . . . a cigarette never tasted
like that. You know, share a cigarette with your lover . . .
AUGGIE: That's bliss.
BOB: That's what I'm going to miss . . . also with coffee. Coffee and
cigarettes, you know? That's like 'breakfast of champions.'
'Blue in the Face' in *Smoke and Blue in the Face: Two Films by Paul Auster*, 1995

And inevitably . . .

To cease smoking is the easiest thing I ever did; I ought to know
because I've done it a thousand times.*
Mark Twain, in Bruce Bohle, editor, *The Home Book of American Quotations*, 1967

If you resolve to give up smoking, drinking and loving, you don't live
longer; it just seems longer.
Clement Freud quoting 'a third-rate comedian in Sloane Square' in *The Observer*, 27
December 1964

* Interestingly enough, this may not be true – see the last entry in Chapter Eleven.

CHAPTER TWENTY

A Final Mixed Bag

[Literature's most famous hangover? Jim Dixon wakes up in the
guest-room at the house of his boss, Professor Welch]

Dixon was alive again. Consciousness was upon him before he could
get out of the way; not for him the slow, gracious wandering from the
halls of sleep, but a summary, forcible ejection. He lay sprawled, too
wicked to move, spewed up like a broken spider-crab on the tarry
shingle of the morning. The light did him harm, but not as much as
looking at things did; he resolved, having done it once, never to move
his eyeballs again. A dusty thudding in his head made the scene before
him beat like a pulse. His mouth had been used as a latrine by some
small creature of the night, and then as its mausoleum. During the
night, too, he'd somehow been on a cross-country run and then been
expertly beaten up by secret police. He felt bad.

He reached out for and put on his glasses. At once he saw that
something was wrong with the bedclothes immediately before his face.
Endangering his chance of survival, he sat up a little, and what met
his bursting eyes roused to a frenzy the timpanist in his head. A large,
irregular area of the turned-back part of the sheet was missing; a
smaller but still considerable area of the turned-back part of the
blanket was missing; an area about the size of the palm of his hand
in the main part of the top blanket was missing. Through the three
holes, which, appropriately enough, had black borders, he could see
a dark brown mark on the second blanket. He ran a finger round a
bit of the hole in the sheet, and when he looked at his finger it bore
a dark-grey stain. That meant ash; ash meant burning; burning must
mean cigarettes. Had this cigarette burnt itself out on the blanket? If
not, where was it now? Nowhere on the bed; nor in it. He leaned
over the side, gritting his teeth; a sunken brown channel, ending in a
fragment of discoloured paper, lay across a light patch in the pattern
of a valuable-looking rug. This made him feel very unhappy, a feeling
sensibly increased when he looked at the bedside table. This was

marked by two black, charred grooves, greyish and shiny in parts, lying at right angles and stopping well short of the ashtray, which held a single used match. On the table were two unused matches; the remainder lay with the empty cigarette packet on the floor. The bakelite mug was nowhere to be seen.

Had he done all this himself? Or had a wayfarer, a burglar, camped out in his room? Or was he the victim of some Horla fond of tobacco? He thought that on the whole he must have done it himself, and wished he hadn't. Surely this would mean the loss of his job, especially if he failed to go to Mrs Welch and confess what he'd done, and he knew already that he wouldn't be able to do that. There was no excuse which didn't consist of the inexcusable: an incendiary was no more pardonable when revealed as a drunkard as well – so much of a drunkard, moreover, that obligations to hosts and fellow-guests and the counter-attraction of a chamber-concert were as nothing compared with the lure of the drink. The only hope was that Welch wouldn't notice what his wife would presumably tell him about the burning of the bedclothes. But Welch had been known to notice things, the attack on his pupil's book in that essay, for example. But that had really been an attack on Welch himself; he couldn't much care what happened to sheets and blankets which he wasn't actually using at the time. Dixon remembered thinking on an earlier occasion that to yaw drunkenly round the Common Room in Welch's presence screeching obscenities, punching out the window-panes, fouling the periodicals, would escape Welch's notice altogether, provided his own person remained inviolate. The memory in turn reminded him of a sentence in a book of Alfred Beesley's he'd once glanced at: 'A stimulus cannot be received by the mind unless it serves some need of the organism.' He began laughing, an action he soon modified to a wince.

Kingsley Amis, *Lucky Jim*, 1954

What this country really needs is a really good five-cent cigar.*

US Vice-President, Thomas R. Marshall, quoted in *The New York Tribune*, 4 January 1920

Four months after the Bay of Pigs, the President called me into his office at five o'clock in the afternoon and he said, 'Here, I need help.'

* 'Our country has plenty of good five-cent cigars, but the trouble is they charge fifteen cents for them.' – Will Rogers (1879–1935)

And I said, 'Well, what is it?' He said, 'I need some Cuban cigars.' I said, 'How many do you need?' He said, 'A thousand.' 'Oooh,' I said, 'and when do you need them?' He said, 'By tomorrow morning.' I said, 'That's a pretty tough assignment, but I'll do my job.' . . .

I got to the White House at eight o'clock the next morning. 'How did you do?' [he said]. I said, 'I did great. I got twelve hundred.' 'Oh, that is so good,' [he said] and he opened up his drawer, pulled out a paper and signed it – and it was the embargo against Cuba.

Pierre Salinger, John F. Kennedy's former press secretary, speaking on *Cigars: Out of the Humidor* (BBC2 *Arena*), 1997

Don't think of it as smoking illegal contraband; more like we're burning their fields.

Kinky Friedman presenting President Clinton with a Cuban cigar at a White House dinner party – in the press release to *Cigars: Out of the Humidor* (BBC2 *Arena*), 1997

By all odds the most interesting feature of the cigar circuit to the average tourist is the spectacle of the paid reader who entertains the workers by reading aloud to them by means of his own wonderful 'bellows'. He reads them three hours a day and he 'had better be good', for the workers themselves pay him . . . In the rooms where men predominate the reader gives surprisingly solid fare including news bulletins . . . and even the classics of Spain and Cuba, not omitting *poetry*, a thing which would be unimaginable in an American factory but is entirely natural in Cuba. The girl workers, especially the strippers (who strip not themselves but the tobacco leaves – of their undesired central stems) prefer romantic novels, usually of the stickiest sort.

Sydney Clark, *All the Best in Cuba*, 1956

Oleg greeted this news with disconcerting equanimity. He stirred his tea slowly, gazing thoughtfully into the cup. He sighed. His sausagey fingers were deeply stained by nicotine; one does not see that kind of stain any more, even on the fingers of the heaviest smokers – I wonder why?

John Banville, *The Untouchable*, 1997

I toyed with my cigarette case – what would I do without my props? – and selected another cigarette and tapped it on the lid. No one taps cigarettes like that any more; why did we do it, anyway?

John Banville, *The Untouchable*, 1997

Beside the paperseller was a cigarette-machine, which gave ten cigarettes, for sixpence and twenty for a shilling (but with the twenty you
got a halfpenny back under the cellophane): one of my fantasies was
to unlock it and rifle the packets for cigarette cards. I sometimes think
the slight scholarly stoop in my bearing today was acquired by looking
for cigarette cards in Coventry gutters. There seemed to be a 'Famous
Cricketers' series every summer then: Woolley, A. W. Carr, R. E. S.
Wyatt (who went to my school), Kenneth Farnes, Freeman, Ames,
Duckworth, Chapman, Hammond, all on green fields against cloudless
blue skies; and then the Australians, the bland Woodfull in his blue
Victorian cap, burly Ponsford, swarthy Wall, and Bradman, with his
green Australian cap and crisp white shirt-collar, enclosed in a legend
that grew bigger daily, like a gigantic indestructible crystal.

Philip Larkin, *Not the Place's Fault*, 1959

An echo of the papal prohibitions was heard, some years later, during
the elaborate, formal proceedings associated with the proposed canon-
ization of Father Joseph Desa of Cupertino. The devout father was a
mystic monk and of the Order of St. Francis. The proceedings, begun
in 1686, instituted a careful examination into the life and habits of
the candidate. During the various assemblies of ecclesiastical courts the
'devil's advocate' advised the sitting cardinals that Father Joseph had
been an ardent snuffer. This was, admittedly, a 'trivial objection,' but
the auditors were reminded that several popes had intervened to
restrain the habit and it was clear that snuffing was a sensual and
pleasurable exercise.

During the series of discussions the defending advocates conceded
that the devout priest had been a snuffer. But, on the testimony of his
confessor and other contemporaries, it was shown that Father Joseph
had employed snuff only for pious reasons and out of humility. He had
himself reported that snuff served to keep him alert for prayers and
other holy duties and it restrained carnal desires. Further, he used
scented snuff out of modesty. There was a divine odor peculiar to the
cell he occupied and this Father Joseph sought to conceal. He wished
not to be thought sacrosanct because of the supernatural fragrance,
undoubtedly from the presence of angels, which emanated from his
body. Further, sinners who visited him left such a nauseating stench
in his holy nostrils that the worthy father found it advisable to repel
that odor of impurity through the use of snuff. These arguments, *inter*

alia, served to convince the councils that this Servant of God was sufficiently possessed of the theological and cardinal virtues and was of heroic temperance. He was beatified during the papacy of Benedict XIV, 1753, and canonized by Clement XIII in 1767.

Jerome E. Brooks, *The Mighty Leaf: Tobacco through the Centuries*, 1953

At that moment he put another cigarette in his mouth (his ninth of the evening – I was counting) and discovered he'd finished his matches.

'Give us a Dutch fuck, old chum,' he said.

The expression was new to me, and probably offensive, so I didn't reply. Oliver leaned towards me, reached out and took the cigarette I was smoking from my hand. He knocked off some ash, blew on the end until it glowed red, then lit his cigarette from mine. There was something repulsive in the way he did it.

'That's a Dutch fuck, old chum.' And he gave me a horrible, leering smile.

Julian Barnes, *Talking It Over*, 1991

Next there was Leslie's trick. Between the ninth green and the tenth tee, surrounded by newly planted silver birches, was a little wooden hut like a rustic bird-box. Here, if the wind was in the right direction, Uncle Leslie would sometimes do his trick. From the breast pocket of his tweed jacket with the leather elbows he would take a cigarette, lay it on his knee, pass his hands over it like a magician, put it in his mouth, give Jeanie a slow wink, and strike a match. She would sit beside him trying to hold her breath, trying not to be a shufflebottom. Huffers and puffers spoiled tricks, Uncle Leslie had said, and so did shufflebottoms.

After a minute or two she would ease her glance sideways, taking care not to move suddenly. The cigarette had an inch of ash on it, and Uncle Leslie was taking another puff. At the next glance, his head was tipped slightly back, and half the cigarette consisted of ash. From this point on, Uncle Leslie wouldn't look at her; instead, he would concentrate very carefully, slowly leaning back a little more with each puff he took. Finally, his head would be at right-angles to his spine, with the cigarette, now pure ash apart from the last half-inch where Leslie was holding it, rising vertically towards the roof of the giant bird-box. The trick had worked.

And later . . .

'When we went down the Old Green Heaven, you used to do your cigarette trick.'

'Which one was that?'

'You used to smoke a whole cigarette without any of the ash dropping off. You used to bend your head back slowly until all the ash balanced on top of itself.'

'Did I do that?' Leslie smiled. At least he had some knowledge, some secrets left. Mostly, the only thing people wanted to find out from those in his position was what it was like to die. 'And you want to know the trick?'

'Yes please.'

'The trick is, you put a needle down the middle of the fag. All that business with bending your head back is just to make it look more real. Same reason you don't do it in a breeze, or outdoors if you can help it, and you get everyone to hold their breath. Make them feel they could wreck it if they don't behave. Always helps, that. You could probably smoke it pointing downwards in a gale and the ash wouldn't drop off. Not that I've tried. But it's hardly the best fag you'll smoke. You keep thinking it tastes of metal.'*

Julian Barnes, *Staring at the Sun*, 1986

Jeanne Calment, the world's oldest person, died in Arles in the south of France yesterday, at the fabulous age of 122 years, five months and two weeks.

Mme Calment, who saw the Eiffel Tower under construction and came into the world ten years after the assassination of Abraham Lincoln, died at the nursing home where she has spent the past 12 years.

Several rivals have claimed to be as old or even older than Mme Calment, but only she had a birth certificate, dated February 21, 1876, to prove it.

Blind, almost deaf and increasingly frail, Mme Calment claimed that humour and an abundance of good olive oil were the principal reasons for her survival. Her consumption of alcohol and cigarettes, which she continued until her final decade, gave heart to millions of

* Clarence Darrow, the nineteenth-century American lawyer, used to employ this trick with his cigar when his opponent was talking to the jury

French men and women. Scientists said Mme Calment's age was largely due to genetic factors, pointing out that her ancestors all had histories of longevity.

The Times, 5 August 1997

'Oh, hi. I'm Troy McClure. You might remember me from such self-help videos as *Smoke Yourself Thin* and *Get Confident, Stupid*. Well, now I'm here to tell you about the only real path to mental health. That's right, it's the . . . Brad Goodman . . . something or other.'

'Bart's Inner Child' (episode 1F05, written by George Meyer) in Ray Richmond and Antonia Coffman, editors, *The Simpsons: A Complete Guide to Our Favourite Family*, 1997 (created by Matt Groening)

Her robe was of sea-green silk, with an iris pattern. Snared in the low-cut corsage were beautiful breasts, that seemed as though they longed to burst forth – a flow of imprisoned beauty. Clasped around each of the nude, dark arms was a golden snake, with glittering emerald eyes. Around the throat of darkest cream were two rows of pearls – pearls that had meant the loss of many lives.

'If you remember me it is because we have met in the land of dreams, or in some land of the mind, where it seems that dreams come true. I am Callisto, daughter of Lamia. During eighteen hundred years my tomb has had peace. It is in the flowerful fields and woods of Daphne, near to the hills where were the voluptuous dwelling-places of Antioch. But in these days even the tombs have no abiding home. They took me to Paris, and my shadow or spirit followed. For a long time I slept in the icy caves of the Louvre. I should have been there for ever and ever if it had not been for a great and grand pagan, a really holy man, Louis Ménard. He is the only living man in all this land who knows to-day the signs and symbols of the ancient divinities. Before my tomb he solemnly pronounced the words that of old gave a nightly and transitory life to the unhappy dead! Therefore behold me. For seven hours each night I may go through your miserable city . . .'

'Oh, child of the older world,' I cried, 'how you must see the change the world sorrows under!'

'Yes, and yet no. I find the dwellings dark, the dresses ugly, the sky sorrowful. How oddly you dress for such a climate. I find that life in general is more stupid, and that human beings look much less happy than in the older and more golden days. But if there is one thing that greatly stupefies me, it is to see that you have still so many of the things that I knew of old. What . . . in eighteen hundred years have you all made nothing more, nothing new? Is that so, really and truly? What I have seen in the houses, the open air, the streets, is that all? Have you not succeeded in finding a new thing? If not, what misery, my friend!'

My attitude of astonishment was my sole reply.

She smiled, the lovely red lips parting over her mother-of-pearl teeth most enchantingly. Then she murmured in explanation –

'See how I am dressed. This was my burial attire. Regard it. In my first lifetime one dressed in wool and silk. In returning to the earth I thought that such things would have passed away even from the memory of man. I imagined that after so many years that the human race would have discovered fabrics to dress in more wonderful than a tissue of sun and silk, more pleasurable to touch than the exquisite tender skin of young virgins, of rose-leaves, of downy peaches. But you still dress or clothe yourselves in thread, in wool, in the silk we all had of old. Then look at my shoes of olive morocco, worked with gold like the binding of a rare book. Have you as lovely things for the feet in these days? And so with the gems and jewels of these days. I knew them all, then.'

. . . 'Callisto,' at last I said, 'you give these things too great an importance. A girl is never so beautiful as when she is made as the gods made her.'

She gazed at me, then said very slowly, 'Are you sure now that women themselves, their form, have not changed since my early days of life?'

To my utter amazement she followed her last words by slipping off her jewels and robes. She had the grandeur of a goddess from throat to feet. She curved into a long, deep, easy chair, and said, 'Why have you people of to-day not perfected the woman as you have perfected flowers?' She continued in a soft, dreamy voice, 'Oh, days of the youth of the world, days of the first coming of pleasure! . . . During the nineteen hundred years of my sleep in the grave what new joy have you all discovered? What new pleasure have you found? Invite me to share it with you . . .'

'We need more time, Callisto,' I pleaded.

She smiled in derision. 'Your art and thought have both borrowed from us – parasites of our dead bodies. Descartes and Kant borrowed from our Parmenides, Euclid, Archimedes, Aristotle, Democritus, Heraclitus . . . you have discovered nothing that they had not dreamt. You have discovered nothing, not even America. Aristotle said the earth was round, and indicated the path that Columbus finally took. But, oh! if only you had discovered *one* new pleasure; only one.'

I sighed. I could not combat her arguments any more than I could resist her beauty. Instead, I simply said, 'Will you take a cigarette? Doubtless Aristotle taught you that – '

'No,' Callisto answered; 'but do you offer me that as a new pleasure?'

She consented to take one, and I taught her the best method of getting joy from those tubes of white and gold. There followed a long silence. She held in her hand my packet of cigarettes, and seemed to be deep in the enjoyment of an emotion she would not share. Another cigarette was lit for her, and slowly smoked.

Callisto, at last, had found a new pleasure!

Pierre Louÿs, *Une Nouvelle Volupté*, 1896 (trans. G. F. Monkshood, 1908)

Acknowledgements

I can now see for the first time why people write those hideously gushing acknowledgements. But, for the sake of any readers who've just eaten, I'll try and restrain myself. And so . . . my heartfelt thanks to the following for their help with the book in various ways:

James Hawks, Terry Eccles, Ingrid Keith, Michael Shelden, Tony Quinn, Tim Rostron, Philippa Wright, David Twiston Davies, Robert Gray, Peter Straus, Caspar Llewellyn Smith, John Coldstream, Marsha Dunstan, Kate and Ted Walton, Ursula Doyle, Derek Johns, Annabelle Whitestone, Jordan Goodman, Martin Cropper, Judith Rice, Julian Loose, Camilla Harford, Joanna Mackle, Polly Clark, Nicola Winter and Carrie O'Grady. Above all, thanks to Helen Jones for practical help way beyond the call of duty – although re-reading Chandler must have been fun – and for putting up with hearing me tell the same fascinating and/or hilarious smoking anecdotes on every social occasion.

Finally, serious apologies to anyone who helped, but whom I've forgotten to mention. (It's been a long time since I started this.)

J.W.

The editor and publishers gratefully acknowledge permission to reprint copyright material in this book as follows:

FLEUR ADCOCK: from *Poems 1960–2000*, published by Bloodaxe Books, 2000, reprinted by permission of the publisher. KINGSLEY AMIS: from *Memoirs*, published by Hutchinson, 1991, reprinted by permission of the publisher; from *Lucky Jim*, published by Victor Gollancz, reprinted by permission of the publisher. MARTIN AMIS: from *London Fields*, published by Jonathan Cape, 1989, reprinted by permission of the publisher; from *The Information*, published by HarperCollins, 1995, reprinted by permission of the publisher. JOHN BANVILLE: from *The Untouchable*, published by Picador, 1997, reprinted by permission of the publisher. JULIAN BARNES: from *Staring at the Sun*, published by Jonathan Cape, 1986, and from *Talking it Over*, published by Jonathan Cape, reproduced by permission of the publisher. RICHARD BEARD: from *X20*, published by Flamingo, 1996, reprinted by permission of HarperCollins Ltd. BRENDAN BEHAN: from *The Borstal Boy*, published by Hutchinson, 1957, reprinted by permission of the publisher.

ACKNOWLEDGEMENTS

LOUIS DE BERNIÈRES: from *Captain Corelli's Mandolin*, reprinted by per-mission of Secker & Warburg. ALAIN DE BOTTON: from *How Proust Can Change Your Life*, published by Picador, 1997, reprinted by permission of the publisher. WILLIAM BOYD: from *Armadillo*, first published by Hamish Hamilton, 1998, copyright © William Boyd, 1988, reprinted by permission of the publisher. DENIS BRIAN: from *Einstein: A Life*, published by John Wiley & Sons Inc, 1996, reprinted by permission of the publisher. JEROME E. BROOKS: from *The Mighty Leaf: Tobacco Through the Centuries*, published by Little Brown & Co, 1952. CHRISTOPHER BUCKLEY: from *Thank You for Smoking*, published by Andre Deutsch, 1995. LUIS BUNUEL: from *My Last Breath*, translated by Abigail Israel, published by Jonathan Cape, 1982, reprinted by permission of the publisher. ANTHONY BURGESS: from *You've Had Your Time, Little Wilson and Big God*, copyright © Estate of Anthony Burgess, reprinted by permission of Artellus Limited. ALLEN CARR: from *The Easy Way to Stop Smoking*, published by Penguin Books, 1987, copyright © Allen Carr, 1985, reprinted by permission of the publisher. RAYMOND CHANDLER: from *Farewell My Lovely*, first published by Hamish Hamilton, 1940, copyright © 1940 by Raymond Chandler, reprinted by permission of Penguin Books Ltd; from *The Lady in the Lake*, first published by Hamish Hamilton, 1944, copyright © 1944 by Raymond Chandler; from *The High Window*, first published by Hamish Hamilton, 1943, copyright © 1943 by Raymond Chandler; from *The Little Sister*, first published by Hamish Ham-ilton, 1949, copyright © 1949 by Raymond Chandler. WENDY COPE: from *Making Cocoa for Kingsley Amis*, published by Faber and Faber, 1986, reprinted by permission of the publisher. ROBERTSON DAVIES: from *A Cunning Man*, first published by Viking, 1995, copyright © Robertson Davis, 1994, reprinted by permission of the publisher. JOHN DIAMOND: from *C: Because Cowards get Cancer Too*, first published by Vermillion in 1998, copyright © John Diamond 1998, reprinted by permission of the publisher. RODDY DOYLE: from *The Woman Who Walked into Doors*, first published by Jonathan Cape, 1996, copyright © 1996 by Roddy Doyle, reprinted by permission of the publisher. T. S. ELIOT: © 'Cousin Nancy', reprinted by permission of Faber and Faber Ltd. SEBASTIAN FAULKS: from *Birdsong*, published by Hutchinson, 1993, reprinted by permission of the publisher. HELEN FIELDING: from *Bridget Jones's Diary*, published by Picador, 1996, copyright © Helen Fielding, 1996, reprinted by permission of the author. STANTON GLANZ: from *The Cigarette Papers*, published by University of California Press, 1996, reprinted by permission of the publisher. JORDAN GOODMAN: from *Tobacco in History*, published by Routledge, 1993, reprinted by permission of the publisher. PHILIP GOUREVICH: from *We Wish to Inform You That Tomorrow We Will Be Killed With Our Families*, published by Picador, 1998, reprinted by permission of the publisher. JOHN GRISHAM:

ACKNOWLEDGEMENTS

from *The Runaway Jury*, published by Hutchinson, 1996, reprinted by permission of the publisher. GRAHAM GREENE: from *The End of the Affair*,
reproduced by permission of David Higham Associates. RALPH HARRIS and
JUDITH HATTON: from *Murder a Cigarette*, published by Duckworth & Co,
1998, reprinted by permission of the publisher. JAMES HAWES: from *A White
Merc with Fins*, published by Jonathan Cape, 1996, reprinted by permission of
the publisher. CHRISTOPHER HITCHENS from *For the Sake of the Argument*,
published by Verso, 1993, reprinted by permission of the publisher. RICHARD
HOGGART: from *The Uses of Literacy*, published by Chatto & Windus, 1957,
reprinted by permission of the publisher. NICK HORNBY: from *About a Boy*,
first published by Victor Gollancz, 1998, copyright © Nick Hornby, 1998,
reprinted by permission of Penguin Books Ltd; from *Fever Pitch*, first published by Victor Gollancz, 1992, copyright © Nick Hornby, 1992, reprinted
by permission of Penguin Books Ltd. G. CABRERA INFANTE, from *Holy
Smoke*, published by Faber and Faber, 1985, reprinted by permission of the
publisher. ANNETTE INSDORF: from *Smoke and Blue in the Face: Two Films
by Paul Auster*, published by Faber and Faber, 1995, reprinted by permission
of the publisher. HOWARD JACOBSON: from *No More Mr Nice Guy*, published
by Jonathan Cape, 1998, reprinted by permission of the publisher. JAMES
JOYCE: from *A Portrait of the Artist as a Young Man*, reproduced with the
permission of the Estate of James Joyce, copyright © Estate of James Joyce.
GARRISON KEILLOR: from *We Are Still Married*, published by Faber and
Faber, 1989, reprinted by permission of the publisher. THOMAS KENEALLY:
from *Schindler's List*, published by Hodder & Stoughton Publishers, reprinted
by permission of the publisher. V. G. KIERNAN: from *Tobacco: A History*,
published by Hutchinson, 1991, reprinted by permission of the publisher.
RICHARD KLEIN: from *Cigarettes Are Sublime*, published by Picador, 1993,
reprinted by permission of the publisher. RICHARD KLUGER: from *Ashes to
Ashes*, copyright © 1996 by Richard Kluger, reprinted by permission of Alfred
A Knopf, a Division of Random House Inc. DENIS LEARY: from *No Cure for
Cancer*, published by Picador, 1992, reprinted by permission of the publisher.
JOHN LANCHESTER: from *Mr Phillips*, published by Faber and Faber, 2000,
reprinted by permission of the publisher. JAMES LEAVEY: from *The Forest
Guide to Smoking in London*, published by Quiller Press, 1996, reprinted by
permission of the author. LAURIE LEE: from *Cider With Rosie*, published
by the Hogarth Press, 1959, reprinted by permission of Random House Group
Ltd. S. LOCK et al: from *Ashes to Ashes: The History of Smoking*, published
by Editions Rodopi, 1998, reprinted by permission of the publisher.
JONATHAN LYNN and ANTONY JAY: from *The Complete Yes Prime Minister*,
reproduced with the permission of BBC Worldwide Limited, copyright The
Complete Yes Prime Minister © Jonathan Lynn and Antony Jay. COMPTON
MACKENZIE : from *Sublime Tobacco*, reprinted with the permission of the

ACKNOWLEDGEMENTS

Society of Authors as the literary representative of the estate of Compton Mackenzie. EDWIN MORGAN: from *The Second Life*, published by Carcanet Press, 1968, reprinted by permission of the publisher. LESLEY STERN: from *The Smoking Book*, published by the University of Chicago Press, 1999, reprinted by permission of the publisher. P. J. O'ROURKE: from *Republication Party Reptile: Essays and Outrages*, published by Picador, 1987; from *Eat the Rich*, published by Picador, 1998; from *Holidays in Hell*, published by Picador, 1998, reprinted by permission of the publisher. GEORGE ORWELL: from *Keep the Aspidistra Flying* and *Down and Out in Paris and London*, copyright © George Orwell, reprinted by permission of Bill Hamilton as the Literary Executor of the late Sonia Brownell Orwell and Secker & Warburg Ltd. DOROTHY PARKER: from *The Collected Dorothy Parker*, published by Penguin Books, reprinted by permission of Duckworth & Co. FIONA PITT-KETHLEY: from *No Smoking*, 1989, reprinted by permission of the author. J. B. PRIESTLEY, from *Delight*, copyright © J. B. Priestley, 1949, reprinted by permission of PFD on behalf of the estate of J. B. Priestley. SIMON RAE: from *W. G. Grace: A Life*, published by Faber and Faber, 1998, reprinted by permission of the publisher. RAYMOND RICHMOND and ANTONIA COFFMAN: from *The Simpsons*, published by HarperCollins, 1997, reprinted by permission of the publisher. JEAN-PAUL SARTRE: from *Being and Nothingness: An essay on Phenomenological Ontology*, published by Methuen, 1943, reprinted by permission of the publisher. SEIGFRIED SASSOON: from *The Memoirs of an Infantry Officer*, first published 1930, reprinted by permission of Barbara Levy Literary Agency. JENNIFER SAUNDERS: from *Absolutely Fabulous*, reproduced with the permission of BBC Worldwide Limited, copyright Absolutely Fabulous 2 © Mr and Mrs Monsoon, 1994. ALEXANDER SOLZHENITSYN: from *One Day in the Life of Ivan Denisovich,* translated by Ralph Parker, published by Victor Gollancz, reprinted by permission of the publisher. TOM STOPPARD: from *Travesties*, published by Faber and Faber, 1974, reprinted by permission of the publisher. JOHN UPDIKE: from *Roger's Version*, published by Penguin Books Ltd, copyright © John Updike, 1986, reprinted by permission of the publisher. KENNETH WILLIAMS: from *The Kenneth Williams Diaries*, published by HarperCollins, 1971, reprinted by permission of the publisher.

The publishers have made every effort to secure permission to reprint material protected by copyright. They will be pleased to make good any omissions brought to their attention in future printings of this book.

Index